D1090857

THE SEVENTIES

THE SEVENTIES

The Decade That Changed American Film Forever

Vincent LoBrutto

ROWMAN & LITTLEFIELD
Lanham • Boulder • New York • London

Published by Rowman & Littlefield
An imprint of The Rowman & Littlefield Publishing Group, Inc.
4501 Forbes Boulevard, Suite 200, Lanham, Maryland 20706
www.rowman.com

6 Tinworth Street, London SE11 5AL, United Kingdom

Copyright © 2021 by The Rowman & Littlefield Publishing Group, Inc.

All rights reserved. No part of this book may be reproduced in any form or by
any electronic or mechanical means, including information storage and retrieval
systems, without written permission from the publisher, except by a reviewer
who may quote passages in a review.

British Library Cataloguing in Publication Information Available

Library of Congress Cataloging-in-Publication Data

Names: LoBrutto, Vincent, 1950– author.
Title: The seventies : the decade that changed American film forever / Vincent LoBrutto.
Description: Lanham : Rowman & Littlefield, [2021]. | Includes bibliographical references
    and index. | Summary: "This book tracks the changing of the guard in the 1970s from the classic
    Hollywood studio system to a new generation of filmmakers who made personal movies targeted
    primarily to a thirty-and-under youth audience. These filmmakers reinvented the content and
    aesthetics of the medium to show that movies can be more than entertainment"— Provided by
    publisher.
Identifiers: LCCN 2020042188 (print) | LCCN 2020042189 (ebook) | ISBN 9781538137185 (cloth) |
    ISBN 9781538137192 (ebook)
Subjects: LCSH: Motion pictures—United States—History—20th century. | Motion picture indus-
    try—United States—History—20th century.
Classification: LCC PN1993.5.U6 L56 2021 (print) | LCC PN1993.5.U6 (ebook) | DDC
    791.430973—dc23
LC record available at https://lccn.loc.gov/2020042188
LC ebook record available at https://lccn.loc.gov/2020042189

♾ ™ The paper used in this publication meets the minimum requirements of
American National Standard for Information Sciences Permanence of Paper for
Printed Library Materials, ANSI/NISO Z39.48-1992.

To
Peter Fonda (1940–2019)
Dennis Hopper (1936–2010)
Sam Peckinpah (1925-1984)
Captain America, Billy, and El Jefe—
they didn't leave motion pictures the way
they first found them.

CONTENTS

PROLOGUE

The sixties did not end at the stroke of midnight on December 31, 1969, but on Saturday December 6, 1969. The Woodstock music festival held that summer kindled hope that people could live together in peace and harmony. A free concert on December 6 by the Rolling Stones at California's Altamont Speedway was planned to celebrate the end of the decade. The Hells Angels were asked to provide security. Instead of Woodstock's peace and love, chaos, confusion, and terror reigned. There were injuries and a man was stabbed to death by one of the Angels. The sixties ended before its time, slaughtered in the night by hate and violence. All of this was captured on film by Albert and David Maysles and Charlotte Zwerin for the documentary *Gimme Shelter*, which was released on the anniversary of the tragic event.

The 1960s started with hope and transformation. The 1970s had a gloomier outlook. A severe economic downturn impacted jobs and personal incomes. In this climate, a cultural and cinematic movement would grow.

ACKNOWLEDGMENTS

Since the seventies, my wife Harriet Morrison and I began going to every movie we could possibly see. I thank her for inspiring and elevating every book I've written and for her wise counsel and fine literary hand. She will always be the love of my life.

My son Alex Morrison screened hundreds of films (maybe thousands) with me and became my first film student. My six-year-old grandson Noah is already an avid watcher of shows and my granddaughter Callie is a liberated four-year-old; they are both signs of hope for the next New Wave. My daughter Rebecca Roes has been a continual source of inspiration for her accomplishments and her support for me and my work. My daughter-in-law Sharon Morrison has a discriminating eye for moving images, my son-in-law Jürgen Roes is a man of few words, and when he speaks, I listen intently.

I have been affiliated with the School of Visual Arts (SVA) from 1970 to 2019, which includes my student years and a teaching career of more than twenty-five years. I thank all my students for engaging in a Socratic learning experience in each and every class.

At William Cullen Bryant High School, a substitute teacher found out I was in one of the only high school film classes in the country and gave me my first Museum of Modern Art (MOMA) schedule; he penciled off what I should see. MOMA became my second home for the first four years of the seventies. Thanks for giving me a start in alternate venue screenings.

The New York Film Festival, especially under festival director Richard Roud, exposed me to films I never would have seen elsewhere and served as my yearly fall celebration. Third Avenue on the east side of Manhattan was a haven for cinema lovers. There was Cinema 1, Cinema 2, the Coronet, and the Baronet; at times I went from one theater to the next to catch the 12:00 to 2:00 and the 4:00 to 6:00 shows. Thanks to Anthology Film Archives, Film Forum, the Thalia, and the many venues that were a cinema university of their own.

All the bookstores in New York were special to me. There were two that featured movie books that were out of the ordinary—both Cinemabilia and Coliseum Books nurtured writers on film.

Thanks to author and critic Peter Tonguette. Although he was not yet born in the seventies, he knows more about that magical decade than most his age. To Everett Aison, then chairman of the School of Visual Arts film school who claimed in a film class that *The Exorcist* was a poorly made movie and then, with patience, wisdom, and a smile on his face, asked me to stand up and argue him down point by point while a handful of bewildered students looked on. To John Donovan for being a great friend who is on the side of the angels, understanding that film is a wider medium than most people can comprehend. My gratitude to my friend Carl Perini for joining me on countless excursions to Manhattan to see seventies movies. I treasure your insight and companionship.

Thanks to Henry Jaglom who screened for a small band of cinematic warriors his daring Vietnam experimental film *Tracks*. After the viewers were gone, he stayed and talked with me about what I should do with my life, leading to an after-midnight self-revelation to quit my messenger job and do what I was born to do.

For Gary Carey, my thesis mentor in the first SVA class to receive BFAs, you'll never know the gift you gave me, spending hours and hours poring over the first book manuscript to qualify as a BFA thesis. We lost you too young.

My gratitude to everyone at Rowman & Littlefield for their unconditional support, professionalism, and care for this author and this book during times that challenged us all.

My sincere thanks to all the filmmakers who were part of the Hollywood New Wave and seventies American cinema. They continue to inspire and remind me that film is truly an art.

INTRODUCTION

Before the creation of the Classical Hollywood Studio System, small studios such as Biograph, Essanay, and Nestor Studios existed. Walt Disney created his animation studio in 1923 and for four years he made the *Alice* comedies before creating animated features including a landmark experiment about the relationship between animation and classical music, *Fantasia* (1940). In the thirties, African American Oscar Micheaux created all-black films and personally distributed them in theaters where Negroes (so referred to at the time) could appreciate the kind of genres that mainstream Caucasian audiences enjoyed. In the forties, Monogram Pictures turned out low-budget Westerns and crime films. The fifties were a politically dire time in America. The post–World War II Red Scare was in full swing and everyone in the industry and their films were scrutinized for Communist infiltration. A prominent example was *Salt of the Earth*, released in 1954 by three film artists who were on the government blacklist. The blacklist signaled that the studios could not hire these individuals. Screenwriter Michael Wilson, producer Paul Jarrico, and director Herbert Biberman were all unable to continue working in Hollywood. *Salt of the Earth*, a low-budget film distributed by Independent Productions, was considered one of the first motion pictures to put forth a feminist point of view. Based on a true story, the narrative concerns a long and contentious labor strike focused on worker solidarity, with New Mexican strikers. The theme was considered left wing and taboo and ultimately only found acceptance when released in Europe. The blacklist had a chilling effect on filmmaking throughout the decade.

The Classical Hollywood Studio System, which was in operation from the twenties to the mid- to late sixties, was founded by immigrants: Harry Cohn, Carl Laemmle, Louis B. Mayer, the Warner brothers—Jack L., Harry, Sam, and Albert—and Adolph Zukor. The five studios at the heart of the system were Metro-Goldwyn-Mayer (MGM), Paramount, 20th Century Fox, Universal, and Warner Bros. The system was able to create entertainment of myriad flights of fantasy and imagination that would reach far and wide. This was no small undertaking; a motion picture is a complex and at times magical product that is a way to pass the time and creates a dreamlike impact on the viewer.

Thousands of movies were released during the Classical Hollywood era, with programmers supplying movie palaces weekly. Audiences were offered diverse examples of film art and entertainments such as *Sunrise: A Song of Two Humans* (1927), *The Crowd* (1928), *King Kong* (1933), *Bride of Frankenstein* (1935), *Citizen Kane* (1941), *Double Indemnity* (1944), *Casablanca* (1944), *Some Like It Hot* (1959), and *To Kill a Mockingbird* (1962).

The mogul was the head of his studio. He would assign a capable producer or executive to oversee a unit or production. These were executives who knew every aspect of film production and meticulously watched for budget overruns. They were in discussion with the director, the stars, and crew and reported directly to the mogul.

The moguls operated their studios utilizing the factory assembly line system akin to the system devised by Henry Ford to manufacture cars. The moguls planned each production and shaped and executed it to specifications based on the house method and style. Their version using this model involved having all the equipment necessary to make movies in-house, with separate departments and facilities for teams of directors, producers, screenwriters, cinematographers, production designers, editors, sound, and music. Sets were constructed specifically for a picture and later modified and reused for other movies. There were soundstages of varying size and backlots for shooting exteriors. Additionally, there were standing sets such as a New York street or a Western town, which were used in many pictures. Each studio had a stable of actors and actresses that contained stars, costars, character actors, and background extras. Everyone was under contract and compelled to work in the representational style of each individual studio.

MGM movies emphasized glamour and beauty. The settings were lavish, detailed, and lush. They had a bevy of stars including Clark Gable, Jean Harlow, Katharine Hepburn, Norma Shearer, Jimmy Stewart, and Spencer Tracy. Directors working for this studio included George Cukor, Victor Fleming, and King Vidor. Paramount had a style often described as European. Its stars included Marlene Dietrich, Cary Grant, Ray Milland, George Raft, Ginger Rogers, Barbara Stanwyck, and Fay Wray. Directors working for the studio included Josef von Sternberg and Preston Sturges. The distinction of 20th Century Fox was presenting realistic films geared to adults that emphasized social and cultural issues. Actors under contract there included Don Ameche, Henry Fonda, Rita Hayworth, Carmen Miranda, Maureen O'Hara, Gregory Peck, and Tyrone Power. Directors included John Ford, Henry Hathaway, Henry King, and Fritz Lang. Although Universal produced a range of film styles, the studio was best known and remembered for horror films such as *Dracula*, *Frankenstein*, and *The Wolf Man*. The art direction and camera style were in the German Expressionism vein. Actors in these films included Boris Karloff, Bela Lugosi, and Lon Chaney Jr. Warner Bros. house style was gritty realism with a cynical life view. Many stories were "torn from today's headlines." Actors under contract to this studio included James Cagney, Bette Davis, Ruby Keeler, Paul Muni, and Edward G. Robinson. Directors included Michael Curtiz, Roy Del Ruth, William Dieterle, Mervyn LeRoy, and Archie Mayo.

With a hierarchy of executives using an American business model, every aspect and step of development, production, postproduction, and distribution were scrutinized, rewritten, retooled, reshot, and reedited as necessary.

The screenplay during the Hollywood Studio System was written by an in-house group, including some famous novelists like William Faulkner, F. Scott Fitzgerald, and Ernest Hemingway, who did poorly with the screen form but were put on the rosters for prestige. Others were pros who understood the form that they helped invent, such as Ben Hecht, Anita Loos, and Francis Marion. Every aspect of the construction of a motion picture flowed from the screenplay—actors and actresses played their characters and the story from the script. Their names on a marquee and the personas that they created brought in audiences. Producers were assigned by the studio mogul to oversee every aspect of the motion picture product. Everyone served what was known as the house style—the genre, physical look, and the feeling tone. Some of the moguls were kings, others were dictators. Everyone obeyed the omniscient mogul. The moguls had learned this nascent business by the seats of their pants, having originally come from divergent occupations such as the fur and garment industries. Their tenacity and astute instincts were largely responsible for the success of this burgeoning industry.

THE RULES

The rules for creating a movie in the Classical Hollywood Studio System controlled narrative clarity, continuity, and storytelling that audiences could follow, understand, and in which they became deeply involved. They were entertained and wanted to see another picture (often a double bill with extras, such as a newsreel, cartoons, and selected short subjects). These technical, aesthetic, and content guidelines influenced how a movie was written, designed, photographed, edited, sounded, acted, and directed. Content was carefully selected and tightly controlled. Studio films were adaptations of hit plays or musicals, bestselling novels, and original screenplays written by a staff scribe from a stable of screenwriters under contract to the studio. Entertainment was king, musicals and comedies were considered a good bet. Dramas were watched carefully for preachy messages and for how sensitive topics were presented. Comedies were engineered for maximum entertainment and diversions.

Act 1 of a screenplay was the setup of the story. Act 2 contained a confrontation between characters, and act 3 was the resolution. Plot points propelled the narrative and kept it engaging. Rising and falling action sustained drama, and a crisis and stumbling blocks kept the audience involved in its outcome. The front office expected a screenplay without elaborate descriptive prose, unlike in a novel; it was a blueprint from which a film could be shot that defined location, time, action, and dialogue. Tried-and-true formulas were encouraged, but the better screenwriters came up with new ways to tell a story within that framework.

The audience had a hero or heroine to whom they could relate and wish for his or her success. They could also count on a happy ending, which resolved the story favorably for the protagonists. The studio's schools and instructors trained actors in diction, movement, and other acting disciplines.

Continuity was essential to create a sense of believability. The position of actors and the look of their costumes, hair, and makeup had to match from shot to shot. This also applied to the set, decoration, and props. In order to believe a character was looking at or talking to another character in a separate shot, the direction of his or her gaze had to be established and properly positioned. This is called eyeline match.

Screen direction was maintained. The audience needed to follow the movement of the characters and vehicles without confusion as to what direction they were traveling, even if it violated the reality of such movement.

A master shot, also known as an establishing shot, is a wide shot in which the entire scene, actors, and environment could be revealed and played out with all the dialogue and action within. Then the production unit could make whatever angles and close-ups were necessary.

The match cut matched the action from one shot to the next. It was an invisible technique, so it did not interfere with the story. The match could be made by a body movement, a piece of action, positioning in the frame, or someone or something entering or leaving the frame.

Shot/reverse shot was a technique that convinced the viewer that two characters in separate shots were looking at each other. This was accomplished with framing and the screen direction in which the actors were looking. When cut together, the continuity between the individual shots of the two speakers was achieved.

Color systems were monitored by consultants from companies such as Technicolor. They dictated what colors could be used in a scene and which would not work. Generally, there was a push for very saturated colors, regardless of whether it suited the story. These consultants often received an on-screen credit.

GENRES OF THE CLASSICAL HOLLYWOOD STUDIO SYSTEM

The moguls quickly realized that audiences responded to movies in a category or form. Genre films had great appeal because of their familiarity to the audience. They suited the factory system because genre films have common elements, which made production cost-effective and speedy. The basics included crime, horror, musicals, science fiction, war, and Westerns.

As the sixties unfolded, the Classical Hollywood System began to unravel. The moguls were ready to move on, and the studios could not find the right properties: the books and plays to make successful motion pictures. They turned to the musical, which had brought cash back to them since the forties. *My Fair Lady* (1964) and *The Sound of Music* (1965) were extravaganzas, and the studios desperately tried to duplicate this kind of success. A long string of failures including *Doctor Dolittle* (1967), *Star!* (1968), *Chitty Chitty Bang Bang* (1968), *Paint Your Wagon* (1969), *Hello, Dolly!* (1969), and *Darling Lili* (1970) exposed that times had changed. The losses from these big budget fiascoes were damaging. Studios were bought out by conglomerates with other concerns than the entertainment business. The era of the moguls, with their total passion for and understanding of how to make movies was over. The audience who regularly attended the local movie theater for decades began to stay put and watch television series and movies at home.

A major catalyst for cinematic change during the seventies was the next generation, codified as the baby boomers, who were younger than thirty at the time and weaned on fifties and sixties television and movies of that era. They understood and embraced media. Films like *Bonnie and Clyde* (1967), *The Graduate* (1967), and *Easy Rider* (1969) spoke to them as youth films, and they were the ones who went to the movies continually.

In 1939 *Gone with the Wind, Stagecoach, The Wizard of Oz,* and many other classic films became part of what was known as the Golden Age of Hollywood. *The Seventies: The Decade That Changed American Film Forever* is about the second golden age that occurred during the 1970s. Often this subject is isolated as the American New Wave, a movement that involved a specific group of filmmakers who had an enormous impact on the American cinema and our culture—it revolutionized the art of the movie. As the American New Wave burgeoned, concurrently, there were films and filmmakers not identified as part of this movement that evolved and broke away from almost everything that came before. They also populated the seventies. They are identified as part of the decade. The focus of this book is the story of a decade of filmmaking whose impact we still feel and whose history and legacy are part of the American story.

I

HOW OLD HOLLYWOOD BECAME NEW HOLLYWOOD

"That's all gone, now, the old Hollywood."—Warren Beatty[1]

"There's the generation that made the rules, the generation that codified them. The generation that broke them—that's mine. The generation that laughed at them—that's Tarantino's. And now there's a generation that doesn't know that there were any."—Paul Schrader[2]

"Ninety-five percent of films are born of frustration, of self-despair, of
ambition for survival, for money, for fattening bank accounts. Five
percent, maybe less, are made because a man has an idea which he
must express."—Sam Fuller[3]

The Golden Age of Hollywood was an era from the twenties to the mid-
to late sixties in which motion pictures entertained and greatly influenced
American life. After the dissolution of the Classical Hollywood Studio
System, there was a second Golden Age of American Cinema, which
took place in the seventies, during which a wide range of filmmakers
presented movies that reflected the times, were unflinching in their approach to difficult content, found new ways of telling cinematic stories,
wrote a new aesthetic Bible, and supplied fresh blood in front of and
behind the camera. Within this was the American New Wave, but the
impact of this decade that changed American film forever was larger than
New Wave—moviemakers in the seventies took the rich history and the
ashes of the Classical Hollywood film and redefined an art form that

forged a significant break between the old and the new, which seemed limitless in its reach.

The American New Wave, also known as "New Hollywood," was a cinema movement that had its precursors in the United States in 1967, was active throughout the seventies, and ended in the early eighties. Members of the New Wave were young filmmakers who felt shut out of Hollywood. They created movies that evolved in reaction to the Classical Hollywood Studio System method and style. The sixties were already a tumultuous time socially and politically, as manifested in a revolution in all forms of art. The seventies took a large next step forward.

In 1967 the erudite film critic Stanley Kauffmann coined the phrase the "film generation," which has come to be defined as the baby boomers who, through television, going to the movies, and educational study, were the most prepared to understand the visual language of film. This generation became the core of the American New Wave and the audience to whom the films were marketed. This wave would shape the American cinema into its own likeness and become a reflection of its culture and country.

Ironically, this group of young filmmakers was brought up on old Hollywood movies that they viewed in neighborhood theaters and on television. They revered and studied these movies. What they were to do in the seventies was to create a cinema inspired by the old but crafted for a new and evolving audience in a rapidly changing country. To accomplish this, they would break every rule, tear down every wall, and destroy the Hollywood myth factory.

Many of the core filmmakers of the Hollywood New Wave attended film schools and were well versed in the canons of Classical Hollywood filmmaking, European cinema, avant-garde/experimental film, documentaries, and independent filmmaking. Museums and other venues ran retrospectives that informed them of the many layers of film history. New forms on television created a language that entered the mix of influences. *The Spike Jones Show* featured a jokester who led his band into burlesque and surreal comedy routines while playing an eclectic mix of classical and other musical genres. *The Steve Allen Show* featured the clever, zany host who assembled one of the funniest ensembles of comedians imaginable, including Don Knotts, Tom Poston, and Louis Nye. *Omnibus* featured sophisticated and diverse programs on topics such as the arts, science, and the humanities, including the televised lectures by maestro

Leonard Bernstein. *Playhouse 90* performed high-quality adult dramas on live television. *The Ernie Kovacs Show* was a lab of television comedy in which the very medium itself was the source of the content. Rod Serling's *The Twilight Zone* stimulated the outer reaches of the imagination, employing what would later be called speculative fiction.

Members of the American New Wave were the spiritual children of the French New Wave, an inestimable movement comprised of many significant filmmakers and film critics who adored the Hollywood film, including François Truffaut, Jean-Luc Godard, and Jacques Rivette. They catapulted the French film into a new era that was committed to the reinvention of the French cinema, themselves inspired by Classical French and Classical Hollywood cinema. A major contribution of the French New Wave was support of the auteur theory, which decrees that the director is the sole author of a film. The concept became a prototype for the American New Wave.

The American New Wave was comprised of a diverse group of mostly young men. Peter Bogdanovich, a living, breathing encyclopedia of Classical Hollywood who lived more in the past than the present, received hands-on experience in every facet of filmmaking working with the king of B movies, low-budget film guru Roger Corman. Robert Altman had directed few feature films but established a long résumé of industrials and television shows including *Combat!*, *Bonanza*, and *Whirlybirds* for the three major networks. Hal Ashby, who looked like a counterculture scruffy hippie, was trained as a film editor in Classical Hollywood. He was nominated for an Oscar in 1966 for *The Russians Are Coming, the Russians Are Coming* and took home the statue in 1967 for *In the Heat of the Night*, both directed by Norman Jewison. Infatuated with movies from a young age, Steven Spielberg made elaborate 8mm films. Rejected from University of California Film School (USC) because of poor grades, he attended California State University, Long Beach, instead. He learned a lot about his craft by continually sneaking onto the Universal Studios lot, convincing the staff he belonged there. He received a number of professional credits working on television series including *Night Gallery*, which featured Rod Serling. He directed legendary actress Joan Crawford in the pilot episode in 1969. He also directed episodes of *Owen Marshall: Counselor at Law* and *Marcus Welby M.D.* Francis Ford Coppola was the first New Waver to go to a film school, the University of California at Los Angeles and direct a Hollywood studio movie, *Finian's Rainbow* in

1968. Paramount later assigned him *The Godfather* after established film directors such as Otto Preminger and Costa Gravas turned it down. Producer Robert Evans selected Coppola because he wanted the film to be authentically ethnic and Coppola was, as an Italian American, even though he knew next to nothing about the mafia and didn't want to glorify it. George Lucas attended USC, where he became fascinated with the experimental film movement and international cinema. Lucas won a scholarship from Warner Bros./Seven Arts to observe and participate on a film of his choice—and he chose *Finian's Rainbow*. In 1968 Lucas wrote and directed a short entitled *Filmmaker* about the making of *The Rain People* (1968) directed by Francis Ford Coppola. In 1969 he cofounded American Zoetrope in San Francisco with Coppola to encourage aspiring filmmakers. He adapted his short film *Electric Labyrinth: THX 1138 4EB* into the feature film *THX 1138* starring Robert Duvall. Martin Scorsese was sickly as a child with severe asthma. He could not play outside with other children, so his father took him to the movies as often as possible to ease his wheezing and entertain him. Scorsese is considered New York University's (NYU) most prestigious former student, but the primary sources for his encyclopedic knowledge and love of film were the cool interiors of movie palaces and his television set, where he endlessly watched movies on local New York channels. John Milius attended USC and was in high demand as a screenwriter for his scripts, which included *Dirty Harry* (1971), *Jeremiah Johnson* (1972), and *The Life and Times of Judge Roy Bean* (1972). Milius was a California surfer who was obsessed with firearms and crafted a tough guy persona—a chronicler of the art of war and a rabid supporter of combat. Milius made his directorial debut with *Dillinger* (1973). The talented Brian De Palma was obsessed with Alfred Hitchcock, especially *Psycho* (1960). Because he worked in the horror genre, long considered a subbasement film category, he was often not taken seriously; nevertheless, he skillfully reinvented Hitchcock's auteur form as both an homage and a new cinematic art form. In the sixties De Palma directed *Murder á la Mod* (1968), *Greetings* (1968) with an early performance by Robert De Niro, and *The Wedding Party* (1969) with a young Jill Clayburgh and De Niro.

In addition to those identified as the core of the American New Wave were many filmmakers representing a wide range of approaches who were part of the innovation of the medium, which occurred during the seventies. These included Woody Allen *Annie Hall* (1977), John G.

Avildsen *Joe* (1970), Ralph Bakshi *Fritz the Cat* (1972), Paul Bartel *Death Race 2000* (1975), John Boorman *Deliverance* (1972), James Bridges *The Paper Chase* (1973), Emile de Antonio *Milhouse: A White Comedy* (1971), Jonathan Demme *Handle with Care* (1977), Robert Downey (father of Robert Downey Jr.) *Pound* (1970), Darryl Duke *Payday* (1972), Richard Fleischer *Soylent Green* (1973), Peter Fonda *The Hired Hand* (1971), James Frawley *Kid Blue* (1973), William Friedkin *The French Connection* (1971), Monte Hellman *Two-Lane Blacktop* (1971), George Roy Hill *The Sting* (1973), Arthur Hiller *The Hospital* (1971), Dennis Hopper *The Last Movie* (1971), Henry Jaglom *Tracks* (1976), Norman Jewison *Jesus Christ Superstar* (1973), Jonathan Kaplan *Over the Edge* (1979), Irvin Kershner *Eyes of Laura Mars* (1978), Tom Laughlin *Billy Jack* (1971), Barbara Loden *Wanda* (1971), Sidney Lumet *Serpico* (1973), Norman Mailer *Maidstone* (1970), Terrence Malick *Days of Heaven* (1978), Elaine May *A New Leaf* (1971), Albert and David Maysles *Grey Gardens* (1975), Paul Mazursky *Next Stop, Greenwich Village* (1976), Jim McBride *Glen and Randa* (1971), Radley Metzger *Lickerish Quartet* (1970), Paul Morrissey *Heat* (1972), Robert Mulligan *Summer of '42* (1971), Russ Meyer *Beyond the Valley of the Dolls* (1970), Floyd Mutrux *Dusty and Sweets McGee* (1971), Alan J. Pakula *Klute* (1971), Sam Peckinpah *Straw Dogs* (1971), Arthur Penn *Little Big Man* (1970), Frank Perry *Diary of a Mad Housewife* (1970), Bob Rafelson *Five Easy Pieces* (1970), Mark Rappaport *The Scenic Route* (1978), Conrad Rooks *Siddhartha* (1972), Alan Rudolph *Welcome to L.A.* (1976), Richard Rush *Getting Straight* (1970), Richard Sarafian *Vanishing Point* (1970), Jerry Schatzberg *The Panic in Needle Park* (1971), Paul Schrader *Blue Collar* (1978), Joan Micklin Silver *Hester Street* (1976), Raphael Silver *On the Yard* (1978), James Toback *Fingers* (1978), Melvin Van Peebles *Sweet Sweetback's Baadasssss Song* (1971), and Claudia Weil *Girlfriends* (1978). These directors were an equal part of the story of the seventies.

This was the era of the "film director as superstar," but none of these directors made a movie by themselves. The Classical Hollywood Studio System had parameters and strict protocols for how the crafts functioned within their system. Most were considered invisible, such as film editing (although this was a traditional myth); others were bigger than life and expressed a glorious artificiality, such as production design. Craft artists during the American New Wave had studied the traditional methods and ways. They were telling new kinds of cinematic narratives, so they developed their own methods, techniques, and systems to create narrative structures and to work with directors in a freer, more collaborative manner.

In seventies films, the screenplay reflected the voice of the writer with a more personal, poetic, and descriptive approach featuring relevant content. Form was revised in terms of length and the timeline of the narrative. Films became more nonlinear, departing from the traditional three-act logical format of the studio system. Seventies screenwriters included Jay Presson Allen *Cabaret* (1972), Marshall Brickman with Woody Allen *Annie Hall* (1977), Paddy Chayefsky *Network* (1976), Joan Didion and John Gregory Dunne *The Panic in Needle Park* (1971), Elaine May *A New Leaf* (1971), Frank Pierson *Dog Day Afternoon* (1975), Stirling Silliphant *The Poseidon Adventure* (1972), Joan Tewkesbury *Nashville* (1975), Robert Towne *Chinatown* (1974), and Rudy Wurlitzer *Two-Lane Blacktop* (1971).

A new generation of actors looked and sounded less like movie stars and more like people the audience might encounter in life. The nature of their performances was realistic, truthful, and accessible to the viewer. Seventies actors included Warren Beatty *Heaven Can Wait* (1978), Karen Black *Five Easy Pieces* (1970), Jeff Bridges *The Last American Hero* (1973), Robert De Niro *Taxi Driver* (1976), Faye Dunaway *Chinatown* (1974), Jane Fonda *Klute* (1973), Elliot Gould *The Long Goodbye* (1973), Dustin Hoffman *Straw Dogs* (1971), Sissy Spacek *Carrie* (1976), and Meryl Streep *Kramer vs. Kramer* (1979).

Some cinematographers were European; many American cameramen worked in a style inspired by international cinema. Cameras became lighter and more mobile, lighting more natural, and compositions more artful.

The director/cinematographer (director of photography) collaboration was closer than ever, and directors often knew lenses and what they could do and generally understood the art of cinematography. Seventies cinematographers included Néstor Almendros *Days of Heaven* (1978), John Alonzo *Chinatown* (1974), William Fraker *Looking for Mr. Goodbar* (1977), Conrad Hall *Fat City* (1972), László Kovács *Five Easy Pieces* (1970), Owen Roizman *The Exorcist* (1973), Bruce Surtees *Blume in Love* (1973), Haskell Wexler *Bound for Glory* (1970), Gordon Willis *The*

Godfather and *The Godfather: Part II* (1972), and Vilmos Zsigmond *McCabe & Mrs. Miller* (1971).

During the seventies, filmmakers often utilized location shoots rather than studio stage work. Finding and selecting the right location was critical to the veracity of the narrative. Often a location was dressed and altered by the production designer and the art department to be transformed into the director's conception and vision of the story. Color palettes expressed the atmosphere as did the created interior environments.

Seventies production designers included Ken Adam *Barry Lyndon* (1975), Mel Bourne *Interiors* (1978), Leon Eriksen *Images* (1972), Harry Horner *The Driver* (1978), Richard MacDonald *The Day of the Locust* (1975), Polly Platt *The Last Picture Show* (1971), Paul Sylbert *One Flew over the Cuckoo's Nest* (1975), Richard Sylbert *Chinatown* (1974), Dean Tavoularis *Apocalypse Now* (1979), and Patrizia Von Brandenstein *Girlfriends* (1978).

During the Classical Hollywood Studio System era, costume designers first and foremost provided beauty and glamour. A common credit was "gowns by." The artist often used one name such as "Adrian." Everyday women's and men's clothes were of designer quality and rarely looked store-bought. During the seventies, the wardrobe of the actors suited the characters more realistically. There was a focus on period accuracy and what was right for the story and less emphasis on glamour. On low-budget films, the actors were sometimes asked to select costumes from their own wardrobes.

Seventies costume designers included Theoni V. Aldredge *Three Days of the Condor* (1975), Milena Canonero *Barry Lyndon* (1975), Aggie Guerard *American Graffiti* (1973), Anna Hill Johnstone *The Godfather* (1972), Jules Melillo *Three Women* (1977), Ruth Morley *The Brinks Job* (1978), Ann Roth *The Owl and the Pussycat* (1970), Anthea Sylbert *Shampoo* (1975), and Theodora Van Runkle *The Godfather: Part II* (1974).

Makeup in Old Hollywood served several purposes: making performers camera ready and beautiful, defining characters, aging, and special makeup for Universal horror films. Seventies makeup artists broke new ground in makeup and special effects makeup. Leading the way was Dick Smith, who achieved landmark work, notably on *Little Big Man* (1970), *The Exorcist* (1973), and *Taxi Driver* (1976). Other makeup artists include Rick Baker *It's Alive* (1974), Rob Bottin *Piranha* (1978), John

Chambers, the *Planet of the Apes* franchise during the decade, Barbara Daly *Barry Lyndon* (1974), Stewart Freeborn *Star Wars* (1977), Frank Griffin *Westworld* (1973), Dorothy J. Pearl *The Texas Chainsaw Massacre* (1974), Tom Savini *Martin* (1977), Tommy Thompson *Battlestar Galactica* (1978), and William Tuttle *The Fury* (1978).

Hair styles and stylists contribute to the definition of a character. In Old Hollywood, the emphasis was more on glamour and less on the accuracy of the period or the nature of the characters. In New Hollywood, the emphasis was on realism and accuracy of period and style. Sydney Guilaroff started in Classical Hollywood as a hair stylist in 1937 and worked for decades designing the hair for superstars such as Ann-Margret in *Carnal Knowledge* (1971), Ava Gardner in *The Blue Bird* (1976), and Liza Minnelli in Scorsese's *New York, New York* (1977). He practiced his craft on more than a thousand movies and set a new standard for his craft. Hair styling professionals in the seventies included Kathryn Blondell *Harold and Maude* (1971), Naomi Calvin *The Godfather: Part II* (1974), Vern Caruso *Heaven's Gate* (1980), Grazzi De Rossi *Daisy Miller* (1974), , Betty Glasow *Sunday Bloody Sunday* (1971), Raymon Gow *The Rocky Horror Picture Show* (1975), Bette Iverson *American Graffiti* (1973), Phillip Leto *The Godfather* (1972), and Marlene D. Williams *The Day of the Locust* (1975).

The Old Hollywood studio chiefs demanded that editing be invisible so it would not interfere with the story. In New Hollywood, the traditional Moviola was still employed to edit film, but a flatbed editing table made screening and changes in structure easier. Francis Ford Coppola was one of the first to purchase a KEM and put it into operation. Editing was Old Hollywood's way of controlling a film and how it was released in theaters. During the seventies editing was no longer invariably invisible, but visible at times and used as an expressive tool. This was especially critical as the director relied on the film editor to keep the scene structure and narrative flow consistent with the director's vision. The editor became a recognized collaborator who worked with the director to shape and finalize the movie. Storytelling abilities were broadened by a new freedom to interpret a story editorially. Editorial structure was accepted as the "final rewrite of a film."

Seventies editors included Dede Allen *Little Big Man* (1970), Donn Cambern *Blume in Love* (1973), Verna Fields *Jaws* (1975), Jerry Greenberg *The French Connection* (1971), Tina Hirsch *The Driver* (1978),

Michael Kahn *Close Encounters of the Third Kind* (1977), Marcia Lucas *American Graffiti* (1973), Sam O'Steen *Chinatown* (1974), Tom Rolf *Black Sunday* (1977), Ralph Rosenblum *Annie Hall* (1977), and Robert L. Wolfe *All the President's Men* (1977).

As the history books state (although there were precursors) the first synchronized sound film was *The Jazz Singer* (1927), and the film industry was never the same. Early sound films were mainly dialogue. In New Hollywood sound design, the art of supporting the film with a palette of audio elements to contribute and support the narrative and characters flourished as an expressive storytelling tool. Technology delivered digital recording in which sound not only supported the images but provided emotional and experiential aural environments to the movies. Sound artists included recordists, mixers, designers, and sound effects creators who had an artistic impact on the soundtrack and its relationship to the images.

Seventies sound creators included Ben Burtt *Invasion of the Body Snatchers* (1978), Cecilia Hall *Star Trek: The Motion Picture* (1979), Walter Murch *The Conversation* (1974), Chris Newman *The Taking of Pelham 123* (1974), Arthur Piantadosi *The Yakuza* (1974), Richard Portman *Stay Hungry* (1976), Jack Solomon *Meteor* (1979), Ross Taylor and Kitty Malone *Apocalypse Now* (1979), Frank Warner *The Trial of Billy Jack* (1974), and Jim Webb *Nashville* (1975).

Music in Old Hollywood consisted of orchestra music performed virtually from the beginning to the end of a film. Most of the music was composed to indicate to the audience how they should feel at any point in the story. The seventies delivered a new kind of composer well versed in all sorts of musical genres; the music was experiential, atmospheric, and emotionally truthful for the story. There were also song scores structured by previously recorded tracks edited into the soundtrack to provide ambiance and specific storytelling information. Seventies composers included Elmer Bernstein *Report to the Commissioner* (1975), Bill Conti *Rocky* (1976), Pino Donaggio *Carrie* (1976), Jerry Fielding *Straw Dogs* (1971), Jerry Goldsmith *The Wind and the Lion* (1975), Dave Grusin *The Yakuza* (1974), Bo Harwood *A Woman under the Influence* (1974), Johnny Mandel *M*A*S*H* (1970), Michael Small *Klute* (1971), and John Williams *Jaws* (1975).

Old Hollywood created special effects that were handmade, actual, and real. There was no CGI (computer-generated images), so everything was practical or done with stage effects or cinematic technique. When computers arrived and specific programs were designed to realize visual effects for movies, anything was possible, from selective images to full-frame visualizations. Some of the effects magicians included Nick Allder, Brian Johnson, and H. R. Giger *Alien* (1979), Greg Auer and John Frazier *The Hills Have Eyes* (1977), Fred Cramer *The Deer Hunter* (1979), John Dykstra *Star Wars* (1977), Joe Eisner and Al Griswold *Rabid* (1977), Frederick Elmes and David Lynch *Eraserhead* (1977), A. D. Flowers, L. B. Abbott, and Matthew Yuricich *The Poseidon Adventure* (1972), Milt Rice *The Last Movie* (1971), Tom Savini, *Dawn of the Dead* (1978), and Brent Sellstrom, Matthew Yuricich, and John Whitney Jr. *Rabid* (1977).

In New Hollywood, most producers were connected to a corporation that owned one of the original studios, which were often bought as business propositions. The corporations viewed the movie studios as viable businesses, but they didn't really know how to make motion pictures. These producers were often freelance, brought in to contribute to the budget, connected to the star of the film, or had a specific skill, such as being a liaison between a novelist and a property or a star or director about whom there was interest. They often worked independently and reported to the studio in a disorganized manner. These personnel could add up to a sizeable number, as opposed to the studio system, in which a single person often produced a movie. There is a solid argument that a savvy producer was as much an auteur of a film as the director. Examples included Phillip De Antoni *The French Connection* (1971), Robert Evans *Chinatown* (1974), Jerome Hellman *Coming Home* (1978), Frank Marshall *Nickelodeon* (1976), Paul Monash *Carrie* (1976), Edward R. Pressman *Sisters* (1972), Albert Ruddy *The Godfather* (1972), Robert Stigwood *Saturday Night Fever* (1977), Jonathan Taplin *Mean Streets* (1973), and Irwin Winkler and Robert Chartoff *Rocky* (1976).

Since most of the filmmakers had formal or experiential training, they understood the early principles and were equipped to invent a new set of rules to suit the personal films that reflected their times. As products of the rebellious sixties, they were temperamentally inclined to rebel, but what they really did was to change Hollywood art to create a new, vital, and reflective cinema. Before *Easy Rider*, Dennis Hopper talked publicly about violating the rules of screen direction, creating alternates to the dissolve, fade in, fade out, and time transitions. During the making of the film, they flipped the celluloid on a shot to change the position of an actor so the actor appeared to be facing in the right direction, applied shock cutting, and staged a commune meal prayer sequence in a 360-degree shot.

The American New Wave tackled content that was rarely investigated or presented in a less than bold fashion by Old Hollywood. Race issues, sexuality, and other controversial subjects were now explored in depth, with full candor.

Cinematographers were more painterly and developed a style for each picture. Contemporary films were adaptations of books that interpreted literary style into a full cinematic medium and the original screenplays were more personal. The three-act structure was still in place, but the presentation of time and space was modern and progressive. Sound became more realistic, with systems that surrounded the audience and signaled specific sounds at specific places and times. Robert Altman presented extensive overlapping dialogue, unheard of in the Old Hollywood era. This was more like life. He also created sound layers, especially for noisy locations such as restaurants and clubs, so the main characters appeared to talk over the din. Music often featured song scores in which previously recorded and released numbers were placed on the soundtrack for atmosphere, narrative, and character connections.

The three forms of moviemaking radically changed by the seventies. These were documentary, animation, and avant-garde, which during the sixties began to be called experimental filmmaking.

In the sixties, French cinema verité recorded life as it was. Rather than narration, there was natural sound. In America this became the nonfiction form, direct cinema, in which filmmakers utilized lightweight and portable equipment to explore truth as they saw it.

Albert and David Maysles were brothers who worked as a team, both directed, Albert was the cameraman, and David was the soundman. When they realized the impact film editor Charlotte Zwerin had on their work, they embraced her as a director as well. They began the seventies with *Gimme Shelter*, which captured rock and cultural history and set a high standard for nonfiction filmmaking. In 1974 they became fascinated with the conceptual environmental artist Christo, releasing *Christo's Valley Curtain*. In 1975 *Grey Gardens* focused on a mother and daughter both named Edith Beale. Although they were the aunt and cousin of former First Lady Jacqueline Kennedy Onassis, these idiosyncratic personalities lived in squalor.

D. A. Pennebaker was a pioneer of direct cinema, with a long résumé during the 1960s including the seminal *Don't Look Back* (1967), profiling a young Bob Dylan. *Town Bloody Hall* was released in 1971, a raucous debate on feminism between Germaine Greer, Norman Mailer, and other women's rights leaders. *Ziggy Stardust and the Spiders from Mars* (1973) is a concert film, the last time David Bowie appeared as his invention, Ziggy Stardust. *The Energy War* (1978) was a three-part PBS special including all sides in a fierce legislative battle over President Jimmy Carter's energy policy.

Frederick Wiseman is a documentary auteur. He graduated Yale Law School in 1955 and taught law at Boston University before becoming a documentary filmmaker. His original purpose was to explore American institutions. Wiseman employed long takes and was patient, waiting to shoot until he saw what he wanted. In 1970 he made *Hospital*, which probed the activities in a large city's outpatient emergency room. *Basic Training* (1971), shot during the Vietnam era, is a detailed examination of that military process. In *Juvenile Court* (1973), young people face the law. *Welfare* (1975) examines the wide range of issues that are part of that social service system.

Barbara Kopple assisted the Maysles Brothers on *Salesman* (1969), their film about Bible salesmen, and appeared on camera for *Gimme Shelter*. She worked in many capacities in nonfiction films for other filmmakers and then set out to make her own feature-length documentary. *Harlan County U.S.A.* (1976) was a hard-hitting look at the lives of Appalachian miners. Kopple and her crew lived with the miners, who were fighting for union recognition. *Harlan County U.S.A.* won the Academy Award for Best Documentary.

Animation had been dominated by Walt Disney. The studio released four features during the 1970s: *The Aristocats* (1970), *Robin Hood* (1973), *The Many Adventures of Winnie the Pooh* (1977), and *The Rescuers* (1977), but the rich, detailed style of animation created while Disney was alive (he died in 1966) was dramatically simplified and not up to the high standards of *Snow White and the Seven Dwarfs* (1937) or *Pinocchio* (1940).

Ralph Bakshi adapted the underground comic *Fritz the Cat*, released in 1972, which became the first animated film to get an X rating. *Heavy Traffic* (1973) contained content that was rough around the edges and continued an animation style that reflected the times more than tradition.

Some viewed the presentation of racial issues as stereotyping; others thought it was honest and brave. *Coonskin* (1975) was a crime film in which an African American rabbit, fox, and bear confront the Italian Mafia. In 1975 an initial version of *Hey Good Lookin'*, a fifties coming-of-age film, was rejected by Warner Bros., which was still reeling from the backlash from *Coonskin*, but it eventually was released in 1982. For the fantasy film *Wizards* (1977), Bakshi created battle sequences by utilizing material from Sergei Eisenstein's *Alexander Nevesky*, *Battle of the Bulge*, *El Cid*, and *Patton*. He rotoscoped this material, a technique in which animators trace over an image to achieve a realistic, fluid effect. Next Bakshi selected J. R. R. Tolkien's trilogy, *The Lord of the Rings*. Released in 1978, it made money even though the studio forced its release before Bakshi had finished covering the breadth of the story.

Andy Warhol, born Andrew Warhola, began as a shoe designer and commercial illustrator in the fifties and became one of the most influential artists of the twentieth century, a major figure behind pop art in the sixties who created a working environment called "The Factory" in New York where he made silk screens of celebrities and in-house independent movies. These ranged from epic-length studies such as *Sleep* (1963), which ran five hours and twenty-one minutes and was constructed out of film loops of performance artist and poet John Giorno. The eight-hour *Empire* (1964) was a study of the iconic Empire State Building. Both films investigated the nature of film time. He also filmed more than four hundred screen tests, which were short films that were Warhol's take on the Hollywood auditioning process. Auditions included visitors to The Factory, namely Dennis Hopper and Bob Dylan and Warhol regulars Nico, Lou Reed, and Edie Sedgwick. The tests were short, silent, and in black and white. The subject addressed the camera without performing a scene, but like their Hollywood counterparts, they still revealed their personalities. Creating an alternate Hollywood, Andy Warhol assembled a group that he called superstars; they represented the subculture of the sixties and seventies and included Candy Darling, a transsexual actress, Joe D'Alessandro, a wild child who had trouble with the law and later became a nude model and sex symbol, and Viva, who was a model and painter before Warhol discovered her and cast her in his films. His influence as a filmmaker is incalculable. In the seventies he collaborated with Paul Morrisey to make films beyond the limited venues such as the commercially viable films *Trash* and *Flesh*, both released in 1970, which had both notoriety and success in general release.

The avant-garde film movement began practically at the beginning of film history and developed and expanded its cinematic language during the 1960s, when it began to be called experimental film. The seventies was a vibrant era in which there were many great films and filmmakers. They were nonnarrative and communicated in many visual modes, including abstraction, mythic, and symbolic. These films did not play in commercial movie theaters, but rather in museums, specialty theaters, lofts, and other gatherings. It was truly a different kind of cinema with little relationship to what came out of Hollywood.

Stan Brakhage was the most influential and prolific experimental filmmaker. His films, with few exceptions, were silent, rooted in poetry and myth, full of texture and abstract autobiographical views. In the sixties Brakhage created *Dog Star Man*, a multipart film considered a masterwork. During the seventies he created as many as sixty films. He continued a series of films he categorized as "songs" and a Roman numeral series. Most if not all in the field were influenced by him.

Bruce Baillie founded Canyon Cinema in 1961, which became the San Francisco Cinematheque in 1975, to exhibit independent films that were experimental in nature. As a filmmaker he worked extensively in the 1960s. In the seventies Baillie created his masterpiece, the influential *Quick Billy* (1970), a near feature-length film about the transformation between life, death, and rebirth. Baillie is a master of layering images that move in, out, back, and forth for a total cinematic experience.

In the seventies the scholar P. Adams Sitney identified a trend he eventually named Structural film. The characteristics are fixed framing, flickering or strobing effects, printing film in circular patterns, and the rephotographing of images off-screen.

Hollis Frampton was a multidisciplinary media artist whose film work defined Structural film. During the seventies Frampton made as many as thirty films. Notable was *Nostalgia* (1971), in which black-and-white photographs were burned one at a time on a hot plate. On the soundtrack, a voice talks about the content of the pictures, allowing the viewer to be involved with the past and present.

A vibrant form of experimental filmmaking from the sixties into the seventies was the diary film. Filmmakers picked up an inexpensive Bolex film camera and kept plenty of Kodak film on hand so that when the spirit moved them, they recorded what they experienced or what was in front of them. These films were often silent and long. Editing was done in-camera and the punch holes at the beginning of a reel were often left intact. One of the major figures in this field is Lithuanian-born Jonas Mekas, who documented his early years discovering an arts community in New York in *Lost, Lost, Lost* (1976), and is often referred to as the pope of avant-garde/experimental film. Mekas founded the Film-Makers' Cooperative and *Film Culture Magazine* with his brother Adolphus in the sixties. On December 1, 1970, Anthology Film Archives, a showcase for avant-garde/experimental film, opened with Mekas as director. The other key diary filmmaker was Andrew Noren, who chronicled *The Adventures of the Exquisite Corpse*, a career work consisting of eight films exploring how the ordinary is extraordinary and magical. Freude Bartlett made poetic diary films that explored her life in the home and in the natural world, which included *Folly* (1972). Tom Chomont's approach was to make the banality of life mystical in *Love Objects* (1971). Robert Huot was a painter who started as an abstract expressionist and transitioned to a minimalist then to diary films that searched the smallest details. He filmed the relationship between him and his wife, choreographer and dancer Twyla Tharp, in *Snow* (1971).

The list of experimental filmmakers who worked in the seventies is vast. They included Kenneth Anger *Lucifer Rising* (1972), Shirley Clarke *Mysterium Intimation* (1978), Bruce Conner *Valse Triste* (1977), Guvnor Nelson *Moon's Pool* (1973), Carolee Schneemann, *Up to and Including Her Limits* (1973–1976), Paul Shartis *Analytical Studies I: The Film Frame* (1976), and Michael Snow *'Rameau's Nephew' by Diderot (Thanx to Dennis Young) by Wilma Schoen* (1972–1974).

New Hollywood film historians and scholars consistently cite three late 1960s films as major catalysts for the American New Wave. *Bonnie and Clyde* (1967), directed by Arthur Penn, takes place in the 1930s and follows bank robbers Bonnie Parker and Clyde Barrow. The film's subtext is a commentary on the 1960s with its violence and complex nonconformist relationships. The slow-motion violence in Sam Peckinpah's *The Wild Bunch* (1969) is a subtext for the bloodshed in Vietnam. *The Graduate* (1967), directed by Mike Nichols, portrays a young college graduate struggling with his future. His father's partner's wife seduces him, and he falls in love with her daughter. This youth film spoke to the new and burgeoning under-thirty moviegoing audience and was shot in an eclectic, derivative style. The graduate, played by newcomer Dustin Hoffman, became a prototype of the antihero of the seventies.

The film with the foremost influence on the American New Wave is the 1969 biker movie, *Easy Rider*. In 1966 Roger Corman directed *The Wild Angels*, starring Peter Fonda, which contained the DNA that would provide inspiration for *Easy Rider*. Peter Fonda, son of Henry and brother of Jane, was a counterculture figure and perfectly positioned for *Easy Rider*, in which he costarred with director Dennis Hopper and served as producer. Screenwriter Terry Southern never really received proper recognition for his enormous contribution to the original screenplay. *Easy Rider* set out to make the ultimate biker movie, expanding it into a metaphor for the conditions in America, a culturally and politically torn country. Dennis Hopper, who plays Billy, a reference to Billy the Kid, and Captain America, played by Peter Fonda, are modern desperadoes who have scored a massive amount of cocaine before traveling across America. Jack Nicholson nearly steals the film, playing an alcoholic American Civil Liberties Union lawyer who joins Captain America and Billy on their road trip, during which they experience the prejudice facing the counterculture and, ultimately, death. The cinematography was shot by László Kovács under off-the-cuff circumstances. The editing by Donn Cambern invented a new transition between scenes in which film frames from an outgoing scene were intercut with an incoming scene. *Easy Rider* has a legendary previously recorded song score with contemporary artists such as the Jimi Hendrix Experience, the Band, Steppenwolf, the Byrds, the Electric Prunes, and Bob Dylan. The film also contains a long and vivid acid trip scene in which the main characters and two women they picked up from a brothel take LSD. Such a visually experimental vision had not yet been done in a Hollywood movie. *Easy Rider* also buried the happy ending in place of a new reality. The film was a low-budget production and the reward was a big box office hit. After its financial success, the studios looked for young long-haired directors to make youth films that would bring in *Easy Rider* money.

Three films from the sixties by Hollywood elders who were always ahead of their time kicked off that decade with a premonition of the cinema-changing decade to come. Each of these groundbreakers reveals harsh, realistic, and socially enlightening examples of what American film reality was to be: the horror of violence, the disillusionment, and the moral decline of America. It is significant that the old lead the new—often an occurrence during a renaissance or artistic and cultural upheaval.

Psycho (1960), directed by Alfred Hitchcock, is a graphically violent black-and-white film that explored the psychology of a serial killer who was a twisted version of the boy next door. It contained an iconic set piece early in the picture in which Marion Crane, the main character played by Janet Leigh, was stabbed to death in the shower by Norman Bates, played by Anthony Perkins. It featured an all-strings Bernard Hermann musical score that was as scary as anything in the movie.

John Huston created a model for the dramatic film of the seventies with *The Misfits* (1960). The screenplay was written by distinguished playwright Arthur Miller and starred Hollywood legends: his then-wife Marilyn Monroe, hoping to prove she was a serious actress, and the king of Hollywood, Clark Gable, in his last motion picture appearance. *The Misfits* is a mournful lament for its emotionally lost characters.

Huston, who directed six films during the seventies, searched for the right visual style for each of his movies. Two especially looked like American New Wave films. *Fat City* (1972) was about a down-and-out boxer. Cinematographer Conrad Hall expressed the seedy environment and desperation of the story with lighting and color. *Wise Blood* (1979), adapted from Flannery O'Connor's dark novel, employed the cynicism of the lead character, a religious con man.

Director Billy Wilder, who explored many genres, created an acerbic dramedy about sex and contemporary morals in *The Apartment* (1960). A worker low on the totem pole at a large corporation pushes his way up the corporate ladder by lending out his apartment to company executives for their romantic affairs. Thematically the film was a commentary on urban contemporary society and laid the groundwork for sophisticated and mature movie content that followed.

Other releases during the sixties reveal that American film was changing. *The Hustler*, directed by Robert Rossen, was a black-and-white movie released in 1961 starring Paul Newman, Jackie Gleason, George C. Scott, and Piper Laurie. This gritty movie probes the psychological underpinnings of a pool player with great talent who behaves as if he is unsure whether he is a winner or a loser.

The premise of *Shock Corridor* (1963), directed by Sam Fuller, involves a newspaper journalist who convinces authorities he is insane so he can enter a mental hospital where a murder had taken place in order to solve the crime and win the Pulitzer Prize. He solves the crime but loses his mind in the process. The performances of the inmates are over the top and suit the outrageous narrative. The corridor in the title was where the men congregated and was designed as a metaphor for the depths of the human mind.

In 1966 director John Frankenheimer and veteran master Hollywood cameraman James Wong Howe collaborated on *Seconds*. The duo demonstrated the ability of the camera to distort, contort, and shoot from angles rarely seen on film to capture the story of a man who becomes an unwilling subject for an underground company that transforms older, dissatisfied men into young men. *Seconds* starred John Randolph as the old man looking for eternal youth and, in atypical casting, Rock Hudson as his youthful counterpart.

In Cold Blood, a nonfiction novel by Truman Capote, would seem impossible to adapt with integrity. It was the true story of a brutal, senseless murder committed by two men in rural Kansas. True stories had been filmed often in Hollywood but usually with dramatic alteration. Actors Scott Wilson and Robert Blake as the killers are realistic and chilling. Director Richard Brooks and innovative cameraman Conrad Hall collaborated on the 1967 film, shot in black and white and in the actual Kansas house where the murders occurred. The film challenges the viewer's perceptions of a fictional movie and documentary starkness.

Medium Cool, written, directed, and photographed by Hollywood cameraman Haskell Wexler, was released in 1968. A politically engaged activist, Wexler strongly sensed the dramatic events that would unfold at the Democratic National Convention held in Chicago during the summer of 1968. President Johnson, waylaid by the turmoil during the Vietnam War, announced he would not run for another term. Protests were planned and record crowds were expected. The largely peaceful protesters were met by violence from Mayor Richard Daley's police force. The mayhem was caught live on network television. *Medium Cool* is about the relationship between a cameraman and what he is filming. Wexler put his crew and cast into the middle of the actual events, armed with his handheld camera, shooting film amid the tear gas and violence, with everyone in peril. *Medium Cool* is part fiction with strong elements of Direct Cinema. The immediacy of *Medium Cool* shocked and educated audiences about the new political reality and inspired filmmakers.

The Western was a popular genre during the Classical Hollywood period but eventually fell out of favor because modern audiences in the early seventies couldn't relate to the beginnings of our country portrayed as poetic and mythic rather than the dangerous place it really was. Eventually a subgenre, the revisionist Western was created in the seventies, such as Peter Fonda's *The Hired Hand* (1971) and Dennis Hopper's *The Last Movie* (1971).

John Cassavetes, the father of independent filmmaking, took roles in many studio films, including *The Dirty Dozen* (1967) to finance his films. Cassavetes paid for everything out of pocket and often used his own home (mortgaged several times) as a set for idiosyncratic films. He trained a group of actors who worked in an improvisational or semi-improvisational style. He developed his own aesthetic methods influenced in part by cinema verité/Direct Cinema. On his productions he tried, with everything in his creative and artistic power, to work against what Hollywood considered proper moviemaking. He strived to capture the unexpected. He often manned a handheld camera, moving all over the set to explore the faces and emotions created by the actors. He was fascinated by the common man and woman, and his films are among the most truthful about the human condition.

In 1970 Cassavetes directed himself in *Husbands* with costars Ben Gazzara and Peter Falk. *Husbands* concerns three friends who experience a midlife crisis triggered by the death of a mutual friend. Cassavetes directed *Minnie and Moskowitz* (1971), an unconventional romantic comedy between a female museum curator and a hippie car attendant, and *A Woman under the Influence* (1974), about a woman struggling with her perceived craziness and her everyday reality, played by his wife and muse Gena Rowlands. Cassavetes next directed *The Killing of a Chinese Bookie* (1976), starring Ben Gazzara as an unconventional strip club owner who runs up a big debt to mobsters. Cassavetes finished out the seventies as a director with *Opening Night* (1977), in which an actress is sent into an emotional tailspin after she is involved in an accident that kills a young female fan. During that decade, John Cassavetes continued taking acting assignments to finance his own films, including *Two-Minute Warning* (1976).

Wanda, directed by Barbara Loden, was a revelation when it opened in 1970—independent films directed by women were nearly nonexistent. Loden stated that the story wasn't autobiographical but inspired by a newspaper article she carried with her for years about a woman who thanked a judge for sentencing her to twenty years in prison for her participation in a bank robbery. Her jail sentence took her away from a sad life that plagued her. Although Loden had gained attention as an actress on stage and screen, she suffered a great sense of loneliness and detachment throughout her life. She did not want the film made at a studio because she knew she would have to give up control of the project. She financed it through a wealthy friend, Harry Shuster. The low budget she asked for was $115,000. She approached several male directors but felt that none really understood this complex female character. She decided to direct the film herself, even though she had never directed a movie before. *Wanda* was shot on 16mm film in what is known as run-and-gun or guerrilla filmmaking style, in which the filmmakers work fast, often on location, with an emphasis on truth over cinematic aesthetics. She hired Nicholas T. Proferes, a young man with many movie skills, especially cinematography and editing, crafts he performed on *Wanda*. The credits clearly identify that the film is by Barbara Loden, but on a separate card it states, "with Nicholas T. Proferes." This does not necessarily mean that *Wanda* was codirected, but that a continuous dialogue took place between Loden and Proferes. The story resonates because of the emotional detail Barbara Loden brings to Wanda's characterization and startling realism with which she is brought to life.

Wanda is an unhappy housewife who divorces her husband and relinquishes her rights to her children. She loses her job. After a one-night stand, Wanda is abandoned, broke, and robbed in a movie theater. She goes to a bar and mistakes a hold-up man, Norman Dennis, for the bartender. He convinces her to participate in a bank robbery. Norman is killed by the police. After hitching a ride, a man attempts to sexually assault Wanda. In a raucous roadhouse, strangers supply her with food, alcohol, and cigarettes. As the camera isolates Wanda looking disoriented, emotionally, and spiritually lost, the image freezes, stopping her in time. Ending films with a freeze frame was common during the seventies either because the filmmakers were not sure how to conclude a film or because they wanted to leave the future of the story up to the viewer. In *Wanda* Barbara Loden wants the audience to understand that this character is aimless and doomed to make the same mistakes. *Wanda* is an early landmark of contemporary women's cinema.

No one has done more to advance the creation of youth exploitation genre movies, the independent film industry, and seventies filmmaking than Roger Corman. He was a prolific producer and director who distributed an abundant roster of exploitation films fast and cheap. The real heart of Corman's success was a formula he demanded of all his directors. At specific intervals in a film's timeline, there had to be acts of violence, sex, nudity or the possibility of nudity, as well as car chases, fights, and explosions. Roger Corman understood his under-thirty youth audience and calculated what to give them. Corman's cut-to-the-bone production methods brought in films in record time.

Roger Corman made sub-low-budget monster and science fiction movies, biker movies, exploitation crime flicks, beach romps, and a cycle of films inspired by horror master Edgar Allan Poe. The drive-in was a prime venue for Corman movies. Young filmmakers flocked to him in hopes of making movies of their own. Students of Corman—often referred to as the Roger Corman school of filmmaking—worked for him for little or no money on practically anything he offered, in any capacity, including a list of countless actors and craftspeople that reads like a New Wave and seventies American film roster: Peter Bogdanovich, Francis Ford Coppola, Joe Dante, Robert De Niro, Jonathan Demme, Ron Howard, Jonathan Kaplan, László Kovács, Jack Nicholson, John Sayles, Martin Scorsese, Robert Towne, Vilmos Zsigmond, and many others who were given their first shot in the film business by Roger Corman.

Roger Corman was the top director and producer for American International Pictures, always reliable, grinding out picture after teen picture. He had an unfailing ability to give the youth audience just what they wanted by delivering genres ignored by the establishment. As an independent, Corman has one of the most extensive résumés in Hollywood history, and he claimed in his autobiography that no picture ever lost a dime. From 1955 to the end of the 1970s, he produced as many as fifty movies not including his directing credits. In 1970 Corman founded New World Pictures, responsible for and including *Bloody Mama* (1970), *Private Duty Nurse* (1971), *Death Race 2000* (1975), *Piranha* (1978), and *Rock 'n' Roll High School* (1979), and he bought the American rights to distribute the films of European masters Ingmar Bergman's *Cries and Whispers* (1972), Federico Fellini's *Amacord* (1973), and François Truffaut's *The Story of Adele H* (1975).

American International Pictures (AIP) was formed in 1954 by James H. Nicholson and Samuel Z. Arkoff to make movies for the youth market that rebelled against the Classical Hollywood Studio System. Arkoff's formula for low-budget filmmaking included violence, sex appeal, and controversial themes. The company developed a so-called Peter Pan syndrome, analyzing the market by examining the screening habits of young audiences and female viewers. After reviewing what young groups would and would not watch, it concluded that the nineteen-year-old male audience should be the target for low-budget films.

Director Bob Rafelson and producer Bert Schneider founded the production company Raybert and produced the television series *The Monkees*, which was an American take on *A Hard Day's Night* (1964) and *Help!* (1965), both featuring the Beatles. The show ran only two seasons (1966–1968) but made a lot of money for Raybert. Rafelson and Schneider also created a Monkees feature film, *Head* (1968), written by Jack Nicholson and directed by Bob Rafelson, described as a psychedelic deconstruction of the television show. Schneider and Rafelson then financed *Easy Rider* for Fonda and Hopper, who were having trouble financing the project. In 1970 Schneider and Rafelson produced *Five Easy Pieces*, directed by Rafelson, took on another partner, Stephen Blauner, and expanded their independent production company now named BBS Productions. In 1971 they sold their outstanding shares to Columbia Pictures. They had an arrangement with Columbia Pictures to distribute their films, and the studio would have no influence over production if the budgets came in under a million dollars. The films are part of the essential history of the American New Wave: *Five Easy Pieces* Rafelson (1970), *Drive, He Said* Jack Nicholson (1971), *A Safe Place* Henry Jaglom (1971), *The Last Movie* Dennis Hopper (1971), *The King of Marvin Gardens* Rafelson (1971), and *The Last Picture Show* Peter Bogdanovich (1971). BBS is another example of how filmmakers in the seventies managed to get personal films completed and distributed by traditional Hollywood without any interference.

Robert Altman founded Lion's Gate, which featured state-of-the-art sound facilities that were used for films Altman directed, including *Brewster McCloud* (1970), *Images* (1972), *The Long Goodbye* (1973), and *Welcome to L.A.* (1978) directed by Alan Rudolph.

American Zoetrope (named after an early film device) first produced Francis Ford Coppola's *The Rain People* (1969) then the George Lucas film *THX 1138* (1971) and *American Graffiti* (1973), then Coppola's *The Godfather: Part II* (1974) and *Apocalypse Now* (1979).

George Lucas opened his own shop, Lucasfilm Ltd., in 1971. Later ventures included Skywalker Ranch for top-of-the-craft film sound and Industrial Light and Magic (ILM), a state-of-the-art visual effects house. Lucasfilm Ltd. produced *Star Wars* and *Indiana Jones and the Raiders of the Lost Ark*. Top filmmakers enhanced their movies in those facilities.

When Universal Studios learned that *Easy Rider* was such a box office bonanza, it wanted part of the action. Executive Ned Tanen headed the Universal Studios Young Filmmakers Program, which searched for young filmmakers to make movies that it would finance for less than a million dollars in hopes history would repeat itself. The list contained many significant seventies films but few moneymakers except for George Lucas's *American Graffiti* (1973). Others included *Diary of a Mad Housewife* Frank Perry (1970), *Taking Off* Miloš Forman (1971), *The Hired Hand* Peter Fonda (1971), *The Last Movie* Dennis Hopper (1971), *Silent Running* Douglas Trumbull (1972), and *Two-Lane Blacktop* Monte Hellman (1972). Although the intention of Universal's program was more financial than artistic, the reality was that despite losing money on many of these projects, Universal contributed to the artistic achievements of the American New Wave. It would have been difficult if not impossible to have greenlighted Dennis Hopper's sophomore directorial effort *The Last Movie* (1971), a film in which Hopper explained that he applied the cinematic medium the way expressionist painters used paint.

Genres developed and ripened during the seventies and included the road movie, which takes place during a long car ride, often cross-country, in which the characters go through a deep self-examination.

Blaxploitation was a subgenre of the exploitation film that was popular during the 1970s. Generally, these films were produced on a low budget and only the on-screen talent were black—the crew was white because blacks had been shut out by the industry or hadn't been developed at the time. Their purpose was to provide African American audiences with prototypical characters ignored by conventional Classical Hollywood. Many were action films in which the lead was a hero or antihero, often bigger than life. Types included urban heroes and crime figures and featured violent engagements, sex, and savagery. Primarily, they were black versions of tried-and-true exploitation themes and formats. Many of the African American actors were known sports figures, such as football great Jim Brown. The female characters were strong and capable of dealing with any situation. There were many franchises and a Caucasian crossover audience. There were detective characters but also pimps and underworld types shown in a glamorous and sometimes heroic light, which caused some controversy and negative criticism. Blaxploitation developed its own star system; popular actors included Richard Roundtree, Pam Grier, and Fred Williamson. Some blaxploitation films include *Super Fly*, directed by Gordon Parks Jr. (1972), about a pimp and drug dealer trying to go straight; *Blacula* (1972), directed by William Crain and starring William Marshall, about the vampire legend; Larry Cohen's *Black Caesar* (1973), a remake of *Little Caesar*; the Edward G. Robinson crime classic, *Foxy Brown*; Jack Hill (1974) starring Pam Grier as a nurse who gets revenge on a drug ring for killing her boyfriend, an undercover policeman; and *Truck Turner* (1974), directed by Jonathan Kaplan, with superstar soul singer Isaac Hayes as Mac "Truck" Turner as a pro football player who becomes a bounty hunter. Themes and content covered in blaxploitation included the impact of narcotics in black communities, oppression of black culture and history, and black nationalism.

The antihero dramas were movies with a male lead who had a complex personality, neither all good nor all bad, and often fought against the traditional system and turmoil within themselves. Jack Nicholson almost singlehandedly dominated this character type in the seventies with *Five Easy Pieces* (1970), *The Last Detail* (1973), and *Chinatown* (1974). Other antihero performers were Clint Eastwood and Al Pacino.

The adult film, both explicit pornography and a softcore format, entered an arty realm containing plots with less graphic imagery. It was now marketed to couples and shown at many local movie theaters far away from New York City's Times Square. These films were also called "porno chic." Some multiplex theaters, formerly single movie houses divided into several venues under one roof, often dedicated one screen to adult films during the seventies. Director Gerard Damiano caused a sensation with *Deep Throat* (1972), a hardcore film with an outrageous premise but better acting than most early porn films. It brought in $50 million. Radley Metzger's *Score* (1974) moved back and forth between the softcore art film and those classified as hardcore. With the advent of videotape in the late seventies, this genre was abandoned by movie theaters. Russ Meyer saw himself as a satirist who skewered American morality with films that featured very well-endowed, mostly naked women. Twentieth Century

Fox became interested in Meyer and hired him to make a sequel to the hit film *Valley of the Dolls* (1967). He and his scenarist film critic Roger Ebert turned the original upside down in *Beyond the Valley of the Dolls* (1970) but it did not provide enough of the typical Meyer filmmaking. The picture made money, but Meyer's adaptation of the Irving Wallace bestseller *The Seven Minutes* in 1971 failed at the box office. Russ Meyer went back to the films for which he was known best.

Disaster movies centered around a catastrophic event, such as a burning high-rise building, an earthquake, or an upturned sunken luxury ship, and the struggle for survival, such as *The Poseidon Adventure* (1972), *Earthquake* (1974), and *The Towering Inferno* (1975). Kung fu movies were light on plot and heavy on realistic martial arts fighting. Although he made but a handful of movies during his short life, Bruce Lee was a major icon and star in this popular action-driven genre and dominated this market during the seventies.

No Wave cinema was a brief underground movement that began in 1976. Very often shot in Super 8mm, the films were projected in less than prestigious venues during off-hours. No Wave films included Scott B and Beth B's *The Offenders* (1979), Vivienne Dick's *She Had Her Gun Already* (1978), and Amos Poe's *Night Lunch* (1975).

Without a studio system with a steady source of financing, production and postproduction were no longer standardized. Amid the horror of war in Vietnam, film art flourished. Old Hollywood was vanishing, but as 1969 surrendered the decade, 1970 emerged with the recognition that a change was coming.

The war in Vietnam was a seminal event in contemporary American history. From the early 1960s to 1975, American involvement in Vietnam escalated and left an estimated 58,202 deaths, 304,704 wounded, and 2,646 missing in action. The under-thirty generation was especially fervent in its rage against the war. For most of the seventies, Hollywood was apprehensive about how American moviegoers would react to subject matter about an unpopular war. There were not many movies about Vietnam until late in the decade. The pivotal year was 1978, when films were released that asked vital questions about war, peace, and patriotism. They expressed counterculture views and demands for a new way of life.

In the early seventies, only two films referred to the Vietnam War. *The Losers* (1970), also known as *'Nam's Angels*, directed by Jack Starrett (*Cleopatra Jones* [1973], *Race with the Devil* [1975]), is about a group of Hells Angels–style bikers who are sent on a mission to a Cambodian jungle to rescue an American diplomat/ CIA agent. The biker gang, under the command of an army general, is made up of Vietnam veterans. Driving their bikes through the jungle, they pull off the rescue. Later, the film was an inspiration to John Milius, an American New Wave writer/director in developing the screenplay for *Apocalypse Now*.

There Is No 13 (1974), directed by William Sachs, is a surrealistic approach to a Vietnam veteran who remembers the twelve women he has been with.

When Hollywood ultimately took the chance, the films were bold and examined the war straight on; the results were sobering, numbing, and conveyed deep sadness for the incalculable losses for those who fought, for those at home, and for the country.

2

1970

April 10: The Beatles break up. . . . May 4: The Ohio National Guard opened fire on a student protest rally at Kent State University to express opposition to the Vietnam War, killing four and injuring nine. . . . October 5: Public Broadcasting Service (PBS) debuts commercial, educational, children's, and cultural programs as distinct alternative to the three major networks, ABC, CBS, and NBC.

January 1970 clearly augurs a new era in American film. The year was filled with innovative movies and new filmmakers. The movie generation took the Hollywood movies they had watched when they were young and turned them upside down and inside out and they became something else—subgenres that reflected their times.

Reinventing and subverting genres from the Classical Hollywood era was an essential element of the American New Wave. *M*A*S*H* (1970), directed by Robert Altman, was a service comedy that took place during the Korean War at a hospital unit. Altman intended the film as a sharp criticism of the Vietnam War, which was raging at the time of its release. Placing the film in Korea (as was the 1968 novel it is based on) avoided controversy, although Altman was pressured to acknowledge its true target by putting into the film what was practically a billboard announcing the location. The large cast included David Arkin, René Auberjonois, Bud Cort, Elliot Gould, Sally Kellerman, Michael Murphy, John Schuck, and Tom Skerritt, some of whom became part of Altman's ensemble while others launched their careers through this vehicle. The characters are part of a medical unit tending to the wounded and dying and are

Jack Nicholson in *Five Easy Pieces*. *Columbia Pictures/Photofest* © *Columbia Pictures*

irreverent and outrageous. Albeit a comedy, it is very dark, with bloody scenes of death in the operating area. The filmmaking deftly handles multiple storylines and a range of relationships at a skillful pace.

The director of photography was Harold E. Stein, who was behind the camera for the disaster picture *The Poseidon Adventure* (1972). The production designer was Arthur Lonergan, whose eighty-three credits include TV and feature films such as *Forbidden Planet* (1956) and *Red Line 7000* (1965), directed by Howard Hawks. The editor was Danford B. Greene, who in 1969 cut Altman's *That Cold Day in the Park* and Mel Brooks's 1974 laugh riot *Blazing Saddles*.

Robert Altman directed thirteen feature films during the seventies. He repurposed the zoom lens and employed the long focus lens to flatten images, compressing the levels of action from front to back, so the depth was no longer a distraction and the front plane received the audience's full attention. Altman changed the way films sounded by utilizing separate microphones for each actor. In Old Hollywood, the studios discouraged overlapping dialogue, but Altman encouraged it because it reflected real life.

Hungarian-born cinematographer Vilmos Zsigmond defined cinematography for the American New Wave. He photographed ten motion pictures during the seventies beginning with *McCabe & Mrs. Miller* (1971) directed by Robert Altman, *Images* (1972), and *The Long Goodbye* (1973), again for Altman. He worked with major directors of the 1970s including John Boorman (*Deliverance*, 1972), Jerry Schatzberg (*Scarecrow*, 1973), Mark Rydell (*Cinderella Liberty*, 1973), Steven Spielberg (*The Sugarland Express*, 1974), Brian DePalma (*Obsession*, 1976), and Michael Cimino (*The Deer Hunter*, 1978). A true companion and collaborator, Zsigmond moved the camera artfully and often and brought a European sensibility to every film he shot. Of the many aspects of his cinematography that made a lasting impact, the concept of flashing became part of a director of photography's toolbox during the seventies. The film stock was exposed to light before it was loaded into the film magazine, and a panel painted with a light, warm tone was photographed, resulting in a soft, painterly effect.

Versatile Canadian-born Donald Sutherland acted in more than twenty-five films during the seventies including *M*A*S*H*, *Klute* (1972), *Don't Look Now* (1973), *The Day of the Locust* (1975), *1900* (1976), and *National Lampoon's Animal House* (1978). Sutherland brought a strong physical presence to his roles, a full, resonant voice, and a keen intensity.

Brewster McCloud was Robert Altman's take on the screwball comedy with an experimental and absurdist sensibility. The film features a young man who is building wings so that he can fly. Living on the lower level of the Houston Astrodome, he develops a relationship with an idiosyncratic woman played by Altman regular Shelley Duvall. There is a side movie in which a quirky lecturer (René Auberjonois) talks to the camera about birds and eventually turns into one. *Brewster McCloud* signaled that Robert Altman was going to walk down many cinematic avenues.

Bud Cort, who played the title role in *Brewster McCloud*, was discovered by Robert Altman, who cast him in *M*A*S*H*. Cort immediately established his presence as a misunderstood youth; he looked the part, with a perennial confused facial expression and a delivery that sounded as if he was talking to himself even when he was not. His signature performance came in 1971 with the title role in *Harold and Maude*, directed by

Hal Ashby, as a boy obsessed with death who develops a relationship with a woman the age of his grandmother.

Shelley Duvall was discovered by Robert Altman and was featured in seven of his films. Duvall was a New Wave star. Tall and thin, she was an outsider with a big toothy smile and a kind voice. Although she worked with other directors, most notably Stanley Kubrick on *The Shining* (1980), it was her performances in Robert Altman's films that made her a standout in American seventies cinema.

Lou Lombardo edited five films for Robert Altman in the seventies, including *Brewster McCloud*. In 1970 he cut *The Ballad of Cable Hogue* (1970) for Sam Peckinpah. He had a freewheeling style that flowed for new narrative constructions perfect for seventies films.

In *Five Easy Pieces*, we learn that the title refers to an instruction book for piano beginners. Jack Nicholson, who worked in low-rent movies for a decade until he broke through in *Easy Rider* as a Southern alcoholic American Civil Liberty Union lawyer George Hanson, plays Bobby Dupea, who comes from a wealthy family of classical musicians whom he abandons for a blue-collar existence. The film traces his search for identity, beginning with his job as an oil rigger, to a family confrontation at his home with his dying father, and finally to his solitary journey on the road to continue his search. Directed by Bob Rafelson, the film signifies seventies cinema in content, tone, and style. Nicholson's portrayal is one of the defining roles of the decade and solidifies the antihero, first identified by Paul Newman in the sixties in films such as *Hud* (1963). His encounter with a surly waitress is part of seventies cinema history. Released at the very beginning of the decade, *Five Easy Pieces* positioned Jack Nicholson to become one of the most essential actors of the seventies.

Actress Karen Black appeared in the 1960 movie *The Prime Time*. In *You're a Big Boy Now* (1966), directed by Francis Ford Coppola, she played a woman with a crush on the lead character. During the same year she played a prostitute in *Hard Contract*, directed by S. Lee Pogostin. In 1969 she won notice in the third act of *Easy Rider*, cast as a prostitute who goes on an elaborate LSD trip with Captain America and Billy. In *Five Easy Pieces* she portrays Bobby's prole girlfriend Rayette who doesn't fit in with his family. Karen Black created distinctive characters in numerous other appearances during the seventies including *Cisco Pike* (directed by B. L. Norton, 1971), *Drive, He Said* (Jack Nicholson, 1971),

The Great Gatsby (Jack Clayton, 1974), *The Day of the Locust* (John Schlesinger, 1975), and *Family Plot* (Alfred Hitchcock, 1976).

Five Easy Pieces was shot by László Kovács, who escaped his native Hungary with fellow countryman Vilmos Zsigmond. Both men dominated the decade with innovative cinematography. Kovács was a major director of photography during the seventies, photographing numerous pictures with various American New Wave and other directors. He was versatile and quick to recognize a good shot, angle, or moment. In addition to Rafelson, Kovacs worked with Paul Mazursky on *Alex in Wonderland* (1970), Dennis Hopper on *The Last Movie* (1971), Peter Bogdanovich on *What's up Doc?* (1972), Richard Rush on *Freebie and the Bean* (1974), Hal Ashby on *Shampoo* (1975), and Martin Scorsese on *New York, New York* (1977). Toby Carr Rafelson served as the production designer working with her ex-husband on *Five Easy Pieces* and *Stay Hungry* in 1976. Coeditor Christophe Holmes's long postproduction credits include *Drive, He Said* (1971), Jack Nicholson's directorial debut, and with editor Gerald Shepard, who worked with Rafelson on the TV series *The Monkees*.

After working as a story editor in New York and an associate producer in Hollywood, Bob Rafelson formed Raybert Productions with Bert Schneider, and they created the American answer to *The Beatles—The Monkees* (1966–1968). The television series led to *Head* (1968), a psychedelic-oriented feature film written by Jack Nicholson, who displayed his considerable talent as a screenwriter. *The King of Marvin Gardens* (1972) was a well-crafted art film about two brothers at opposite poles, and *Stay Hungry* (1976) was a quirky comedy about bodybuilding, ruthless real estate agents, and an offbeat romance between characters played by Sally Field and Jeff Bridges. Rafelson and Schneider brought friend Steve Blauner onto their team and turned Raybert into BBS productions, which supported key films in the seventies including *The Last Picture Show* (1971), directed by Peter Bogdanovich.

One of the first major rock concerts on film was *Monterey Pop*, released in 1967, which presented acts as diverse as the Who, Otis Redding, the Mamas and the Papas, and sitar master Ravi Shankar. Held in California and masterfully filmed by D. A. Pennebaker and a team of adroit documentary filmmakers with a great affinity for the music, it opened the door to the rock concert film subcategory, which continued into the seventies with vehicles such as *The Last Waltz* (1978). Others included

Wattstax (1973), held by Stax records to commemorate the 1965 Watts riots, *The Song Remains the Same* (1976), featuring Led Zeppelin, and *The Kids Are Alright* (1979), highlighting the Who.

The Woodstock Music and Arts Festival, held in 1969 with the epic documentary film released in 1970, was the counterculture's answer to a new way of living in peace and harmony. It defined a generation. *Woodstock* was directed by Michael Wadleigh, and at a running length of just over three hours, it featured one of the greatest presentations of rock acts in history, including Jefferson Airplane, Joe Cocker and the Grease Band, Jimi Hendrix, Santana, and the Who. Martin Scorsese's longtime editor Thelma Schoonmaker led the postproduction team with inventive editing. Multiple screens within the frame were employed to display the massive amount of impressive footage captured by the team of cinematographers in order to create interplay between the musicians, performers, and the estimated half-million young people watching them. Postproduction was on film; therefore, opticals were lined up by eye and completed in a laboratory. The documentary included interviews with a range of participants. *Woodstock* won the Academy Award for Best Documentary and the unique project retains the spirit of peace and love that encompassed one of the biggest gatherings of all time.

Woodstock opened in March 1970. *Gimme Shelter* was released in December 1970, allowing viewers to witness events that occurred less than half a year after Woodstock and try to process how peace and love turned into violence and death. *Gimme Shelter*, a concert film about a Rolling Stones tour, demonstrated that documentaries needed to follow the story wherever it took them. Directed by Albert and David Maysles and edited by Charlotte Zwerin, who made a major contribution during postproduction, the film documented the senseless violence at the Altamont Speedway in Tracy, California, in all its fury. The Hells Angels motorcycle gang was given cases of beer and decided to arm themselves with pool sticks filled with lead. They had been assigned as security at the overcrowded venue in California when bedlam broke out and a man was killed. Multiple cameras rolled from all angles. *Gimme Shelter* exemplifies creativity in presenting a true story. The editing room sequences where Mick Jagger watches the film in progress are a window into flashbacks of the concert. The shots of the legendary front man as he viewed the footage attempted to show his reaction to what had happened and to pierce his inner thoughts. It is rare that filmmakers capture a murder on film. The handling of the footage on the editing table, including freeze-frames at key moments, makes it all too deadly clear that the viewer is witnessing the end of peace and love in the sixties. *Gimme Shelter* was released on the anniversary of the tragic event, December 6, 1970.

Paul Mazursky's career began as an actor, appearing in Stanley Kubrick's first feature film, *Fear and Desire* (1953), and then as one of the students in *Blackboard Jungle* (1955). In 1965 he collaborated with Larry Tucker, his writing partner, to create the pilot for *The Monkees*. He received attention in 1969 with his first feature *Bob & Carol & Ted & Alice*, a film about fidelity, infidelity, and a foursome among friends. A new sexual lifestyle is explored in the film, which showed that the audience was open enough to embrace an adult comedy about sex. As a director, Paul Mazursky had a sense for social satire. *Alex in Wonderland* (1970) studies a film director tormented about the topic of his next film, mimicking in spirit Federico Fellini's masterpiece *8½* (1963). Although not a strong visual stylist, Mazursky was pure New Hollywood in theme and approach to narrative and character. *Blume in Love* (1973) was considered a notable film by critics who reacted positively to the way Mazursky handled male-female relationships and the theme of self-discovery. *Harry & Tonto* (1974) is an offbeat road movie for which Art Carney won a best actor Oscar for his portrayal of a dislocated elder and his cat, Tonto. *Next Stop, Greenwich Village* (1976) takes place in 1953 and follows an aspiring young actor who leaves Brooklyn and winds up living in the Village with an eccentric group of his peers. *An Unmarried Woman* (1978), starring Jill Clayburgh, probed the sexual revolution, the plight of women in the seventies, and the mounting number of divorces during the decade.

An Unmarried Woman was photographed by Arthur J. Ornitz, who shot nine films during the seventies including *Minnie and Moskowitz* (directed by John Cassavetes, 1971), *Serpico* (Sidney Lumet, 1973), and *Next Stop, Greenwich Village*, in 1976, also for Mazursky. The production designer was Pato Guzman, who had worked with Paul Mazursky on his directorial debut, *Bob & Carol & Ted & Alice* in 1969.

It would have been unlikely in 1970 to adapt a novel by a postmodern metafiction novelist such as John Barth, but noted film editor Aram Avakian, who worked with Arthur Penn on *Mickey One* (1965) and Francis Ford Coppola on *You're a Big Boy Now* (1966), did just that. *End of the Road* concerns Jacob Horner (Stacy Keach), a young man who has a catatonic episode on a train platform and is taken to an unconventional asylum where he is cured, becomes a lecturer, and begins a disastrous affair with the wife of a colleague.

Joe, directed by John G. Avildsen, gained a lot of attention because of its anti-hippie stance. A well-off advertising man, Bill Compton (Dennis Patrick), kills his daughter Melissa's boyfriend when he learns that the boyfriend was responsible for her drug overdose. Compton later meets Joe Curran (Peter Boyle), a factory worker who rants about hating hippies. Melissa (Susan Sarandon in her first film role) escapes from the hospital and overhears that her dad murdered her boyfriend. She flees and Joe and her father search for her, meeting two hippies and their girlfriends. At an apartment, Joe and Compton are robbed and one of the hippies' girlfriends is beaten until she tells them where Melissa's boyfriend may be. At a commune Compton accidentally kills his own daughter. Joe reflected the hatred of youth culture by some parts of society. Joe is not film art or part of the New Wave except in its contemporary look at youth culture. Joe presented content without cinematic vision or subtlety. It is a film that went against the principles of the under-thirty generation. The low-budget production, which struck a chord with the middle class who reacted negatively to the counterculture, was shot by director John G. Avildsen, who photographed many of his own films. George T. Norris edited Joe as well as light sexploitation films.

After Joe, John G. Avildsen directed Cry Uncle! (1971), a low-budget film with a lot of sex and nudity. Also in 1971, Avildsen made another excursion into the counterculture with Okay Bill, about a stockbroker who ventures into hippie culture. Save the Tiger (1973) starred Jack Lemmon as a garment industry executive struggling with contemporary life. Lemmon won an Academy Award for his performance. In 1976 Avildsen hit movie gold with Rocky, which was nominated for ten Oscars and won three, for editing, best picture, and best director. It is one of the most popular and successful boxing pictures of all time and was followed by seven sequels. It launched the unknown Sylvester Stallone, who starred as Rocky and wrote the screenplay, into superstardom.

Peter Boyle, star of Joe, appeared in nineteen motion pictures during the seventies. Three of his most memorable roles are as the heady Wizard in Taxi Driver (1976), directed by Martin Scorsese, especially for the street scene in which he tries to philosophize with Robert De Niro's Travis Bickle to raise his spirits; as the Monster in Young Frankenstein

(1974), directed by Mel Brooks; and as the sleazy private investigator in Paul Schrader's *Hardcore* (1979).

Susan Sarandon would go on to a career that spanned the seventies and continues in the 2020s. Her credits during the seventies continued with *Lovin' Molly* (directed by Sidney Lumet, 1974), *The Front Page* (Billy Wilder, 1974), *The Great Waldo Pepper* (George Roy Hill, 1975), *The Rocky Horror Picture Show* (Jim Sharman, 1975), *Pretty Baby* (Louis Malle, 1978), and *King of the Gypsies* (Frank Pierson, 1978).

The Strawberry Statement is an adaptation of the 1968 memoir *The Strawberry Statement: Notes of a College Revolutionary* by James S. Kunen. The events in the book follow student protests at New York's Columbia University in reaction to the school's involvement with a government institute for defense analysis. Irwin Winkler and Bob Chartoff, who later had great success with *Rocky* (1976), bought the property because they felt it was a way of bridging the generation gap—explaining how a regular young man became a revolutionary. MGM decided to change the location from Columbia to a school in California. François Truffaut was offered to direct but refused. Stuart Hagmann, a television director, was given the job, and the screenplay was written by noted playwright Israel Horovitz, who struggled with many drafts and fought the studio, which kept diluting and cutting the story line. *The Strawberry Statement* is still an example of youth culture content in the seventies, but the severe changes imposed by the studio made the end product more Old Hollywood than New Hollywood.

In addition, the winning team of Winkler and Chartoff produced many other movies in the seventies including *The Gang That Couldn't Shoot Straight* (directed by James Goldstone, 1971), *The Gambler* (Karel Reisz, 1974), and *Comes a Horseman* (Alan J. Pakula, 1978).

The Revolutionary, directed by Paul Williams, also focused on a student's journey into political radicalism, a more extreme case of a bomber. The time and place are not specific, but it is contemporary. The central role, known simply as "A," was played by Jon Voight. In 1972 Williams directed *Dealing: Or the Berkeley-to-Boston Forty Brick Lost-Bag Blues*, an independent film featuring John Lithgow in his first film role and Barbara Hershey, whose character loses forty bricks of marijuana on a cross-country flight. Also in 1972, Williams directed *Nunzio*, about a grown man with the demeanor of a child who lives with his mother. The title role is played by David Proval, who would have a significant role in Martin Scorsese's *Mean Streets* (1973).

In 1969 Jon Voight was cast as Joe Buck in *Midnight Cowboy*, a naive, good-looking young man from Texas who travels to New York to hustle women and improve his lot. He and costar Dustin Hoffman delivered Academy Award–nominated performances. Voight was a strong actor with considerable technical skills and a natural ability to bring emotional life to a character. Voight appeared in *Catch-22* as the World War II supreme entrepreneur Milo Minderbinder (1970); in *Deliverance* (1972)—along with Burt Reynolds, Ned Beatty, and Ronny Cox—as Ed, a gentle man whose life is changed by a canoe trip in the northern Georgia wilderness; and in *The All-American Boy* (1973) as a young man with great potential who walks away from it all. In *Conrack* (1974), he played Pat Conroy, who is assigned to teach poor black children in the South. Jon Voight won an Academy Award for his searing portrayal of a wheelchair-bound Vietnam vet in *Coming Home* (1978) and closed out the decade in a remake of *The Champ* (1979), portraying boxer Billy Flynn.

In *Puzzle of a Downfall Child*, Faye Dunaway gives an all-out emotional performance as Lou Andreas Sand, a former fashion model who spirals into drugs and experiences a mental collapse. Director Jerry Schatzberg was a top fashion photographer and worked with fifties model Anne St. Marie when she was in decline. The complex narrative structure has its genesis in tapes he made of St. Marie. In 1973 Schatzberg directed *Scarecrow*, featuring Al Pacino and Gene Hackman as vagabonds who leave California for Pittsburgh to start a car wash business. They are waylaid as Pacino's character attempts to reconnect with his ex-wife and his young child. The detour goes awry, and the men's relationship deteriorates. Schatzberg's last film of the seventies was the political drama *The Seduction of Joe Tynan* in 1979, a political drama starring Alan Alda as a senator in conflict.

Al Pacino has an eight-film résumé during the seventies alone that contains some of the strongest portrayals of the decade. After *The Panic in Needle Park* (1971), Al Pacino's professional and private life changed forever when he was cast as Michael Corleone in Francis Ford Coppola's *The Godfather* (1972), the son who wasn't meant to be involved in the family business but would be totally. In 1973 Pacino played real-life figure Frank Serpico in *Serpico*, an honest cop in a corrupt district, directed by Sidney Lumet. In 1973 he costarred with Gene Hackman in

Scarecrow (directed by Jerry Schatzberg), playing Francis Lionel "Lion" Delbuchi, a child-like ex-sailor. *Godfather: Part II* (1974) continued Michael Corleone's descent as he ran the family's operation while distancing himself from those around him. In 1975 Pacino took on the true story of Sonny Wortzik in *Dog Day Afternoon*, who robbed a bank to pay for the sex reassignment surgery of his male lover. His performance is mesmerizing, full of energy, pathos, fear, and bravado. This was another outing with director Sidney Lumet.

Trash was directed by Paul Morrissey, who was the film director associated with Andy Warhol. *Trash* had a general release and received critical and audience attention. Joe Dalessandro, a Warhol underground superstar, plays Joe, a heroin addict on a quest to score more drugs. His sexually frustrated girlfriend is played by another Warhol superstar, Holly Woodlawn. The acting in the film is flat and amateurish, as are the production values. Warhol moved from limited venues to the distribution of films in neighborhood theaters without totally losing his vision of life in New York and America in general.

African American filmmaker Melvin Van Peebles made a series of short films, *Pickup Men for Herrick* (1957), *Sunlight* (1957), and *Cinq cent balles* (1963). He traveled to New York but was unable to find anyone who would hire him as a director; a man who saw his shorts wanted to screen them in Paris. Van Peebles was invited to France by Henri Langlois, archivist of the Cinématèque française. In 1968 he directed his first feature film, *The Story of a Three-Day Pass*, the story of a black U.S. Army soldier who is promoted and receives a three-day pass. He meets a white woman with whom he spends the weekend, and when his superiors find out, the ugly face of racism affects him. At times, the movie is directed in a French New Wave style. *The Story of a Three-Day Pass* caught the eye of Hollywood producers, who thought Van Peebles was a French auteur. Columbia Pictures was impressed with his debut and hired him to direct *Watermelon Man* (1970), in which a bigoted white insurance agent wakes up one morning to find that he is now black. *Watermelon Man* is an early example of contemporary black cinema. Ever the maverick, Van Peebles turned down a three-picture contract from Columbia and moved on to the controversial independent film, *Sweet Sweetback's Baadasssss Song* (1971), which contains violence, sex, and a strong condemnation of race relations in America. Melvin Van

Peebles is a black filmmaker who always looked for new ways to approach racism with outsider cinematic forms.

In the 1950s women fulfilled the traditional gender roles of wife and mother. During the sixties, those molds began to break. In the seventies, American women discovered change as the women's movement developed at the turn of that decade—now more than ever the movies reflected shifting roles for women in America.

Films in the seventies introduced female characters in circumstances that mirrored emerging roles for women in American society. Below are a sample of these films.

In *The Baby Maker* (1970), a young woman is a surrogate for a couple who wants a baby. As she becomes familiar with the couple, she is concerned about their value system and how the child would be raised.

In *Alice Doesn't Live Here Anymore* (1974), a woman's husband dies suddenly. To support herself and her precocious son, she returns to her hometown to restart her fledgling career as a singer. En route she begins a relationship with a man who is revealed as violent and abusive. Forced to flee, she finds work as a waitress and meets a kind and gentle man who is a regular in the diner. They fall in love, but she still wants to fulfill her dream as a singer. The couple comes together, and her aspirations are supported by her partner.

In *A Woman under the Influence* (1974), a working-class woman with a husband and three children believes her role is to be a normal housewife and mother. Her day-to-day behavior is considered eccentric only by her husband. Although she is often confused and disoriented, she is a loving mother. Her perceived aberrant behavior is considered dangerous by her extended family and she is institutionalized. When she returns home, subdued and unhappy, and she is finally alone with her husband, he accepts her as she is, and she is able to continue with her life.

The title character of *Annie Hall* (1977) is a seventies woman with many interests and ambitions and a quirky, insecure, yet believable personality. Actress Diane Keaton blended experiences from her real-life relationship with costar and director Woody Allen and aspects of her own nature. The methodology used by Keaton was uncommon before the seventies, but it was successful. The couple's love story ends when Annie's own needs reinforced by psychoanalysis motivate her to terminate the relationship and seek independence.

In *An Unmarried Woman* (1978), a woman whose husband leaves her for a younger woman sets out, looking for a new life and a new way of living. In the process she travels emotionally from rage to self-exploration to seek a new love and liberation.

In *Coming Home* (1978), a Marine captain is about to be shipped to Vietnam. His wife has been deferential, dresses conservatively, and follows her husband's lead. After he leaves, she volunteers in the local veteran's hospital where she meets a Vietnam vet confined to a wheelchair. The film takes place in 1968, a time of societal transformation. Her activities in the hospital and her exposure to the veteran lead to a physical and emotional evolution. They fall in love, and when her husband comes home and discovers the affair, he holds the two at rifle point in a fury. The vet disrupts the confrontation with an emotional plea for their lives. Later the husband commits suicide. The future of the wife is not resolved, but clearly she has developed as a woman.

In *Norma Rae* (1979), a single mother with two children by different fathers works in a cotton mill under conditions that strain her health. A New York City union organizer involves her in the difficult task of unionizing the shop, which is run by ruthless men who retaliate against her. This strong woman with solid convictions stands her ground by defying the establishment's power. The unionization is successful by about one hundred votes. With the organizer's job done, he prepares to leave for the next challenge, even though he has fallen in love with Norma; they shake hands on their victory, and he leaves, respecting her wishes.

In *Kramer vs. Kramer* (1979), a woman confronts issues of motherhood and identity. Unhappy in her marriage and her role as a mother, she abruptly tells her husband she is leaving him and their son. The husband, without preparation, becomes a single parent. Eventually the wife returns, now feeling whole whereas previously she had not, and sues to gain custody of her son. The divorce proceedings hang on whether a man can raise a child. The father loses the case. On the day their son is to leave with his mother, she recognizes it is right that the boy and his father remain together. The film captures the mother's inner torment, her struggle with gender roles, identity, and consequences, and her painful journey in search of what is right for her son.

The portrayal of women in the seventies not only reflects seismic changes in gender roles, but these progressive characters served as inspiration to men and women that change had arrived, and society and the American cinema were never going to be the same.

3

1971

July 5: The twenty-sixth amendment lowered the voting age to eighteen. . . . September 8: The John F. Kennedy Center for the performing arts opened in Washington, D.C., to celebrate all the performing arts including motion pictures. . . . September 9: Attica prison uprising occurred in New York State involving 1,281 of the approximately 2,200 inmates. Prisoners demanded better living conditions and political rights. Negotiations lasted four days, with authorities agreeing to twenty-eight of their demands but not to amnesty. Governor Nelson Rockefeller ordered authorities to take back the prison by force, leading to the deaths of forty-three people including ten correctional officers and civilian employees and thirty-three inmates.

In 1971 it was a banner year that proved the American New Wave was well underway. Many significant movies were released this year. The composition of movie audiences continued to change, and the under-thirty baby boomer generation was now going to the movies in record numbers because they were the ones reflected on the motion picture theater screen.

Movies throughout the decades imitated or echoed images from prior movies as references or comments to the audience, but by the seventies this practice became an art form: American New Wavers screened so many movies on television, in revival theaters, and in first-run houses and studied them shot by shot that they could duplicate a master's work. This exercise was respected by cineastes, critics, scholars, and avid movie-goers who recognized most references and could put them into context.

Warren Oates, Dennis Wilson, James Taylor, and (in back) Laurie Bird in *Two-Lane Blacktop*. *Universal Pictures/Photofest © Universal Pictures*

The Last Picture Show, based on the novel by Larry McMurtry, takes place in a small town in north Texas in the early 1950s. This 1970s movie, shot in classical black-and-white photography, visually references images recalled from movies of the past, usually made by auteurist directors such as John Ford and Howard Hawks. Director Peter Bogdanovich is a film historian who interviewed and wrote about practically every director from the Golden Age of Hollywood. The continuous flow of references to that era in *The Last Picture Show* is an homage to those directors and represents Bogdanovich's love for bygone days and his rejection of contemporary life—even of the American New Wave itself.

The content of *The Last Picture Show* includes mature subject matter such as loss of virginity, adultery, and mental illness, and contains nudity and physicality virtually never seen with this kind of candor in earlier decades. Bogdanovich handpicked a group of actors, many unknown, including Sam Bottoms, Timothy Bottoms, Eileen Brennan, Jeff Bridges,

Ellen Burstyn, Clu Gallagher, Cloris Leachman, Randy Quaid, Cybil Shepard, and Ben Johnson, who worked with John Ford, Howard Hawks, Sam Peckinpah, and George Stevens and won the Academy Award for Best Supporting Actor playing Sam the Lion, the moral center of the film representing the end of an era for America.

Peter Bogdanovich was a film critic and film programmer at the Museum of Modern Art. He watched upward of four hundred films a year. He featured American directors in his schedule and wrote monographs on Orson Welles, Howard Hawks, Fritz Lang, and John Ford. Bogdanovich's most original film is *Targets* (1968), a story of a serial killer, lean in style and rich in realism. After *The Last Picture Show* came the director's take on screwball comedy with *What's up Doc?* (1972), which was really a retro presentation of *Bringing up Baby* (1938), and was enormously successful at the box office. *Paper Moon* (1973) was about a con artist and a nine-year-old who pretends to be his daughter and gives nods to Old Hollywood. Failure came to the director with *Daisy Miller* (1974), featuring Cybil Shepard who is unable to emote during the film and is swallowed up by the lush period settings. In 1975 Bogdanovich paid tribute to the Hollywood musical with *At Long Last Love*, but even with Cole Porter songs and Burt Reynolds and Cybil Shepard in the cast, the singing was below the standards of the Old Hollywood musical. *Nickelodeon* (1976) is about the early days of Hollywood based on actual stories some of the pioneer filmmakers told Bogdanovich when he interviewed them. *Saint Jack* (1979) was a return to the modern day with a story about an American hustler scheming to build a successful brothel in Singapore so that he can live in luxury in the States. Later, critics pointed out many similarities between this film and John Cassavetes's *The Killing of a Chinese Bookie* (1976), both starring Ben Gazzara.

Cybil Shepard started her career as a popular model. Bogdanovich saw a photo of her on a magazine cover while he was casting *The Last Picture Show* and knew she was right for the part of Jacy, a provocative teenager. The part launched both her acting career and a relationship with Peter Bogdanovich while he was married to Polly Platt, the film's production designer.

Jeff Bridges comes from an acting dynasty. His mother Dorothy was an actress, his dad Lloyd Bridges was a movie actor and star of the innovative television series *Sea Hunt*. His older brother Beau Bridges is also an actor. Jeff Bridges appeared in seventeen movies during the seventies. In 1972 he was directed by John Huston in the boxing drama *Fat City* as Ernie Munger, an eighteen-year-old fighter seen as a comer. In 1972 Bridges acted in the Western *Bad Company*, directed by Robert Benton, and played Jake Rumsey, a leader of petty criminals. In 1973 Bridges portrayed true-life NASCAR driver Junior Johnson in *The Last American Hero*. In 1974 he costarred opposite Clint Eastwood in *Thunderbolt and Lightfoot*, the directorial debut of Michael Cimino, as the young man who by sheer accident rescues the lead character (Eastwood), who is on the run from his own gang. *Rancho Deluxe* (1975) is a contemporary Western written by Thomas McGuane and directed by Frank Perry. In 1975 Bridges appeared in *Hearts of the West*, a Western comedy directed by Howard Zieff. In 1976 he was in *Stay Hungry*, an offbeat comedy about weightlifters directed by Bob Rafelson. In 1979 he was in the political thriller *Winter Kills*, directed by William Richert, which mirrors the circumstances surrounding the assassination of President John F. Kennedy.

For director of photography on *The Last Picture Show*, Bogdanovich chose Robert Surtees, a Hollywood veteran with a long résumé that extended to the beginning of the American New Wave. Surtees understood the chiaroscuro of classical black-and-white film, having shot *Thirty Seconds over Tokyo* (1944). In 1967 he photographed *The Graduate* in color. Production designer Polly Platt, whose marriage to Bogdanovich was dissolving because of the developing romantic relationship with his young star Cybil Shepard, transported an actual town into black-and-white realism, and an environment for the end-of-an-era story. Film editor Donn Cambern is credited onscreen as the editor of *The Last Picture Show*, but Bogdanovich did an edit of the film himself. This was a union picture and was required to have a member of the guild credited. While working on another film in a neighboring room, Bogdanovich explained that Cambern was helpful with some purchasing paperwork. Bogdanovich asked Cambern about taking the credit and the editor agreed. Donn Cambern has refuted Bogdanovich's claims. Cambern seems to have been brought in later in the editing process and there is no record of the editing, revisions, or changes for which Cambern is responsible. From 1968 to 1996 Donn Cambern had thirty-two credits as a film editor including *Easy Rider* (directed by Dennis Hopper, 1968), *Drive, He Said* (Jack Nicholson, 1971), and *Blume in Love* (Paul Mazursky, 1973).

The practice of extensive referencing of older films, also known as quoting, became prevalent throughout the seventies. Martin Scorsese was a practitioner. He has such a broad range of cinematic interests that the references cover a wide spectrum of American and European filmmaking. Brian DePalma has been heavily influenced by the films of Alfred Hitchcock and often worked in a similar genre. Images and content from the master's *Psycho* show up often. For DePalma, quoting is homage and a way of creating contemporary horror films by echoing Hitchcock's approach to the thriller and a way of exploring what was in its time the scariest movie made. Many attribute the practice of cinematic quotes to French New Wave innovator Jean-Luc Godard, starting with his first film, *Breathless* (1959), and moving through his work in the decades that followed. The American practice underlines the movie culture that emerged during the seventies.

Straw Dogs is Sam Peckinpah's most controversial and intensely violent movie. David Sumner, a young man played by Dustin Hoffman, and his wife, played by Susan George, stay at a cottage in England while he is working on a mathematics grant. A situation with hostile locals becomes untenable and an angry group attacks Sumner's house to murder a mentally challenged man that they believe killed a young relative. One by one, Sumner kills all the intruders, proving Peckinpah's point that a man will kill to defend what is his. Sumner is even proud of it. The film was rated X for excessive violence and a double rape of the wife. During the shocking sequence, nearly impossible to watch, it at first appears that she is experiencing some pleasure. Peckinpah was called a misogynist and film critic Pauline Kael writing in the *New Yorker* called it "the first American film that is a fascist work of art."[1]

Sam Peckinpah is a significant American film director who accomplished much of his total output during the seventies. He was not part of the American New Wave in content or style. Although he worked in other genres, he was a director of Westerns. The West intrigued his artistic spirit and he lived his life as a man of the West. In the sixties Peckinpah established himself as a feature film director with *Ride the High Country* (1962), which contains one of Peckinpah's favorite lines, "All I want to do is enter my house justified." He ended the decade with the seminal *The Wild Bunch* (1969), which brought screen violence to new heights and broke down the good guy, white hat, bad guy, black hat Western movie code. The bunch lived above the law and robbed whoever had the money.

The Wild Bunch is violent, sexist, and set during a time defined as the end of the West, as America was moving into the modern era.

Peckinpah admired John Ford, Howard Hawks, and all the great directors of Westerns, but he knew they were all poetry and not reality. Peckinpah was a student of history and a revisionist who transferred his philosophy onto the screen. *The Wild Bunch* is one the most violent films of its time, receiving an X rating. It is not a metaphoric film, but because the nightly news on all three networks broadcast footage from Vietnam and stated the body count for the day, it was in everyone's mind including those who saw *The Wild Bunch.* This film was hated by most film critics during its time; now it is taught in film schools across the country and Peckinpah is deemed a great American film director by scholars and historians. The Western was a major American film genre. *The Wild Bunch* was a revisionist Western in its realistic depiction of the old West.

The Ballad of Cable Hogue (1970) is a Western fable about a man who finds water in the desert and sets up a profitable business. He falls in love with a town "lady of the night" and they try to make their relationship work. There are some Peckinpah touches of signature violence but also warm humor and romance rare in his films. In *Junior Bonner* (1971) Peckinpah moved in an entirely different direction with a film about the life of an aging rodeo rider who returns home, played by Steve McQueen. This is the first of two films directed by Sam Peckinpah that featured the superstar. *The Getaway* (1972) is a chase/caper movie in which Carter "Doc" McCoy (McQueen) is a prisoner who is released due to the efforts of his wife, Carol, portrayed by Ali MacGraw, so that he can pull off a major robbery. *Pat Garrett and Billy the Kid* (1973), featuring James Coburn and Kris Kristofferson in the title roles, is an epic Western about these legendary figures. Bob Dylan plays a small but noticeable role and composed the music for the score. The battle for *Pat Garrett and Billy the Kid* was waged in the editing room when studio executive James T. Aubrey, who had been fighting with Peckinpah throughout the production, began demanding changes. Peckinpah had a bad record with executives and always lost. Aubrey eventually took the film away from Peckinpah and had it cut from 124 minutes to 106 minutes. In 1988 Peckinpah's version of *Pat Garrett and Billy the Kid* became available to the public. Critics called it a lost masterpiece. This radical interference by a major studio with an A-list film director was an early sign that auteur cinema could be in trouble. *Bring Me the Head of Alfredo Garcia* (1974) is just what the title says: a Mexican crime lord sends Bennie, played by Warren Oates, to bring him a severed head. Bennie drives with the head in the passenger seat, pouring tequila on it periodically to keep it fresh. The film contains sex and a lot of violence. *The Killer Elite* (1975) starred James Caan in a drama in which the CIA goes amok. Film critics found it muddled and without purpose. *Cross of Iron* (1977) is Sam Peckinpah's take on World War II from the German perspective. His signature approach to violence is applied to battle. *Convoy* (1978) was made to feed the active CB radio fad in the country at the time and was one of Peckinpah's biggest hits.

Jerry Fielding was a blacklisted musician and film composer who scored twenty-three feature films in the seventies. He often took an atmospheric approach to film music rather than using a conventional lyrical theme-based approach. He is closely associated with Sam Peckinpah, having scored *The Wild Bunch, Straw Dogs, Junior Bonner, Bring Me the Head of Alfredo Garcia*, and *The Killer Elite*. Other directors he worked with included Clint Eastwood *The Outlaw Josey Wales* (1976) and *The Gauntlet* (1977); Gordon Parks *The Super Cops* (1974); Karel Reisz *The Gambler* (1974); Michael Ritchie *The Bad News Bears* (1976); Don Siegel *Escape from Alcatraz* (1979); and *The Nightcomers* (1971), *Chato's Land* (1972), *The Mechanic* (1972), *Scorpio* (1973), and *The Big Sleep* (1978) for director Michael Winner. Jerry Fielding was a true music maverick who contributed to a new era in film scoring.

In the black comedy *Harold and Maude*, directed by Hal Ashby, Harold (Bud Cort) is a young man obsessed with death. He fakes suicides and attends funerals of people he doesn't know. At one funeral he meets seventy-nine-year-old Maude, played by Ruth Gordon, who has the same dark interests. They become friends, then a romantic link is formed. Harold wants to marry Maude, but Maude insists that age eighty is the perfect time to die. After the two celebrate her birthday, Maude reveals she has taken sleeping pills and commits suicide. Ultimately, because of what he has learned about life from Maude, Harold can live. *Harold and Maude* initially was a failure, but later it developed a following in theaters in France, Canada, and the United States for continuous runs and became a cult film.

A notable beginning for the American black comedy is *Dr. Strangelove or: How I Learned to Stop Worrying and Love the Bomb*, released in 1964. By the seventies, black comedy had few limits as to what subjects it could handle. Some black comedies include *Where's Poppa?* (1970), directed by Carl Reiner, about a lawyer and his senile mother; *Gas-s-s-s,* also known as *Gas! Or It Became Necessary to Destroy the World in Order to Save It* (1970), directed by Roger Corman, in which a nerve gas kills everyone older than twenty-five; and *The End* (1978) directed by Burt Reynolds, in which a crooked real estate promoter decides to commit suicide and winds up in a mental institution where he meets an unhinged schizophrenic who assists him in finding the end.

Hal Ashby began his career in a Hollywood editing room, working his way up from assistant to full editor. He was nominated for best film editing for *The Russians Are Coming, the Russians Are Coming* in 1967 and won the Oscar for editing *In the Heat of the Night* (1968), both directed by Norman Jewison. Ashby made the transition to director in 1970 and became synonymous with seventies cinema for films that reflected the times and sensibilities. Born in 1929, he was a hippie from an older generation sporting long hair and a full scruffy beard. In 1970 he directed *The Landlord,* in which a white privileged male purchases a tenement and eventually romances two black women as a rebellion against his parents. After *Harold and Maude,* Ashby directed *The Last Detail* (1973), where two sailors from shore patrol are instructed to take a young sailor to prison though he has committed only a minor infraction. The journey is full of soul searching and adventures so that the naive sailor can experience some of life's joys before his long incarceration. The film is full of profanity, which was apt for sailors on a raucous journey. In 1975 Ashby directed *Shampoo,* starring Warren Beatty as a Beverly Hills hairdresser who moves from one female romantic encounter to another and finds himself in trouble with a powerful man who is going to give him money to set up his own shop. The deal becomes entangled with women connected to his money source. *Bound for Glory* (1976) is an epic biopic of Woody Guthrie. *Coming Home* (1978) is a strong in-country drama about the Vietnam War and its devastating impact on a couple and a veteran. *Being There* (1979) is a whimsical film about a gardener who is misconstrued as intelligent and omniscient but is unaware of why everyone around him, including the president of the United States, listens attentively when he speaks. Sadly, Hal Ashby was a heavy drug user. With his career in decline and suffering from various diseases, Ashby died at fifty-nine in 1988. Hal Ashby's legacy is as social satirist; he was America's observer of the comedy of manners.

The French Connection is a different and vibrant approach to the cop thriller. The film, based on the 1969 nonfiction book *The French Connection: A True Account of Cops, Narcotics, and International Conspiracy* by Robin Moore, is about the real-life detectives Eddie Egan, also known as Jimmy "Popeye" Doyle (Gene Hackman), and his partner Sonny Grosso, known as Buddy "Cloudy" Russo (Roy Scheider), who track a major heroin source from France to New York. Director William Friedkin contrasts the diverse cultures of the drug runners and the police by intercutting the two French connections—kingpin Alain Charnier (Fernando Rey) and his muscle/hit man Pierre Nicoli (Marcel Bozzuffi)—dining inside a fine French restaurant with Popeye sloppily eating pizza out in the cold across the street. The legendary chase scene is not the ordinary car chase, but a car and elevated subway train. *The French Connection* had audiences on their feet, trying to dodge a car coming to the front of the camera lens that they thought might actually hit them, a phenomenon that hadn't occurred since the beginning of cinema when the Lumière brothers in 1895 filmed the arrival of a steam locomotive into a station in France (*L'Arrivée d'un train en gare de La Ciotat*) that panicked audiences. *The French Connection*, which won five Academy Awards, including Best Picture and Best Director, was a box office bonanza grossing $75 million worldwide on a $1.8 million budget. The word in the industry was that a good part of the Best Picture win was for the breathtaking chase scene edited by Jerry Greenberg.

After three feature films in the sixties including an adaptation of Harold Pinter's play *The Birthday Party* (1968), in which a cozy birthday party is interrupted by two menacing unknown men, William Friedkin began the seventies with an adaptation of Mart Crowley's off-Broadway play *The Boys in the Band* (1970), about the lives of gay men in an Upper East Side apartment in New York City in 1968. After shattering the genre of crime film and establishing what became known as the New York style, Friedkin directed one of the most successful horror films of all time, *The Exorcist* (1973). Where *The French Connection* was gritty and edgy, this story of a young girl possessed by the devil was full of terrifying visual effects including the levitation of the child, her head turning around completely, and furniture moving with speed into corners of the bedroom. *The Exorcist* was a towering success, playing to lines stretching around the block, packing in audiences who screamed as if on cue. *Sorcerer* (1977) seemed too big a production for any director, and during production it received bad press. Overindulgent, too picturesque, and lacking a compelling story (even though it appeared to be an adaptation of Henri-Georges Clouzot's *Wages of Fear* [1955], which Friedkin refuted), *Sorcerer* lost money and broke Friedkin's winning streak. *The Brink's Job* (1978), which also failed at the box office, was the story of the famed Brink's building robbery.

Gene Hackman, a powerful physical actor, worked steadily during the sixties including in *Bonnie and Clyde*. In the seventies he became a superstar and audience favorite for his aggressive character work as Popeye Doyle in *The French Connection* (1971), for which he won the Oscar for Best Actor. He was compelling as the radical reverend in *The Poseidon Adventure* (1972), directed by Ronald Neame, and he transformed into Harry Caul in Francis Ford Coppola's *The Conversation*, a master surveillance expert who has the tables turned on him. He appeared in the World War II epic *A Bridge Too Far* (1977) as Major General Sosabowski, a member of the Polish armed forces. In 1978 he played the ultimate villain Lex Luthor in *Superman*, directed by Richard Donner.

Owen Roizman photographed *The French Connection* and contributed inventive techniques to the car chase. He was a leader in the New York school of cinematography—a gritty realistic style often rendered in exciting documentary-inspired handheld camerawork. Jerry Greenberg, who had been an assistant editor to leading film editor Dede Allen on *Bonnie and Clyde*, won the Oscar for editing *The French Connection*. Although William Friedkin was responsible for staging and shooting the legendary chase scene, he then delivered it to Greenberg's editing room. It is in the cat-and-mouse scenes between the French connections and Popeye Doyle and the split-second intercutting that shot-by-shot advanced the tension and excitement. The overall pacing of *The French Connection* is flawless and makes a major contribution to this picture.

Jerry Greenberg would join the postproduction team for Francis Ford Coppola's *Apocalypse Now*, edit the divorce drama *Kramer vs. Kramer* (1979), and work in postproduction on many seventies films including *Electra Glide in Blue* (1973), directed by James William Guercio; *The Taking of Pelham One Two Three* (1974), directed by Joseph Sergeant; and *The Missouri Breaks* (1976), directed by Arthur Penn.

The Panic in Needle Park (1971) was filmed in semi-documentary realism with Al Pacino and Kitty Winn before they became stars in *The Godfather* and *The Exorcist*, respectively. This gritty realistic New York film came closest in the genre to capturing the desolation of young street junkies. It was shot in a semidocumentary style by director of photography Adam Holender, often with long lenses to allow the camera to capture spontaneity. The graphic scenes of heroin addicts shooting up are difficult to watch but achieve a new level of cinematic honesty in depicting this human tragedy. *The Panic in Needle Park* was shot on the Upper West Side of Manhattan—the real location where the novel took place. The collaboration with Adam Holender was especially effective because of Schatzberg's extensive knowledge of still photography. Editing was by Evan Lottman who, among other important directors such as William Friedkin and Alan J. Pakula, often worked with Jerry Schatzberg.

Dusty and Sweets McGee, the directorial debut of Floyd Mutrux, was supported and distributed by Warner Bros. The edgy subject was young drug addicts. The major studio was anxious to exploit the burgeoning youth market. There was no traditional script, but the dialogue was based on interviews with real addicts. The film follows the main characters and their aimless existence. The point seems to be that society has failed these youths. The film never found an audience but became part of seventies cinema legend due to its neorealistic approach. Long after the film's release, controversy developed. Billy Gray, one of the actors who was famous as Bud in the popular television series *Father Knows Best*, played a heroin addict in the film and was labeled by some in the media as an actual addict. Gray believed this started with a misreading of a press release and he launched lawsuits to set the record straight. Some lawsuits were dropped; another resulted in an apology.

Dirty Harry is the legendary take-the-law-in-your-own-hands movie that starred Clint Eastwood as Inspector Harry Callahan. Don Siegel directed the script by Harry Julian Fink, Rita M. Fink, Dean Reisner, and uncredited John Milius and Terrence Malick. A serial killer is loose in San Francisco. Wielding his 44 Magnum, Harry tracks him down without obeying any rules or his superiors. Finally, he has the killer where he wants him and blows him away. He then tosses his badge in the water nearby; he is fed up with the limits restricting him and remains a man who believes in taking the law into his own hands. The film was a huge success and a crowd-pleaser, especially for audiences who believed Harry was right. Four sequels followed.

Don Siegel was the B-movie auteur who in the seventies directed *Two Mules for Sister Sara* (1970) with Clint Eastwood and Shirley MacLaine and *The Beguiled* (1971), set in the South during the Civil War, starring Clint Eastwood and a strong group of actresses who play women jilted by his character and plan their revenge. During the decade Siegel also directed *Charlie Varrick* (1973) starring Walter Matthau as the title character who robs a bank then finds out the money belongs to the mob. *The Shootist* (1976) is a Western that was John Wayne's last film. *Telefon* (1977) starred Charles Bronson, who thwarts attacks that are triggered over the telephone by special codes. Clint Eastwood starred in the taut drama *Escape from Alcatraz* (1979), playing Frank Morris, in a true story filmed at the actual prison.

Dennis Hopper had an accomplished career as an actor prior to the seventies. He appeared in *Rebel without a Cause* (1955), directed by Nicholas Ray and starring James Dean, who greatly influenced Hopper; *Giant* (1956), directed by George Stevens; *Gunfight at the O.K. Corral* (1957), directed by John Sturges; *Night Tide* (1961), directed by Curtis Harrington, in which Hopper plays Johnny Drake, a man who believes a woman he meets is really a mermaid; *The Trip* (1967), an LSD movie directed by Roger Corman in which he plays an acid guide; and *Cool Hand Luke* (1967), directed by Stuart Rosenberg, all before costarring and directing *Easy Rider.*

With that résumé, Hopper could have made almost any film as an under-thirty installment, but instead he made *The Last Movie*, a confusing, obtuse, and meandering film. One of the biggest failures of the American New Wave, it was the only film directed by Dennis Hopper during the seventies. The title *The Last Movie* led to speculation about its meaning. Was Hopper saying this was *his* last movie? Was Hopper saying that he was making the *last* movie? Had American movies after *Easy Rider* reached an end point in terms of content and cinematic aesthetics?

In *The Last Movie*, a Hollywood movie crew is on location in Peru shooting a Western. The director of this movie-within-a-movie is played by legendary maverick Sam Fuller. Dennis Hopper plays a stuntman named Kansas. When the Western is completed and the company leaves for the States, Kansas stays in Peru. The Peruvians build camera equipment out of bamboo and proceed to make their own movie, but instead of staged Hollywood shoot-outs and fistfights, the violence depicted is real. The themes in *The Last Movie* are the perception of movies as reality and comments on the nature of violence. There are "scene missing" cards and other techniques to indicate to the audience that they are watching a film—a self-referential strategy. There are narrative asides and subplots that are barely comprehensible.

Hopper called in chips to nearly every TV and movie cowboy actor and counterculture type he knew. Some are in the background, barely recognizable to the camera and have little to no discernible part that contributes to the story. Some of them include Rod Cameron, Warren Finnerty, Peter Fonda, Henry Jaglom, Kris Kristofferson, John Phillip Law, and Russ Tamblyn.

Regardless of the fine work by director of photography László Kovács, art director Leon Erickson, and editor David Berlatsky, *The Last Movie* was Hopper's picture through and through. Hopper was the only one who perceived he really knew what the picture was about. Even Stewart Stern (*Rebel without a Cause*), who developed the script with Hopper in the early sixties, was unclear because Hopper had departed wildly from the original concept and screenplay. During the shooting in Taos, New Mexico, Hopper indulged in excessive drug use and cavorted with female companions. This and dreams of grandeur clouded his thinking and produced a motion picture beyond understanding that bewildered audiences.

The Last Movie won the Critics Prize at the 32nd Venice Film Festival. Universal Studios ran the film for a week in big cities and then it disappeared from view. Hopper, an artist with an extensive art collection, said that American expressionist painters used paint as paint, so he was using film as film. Hopper certainly experimented with the American Western and the American movie in general. *The Last Movie* became a legend that was almost impossible to see in a movie theater for decades. In 1993 the film was released on VHS. It showed up on the internet and was suddenly removed. In 2018 *The Last Movie* was released on DVD in a fine print and with many bonus features that provided insights into this example of radical American New Wave filmmaking. *The Last Movie* may have stretched the narrative American film to its limit, and for that alone it can be perceived as the last movie of its kind released by a Hollywood studio.

Dennis Hopper was a risk taker and a talented and experienced actor. In 1973 he was in *Kid Blue*, directed by James Frawley, in the lead role as a failed train robber trying to go straight. In 1976 Hopper appeared in *Mad Dog Morgan*, directed by Phillippe Mora, as a man who has a "reverse epiphany" and turns into a robber. Hopper was in *The American*

Friend (1977), directed by German New Wave director Wim Wenders, based on a Patricia Highsmith novel. In 1979 Dennis Hopper played a crazed, waylaid photojournalist in *Apocalypse Now*. Hopper would regain the director's chair in the eighties with *Out of the Blue* and *Colors* but would never again achieve the heights of *Easy Rider*.

Peter Fonda's *The Hired Hand* is a revisionist Western visualized as if it were an experimental film. It appears to be inspired by Bruce Baillie's masterwork *Quick Billy*. It stars Fonda and Warren Oates as two men in the old West who ride from place to place until Harry (Fonda) decides it's time for him to go home to his wife Hannah (Verna Bloom) and daughter Janey (Megan Denver). Hannah is a strong woman and a fully developed character who expresses the difficulty and loneliness of running their homestead. Harry decides to stay home and Arch (Oates) moves on. When the town messenger delivers Arch's bloody, dismembered finger, Harry rides off to save his kidnapped friend, breaking ties with Hannah. Unlike traditional Hollywood Westerns, *The Hired Hand* has no happy ending. The bond between the two men is an essential theme in the film. The acting is realistic and believable. Evil lurks in a town where the people and the place itself are malevolent. Director Peter Fonda is sure-footed with the narrative, performances, and visualization. Cinematographer Vilmos Zsigmond visually reinvents the Western genre and contributes to the layered montages that appear throughout the movie with lyrical grace. The editing, by Frank Mazzola, weaves dissolves and superimpositions into a poetic stream. *The Hired Hand* defines the American New Wave—it is enigmatic and genuine but open for interpretation—a genre buster through and through.

Peter Fonda was the son of actor Henry Fonda, the brother of actress Jane Fonda, and father of actress Bridget Fonda. Peter Fonda became a member in good standing of the counterculture in the sixties by appearing in *The Wild Angels* (1966) and *The Trip* (1967), but his greatest accomplishment was producing and costarring in *Easy Rider*. He began performing in the sixties on television. He started in feature films with *Tammy and the Doctor* (1963) as Dr. Mark Cheswick, costarring with the popular teenage actress Sandra Dee, and was thought of as the boy next door. As a director his credits include *Idaho Transfer* (1973), a science fiction film about teenagers who travel into the future to avoid a coming apocalypse, and *Wanda Nevada* (1979), in which he plays drifter Beaudray Demerille, who wins a young orphan (Brooke Shields) in a poker game and takes her prospecting where they meet with an old prospector played in a cameo by Henry Fonda.

Lawrence G. Paull was the production designer for *The Hired Hand* and would go on to design *Blade Runner* (1982). In the seventies he also designed *The Bingo Long Traveling All-Stars Motor Kings* (1976), directed by John Badham; *Blue Collar* (1978), directed by Paul Schrader; and *FM* (1978), directed by John A. Alonzo, the cinematographer who had photographed *Chinatown* in 1974.

Klute is a film about a high-end New York City call girl who helps a detective solve a murder. In principle, *Klute* could have been produced in the 1960s, though not in its present form. There is some sex talk, a little skin exposure, but nothing explicit. The reason that *Klute* was a seventies film was because audiences were ready to witness a deep psychological study into the mind and life of a call girl, or sex worker (a term coined in the late seventies). *Klute* is complex with investigations into Bree Daniels, played by Jane Fonda, her relationship with the detective John Klute (Donald Sutherland), and the killer at large. *Klute* is a sexy, dramatic thriller with an ending so tense and frightening that Fonda is unable to stop the snotty flow coming from her nose while she shakes with fear. *Klute* was a big success proving that audiences wanted to see mature films with multifaceted subject matter. Jane Fonda won the Academy Award for her lead performance.

Klute was photographed by the so-called prince of darkness Gordon Willis, who forced audiences to look into and beyond the shadows. Gordon Jenkins designed many films for Alan J. Pakula such as *The Parallax View*, *All the President's Men*, and *Comes a Horseman*, always with startling truth, believability, and detail.

Alan J. Pakula first worked as a producer for director Robert Mulligan, including on Best Picture Oscar winner *To Kill a Mockingbird* in 1962. He made his directorial debut in 1969 with *The Sterile Cuckoo* starring Liza Minnelli. In 1974 he began to make political films that explored assassination and abuse of power. Critics dubbed *Klute* and Pakula's next two films his "paranoia trilogy." *The Parallax View* (1974) starred Warren Beatty as a reporter who gets in too deep investigating an underground company whose service is assassinating officials. A taut thriller, *The Parallax View* also features a film within a film that is used to determine whether a man can be trained to murder by assignment. *All the President's Men* (1976), with Robert Redford and Dustin Hoffman as

Washington Post reporters Bob Woodward and Carl Bernstein, uncovered the Watergate scandal and ultimately forced Richard Nixon to resign as president of the United States. The nonfiction book of the same name was adapted by the screenwriter many felt was one of the best of the decade, William Goldman. *Comes a Horseman* (1978) is an atypical Western about two ranchers (James Caan and Jane Fonda) who have economic hardships and are threatened by a land baron played by Jason Robards. *Starting Over* (1979) was a successful comedy featuring Burt Reynolds, Jill Clayburgh, and Candice Bergen.

After appearing in seventeen films in the sixties including *The Chase* (1966), *Hurry Sundown* (1967), *Barbarella* (1968), and *They Shoot Horses, Don't They?* (1969), Jane Fonda continued in the seventies with *Tout Va Bien* (1972), a political drama with Yves Montand directed by Jean-Luc Godard and Jean-Pierre Gorin. In 1973 Fonda played Nora in Joseph Losey's adaptation of Ibsen's *A Doll's House*. It aired on ABC television, played at the New York Film Festival in 1973, and later had a short run at a theater in Los Angeles. *The Blue Bird* (1976), a children's fantasy, was directed by George Cukor. *Fun with Dick and Jane* (1977) is a comedy critical of the American way of life. In *The China Syndrome* (1979), directed by James Bridges, Fonda played a television reporter who learns a nuclear plant is faulty. *The Electric Horseman* (1979), directed by Sidney Pollack, is a romantic comedy with Robert Redford and a free-the-animals theme.

Warren Beatty is a seminal figure in the seventies as an actor, producer, and director. Beatty began in television, appearing on anthology shows, notably as Milton Armitage in *The Many Loves of Dobie Gillis*. He made his feature film debut in Elia Kazan's *Splendor in the Grass* (1961) as Bud Stamper, the son of a wealthy oilman, opposite Natalie Wood, his sensitive girlfriend. He and the film received much acclaim. After several performances, he worked for the first time with director Arthur Penn on *Mickey One* (1965) as the title character, a stand-up comedian who manages to incur the wrath of the mob. Later Beatty became the producer and star of *Bonnie and Clyde* (1967), directed by Penn with considerable input from Beatty about the content and realization of the film. In 1970 he costarred with Elizabeth Taylor in *The Only Game in Town*, the last film directed by the legendary George Stevens. In 1971 he was gambler John McCabe, a cocky entrepreneur in *McCabe & Mrs. Miller*, directed by Robert Altman. McCabe works hard building a

settlement that fits into the modern world. He appeared opposite Julie
Christie, a British madam who sets up shop in the town and, in the
frigidly cold and isolated environment, becomes addicted to opium. Also
in 1971, he and Goldie Hawn appeared in $ (Dollar$), a caper film
directed by Richard Brooks. In 1974 Beatty was newspaper man Joe
Frady in *The Parallax View*, who investigates an underground company
that trains political assassins and becomes caught in their maze. In 1975
Warren Beatty coproduced and cowrote *Shampoo*, a political comedy
about Beverly Hills hairdresser George Roundy, who juggles the romantic and business aspects of his life while continually fighting off consequences. *Shampoo* was directed by Hal Ashby with strong input from
Beatty. In 1975 Beatty and Jack Nicholson were con men in the Mike
Nichols film *The Fortune*. In 1978 Beatty codirected, with Buck Henry,
Heaven Can Wait, an updated version of *Here Comes Mr. Jordan* (1941)
about Joe Pendleton, a backup quarterback for the Los Angeles Rams
who is prematurely plucked from life by an angel. Warren Beatty was
always careful choosing projects. He is a true movie star from the end of
the classical era, and an actor and director in the American New Wave.
He has the looks and is charismatic, smart, and well trained.

Julie Christie is a British actress who began her career in the sixties
and won a Best Actress Oscar for *Darling* (1965) directed by John Schlesinger. In the seventies she was noteworthy for her fully developed characters. *Don't Look Now*, directed by Nicholas Roeg, was released in 1973
with Christie and Donald Sutherland as a couple dealing with the death of
their child. The film contains an explicit sex scene that was controversial
in its time. *Shampoo* (1973) was a sex farce in which she played a former
girlfriend of the hairdresser played by Warren Beatty and the mistress of
a man who wants to finance his shop. *Demon Seed*, directed by Donald
Cammell, was an offbeat science fiction film about impregnation by computer. In *Heaven Can Wait*, Christie plays Betty Logan, a love interest of
a deceased football player who was accidentally plucked by an angel.

In a road movie, characters ride in a car and travel from A to Z. It may
or may not matter where they are going or why. A road movie is an
existential trip through the psyche as the travelers learn about themselves,
the purpose of life, or the hopelessness of existence. What happens scene
to scene reveals something about the characters; it is less about an action
sequence or a big dramatic moment. Instead, the focus is on the charac-

ters, the aimlessness of their lives, and the potential for finding themselves.

Two-Lane Blacktop is a definitive road movie that represents the essence of seventies cinema. Directed by Monte Hellman, an adept film editor, and written by experimental novelist Rudolph Wurlitzer, *Two-Lane Blacktop* is a heightened existential journey through a long automobile race between two young hotshots who live for the road and the character GTO, a degenerate liar with a magnetic personality. In a decade filled with risks, Hellman cast three nonprofessional actors and an essential character actor often seen in Westerns. Non-actors had been cast in movies before, especially by John Cassavetes, and performers from the music business were in movies during the fifties and sixties. In the script for *Two-Lane Blacktop*, the characters are referred to as the Driver, played by singer/songwriter James Taylor, the Mechanic portrayed by Dennis Wilson, drummer of the Beach Boys, and the Girl, portrayed by Laurie Bird, cast for her quintessential hippie look and persona. Warren Oates, as GTO, performed in his fourth film of the seventies, a decade in which he would appear in a total of twenty-four movies.

Oates was the oldest in the cast and played a character with an elusive nature. There is little action or significant dialogue, but *Two-Lane Blacktop* is a journey during a decade that promised that road movie characters could find out who they were and where they should be going. Many of the scenes are cryptic and take place in one of two cars. *Two-Lane Blacktop* was not a success in its time and lasted only a few weeks in first run. Ultimately, it became a cult film.

Monte Hellman was mentored by Roger Corman, who produced Hellman's first feature *Beast from Haunted Cave* (1959), a heist movie about criminals who plan to steal gold bars and are later attacked by a monstrous beast in a cave. In 1964 he directed *Back Door to Hell*, a World War II movie in which Jack Nicholson appeared in the cast. Hellman directed two existential Westerns with Nicholson, *The Shooting* (1966) and *Ride in the Whirlwind* (1966). After *Two-Lane Blacktop*, Monte Hellman directed *Cockfighter* (1974), starring Warren Oates, about the repellant subject of cockfighting, and although admirers of *Two-Lane Blacktop* were anxious to see Hellman's next film, *Cockfighter* did not find an audience. In 1978 Hellman directed *China 9, Liberty 37*, a Western that also starred Warren Oates about a man given a reprieve from hanging if he hunts down and kills a man who won't sell his land to the railroad. Monte Hellman also edited *The Killer Elite* (1975) for Sam Peckinpah.

Warren Oates was a distinctive actor known for his wicked grin and the ability to play characters who fascinated the viewer due to their believability and complexity. Warren Oates began in television anthology shows and Westerns, and on *The Rifleman*, he met director Sam Peckinpah, who would include him in his ensemble of actors. Oates appeared in many of Peckinpah's films, including *The Wild Bunch* (1969), as one of the ornery Gorch brothers.

In 1973 John Milius directed Oates in *Dillinger*, in which he portrayed the infamous 1930s criminal without depicting him stereotypically. As the father in *Badlands* (1973), directed by Terrence Malick, he was protective of his young daughter played by Sissy Spacek and believable in his job as a skilled sign painter. Warren Oates was recognized as a magnetic ensemble character actor.

Legendary character actor Harry Dean Stanton was in more than twenty movies during the seventies. In *Two-Lane Blacktop* he plays a hitchhiker picked up by GTO who is shortly thereafter ejected from the vehicle when he makes an unwanted move toward the driver. Stanton's other performances in the seventies include roles in *Cisco Pike, Pat Garrett & Billy the Kid* (1973), *Dillinger, The Godfather: Part II* (1974), and *Alien* (1979). Stanton had a gaunt, nearly haunted look that distinguished him and the skill to quickly establish a character on screen. In addition to Monte Hellman, Harry Dean Stanton worked with Sam Peckinpah, Francis Ford Coppola, John Huston, and Ridley Scott. His career spanned six decades.

Though uncredited, cinematographer Gregory Sandor, working with Hellman, was essential in achieving the way *Two-Lane Blacktop* was shot. Jack Deerson was credited and was previously credited on *The Dark Side of Tomorrow* as Jacque Beerson, his first as a cinematographer. *Two-Lane Blacktop* is bleak, relentless, and drained of Hollywoodized, saturated color. Monte Hellman edited this film. Road pictures are challenging in postproduction because they contain many more interior moments and expressions of emotion than action pieces.

Carnal Knowledge, directed by Mike Nichols, starred Jack Nicholson as Jonathan Fuerst, a man who aggressively pursues women, and singer-turned-actor Art Garfunkel (Simon & Garfunkel) as Sandy, who takes a somewhat gentler approach to females. Over a twenty-five-year period, the film vividly presents their sex lives as they unfold from the late forties to the early seventies. *Carnal Knowledge* is structured in three parts or acts. The first takes place when the men are college roommates, the second is after college, and the third is when they are middle-aged. The film was frank, often vulgar, and the behavior of the men toward the women in their lives was abusive. Candice Bergen and Ann-Margret also star in the film. There is nudity and implied sex acts, which could not have been shown in an earlier decade. The characters, especially Jonathan, are repugnant and misogynistic. Time had changed the way movies portrayed sexuality, but community standard laws had not. A theater in Albany, Georgia, screened the film and the print was seized by local police. The theater manager was convicted for displaying obscene material. Eventually a higher court found that the film was not obscene. *Carnal Knowledge* supported the right of audiences to see mature material if they chose, but the disparity continued between frank and mature movie audiences who wanted to see these films and those who were more morally conservative.

From 1958 to 1960 Mike Nichols and Elaine May were a sensation on stage, television, and record as the improvisational duo Nichols and May. This improvisational skill and work as an actor served Nichols well in his film career, teaching him to seek new methods and improving his skill in directing actors. After breaking taboos about sex and relationships in the adaptation of Edward Albee's award-winning play *Who's Afraid of Virginia Woolf?* (1966), he directed *The Graduate* (1967). In 1970 he took on what many felt was the great American novel: Joseph Heller's *Catch-22*. Although it was an artistic and box office failure, it did attempt to cinematically interpret a contemporary literary classic. After *Carnal Knowledge*, Nichols directed *The Day of the Dolphin* (1973), which starred George C. Scott as a scientist who trains dolphins to communicate with humans. Later they are stolen by a nefarious organization that plans to retrain them to carry out political assassinations. Nichols was not the intended director; fate struck a blow to the original writer/director Roman Polanski, when his wife Sharon Tate and their unborn child were slaughtered by the Manson family. Nichols did a workmanlike job but the film was another failure at the box office. *The Fortune* (1975) featured Warren Beatty, Jack Nicholson, and Stockard Channing.

A Safe Place is Henry Jaglom's directorial debut featuring Jack Nicholson and Tuesday Weld as a mentally disturbed woman trying to find a "safe place" from her torment. Orson Welles, who eventually enjoyed a long relationship with Jaglom after some heated back and forth, agreed to appear as a magician whose tricks lift Weld's everyday gloom. *A Safe Place* was a BBS production and poorly reviewed, with critics attacking the film as pretentious. It did not last long on the screen in first run and later had to be tracked down in a revival theater to be seen.

Henry Jaglom studied with Lee Strasberg at the Actor's Studio and acted and directed off-Broadway and in cabarets until he went to Hollywood in the late 1960s, where he performed in the counterculture film *Psych-Out* (1968), directed by Richard Rush. Jaglom was involved in postproduction on *Easy Rider*. He appeared in *Drive, He Said* (1971). In *The Last Movie* he played the minister's son. He was in *The Other Side of the Wind*, directed by Orson Welles and shot during the seventies but released in 2018. After *A Safe Place*, Henry Jaglom continued his complex and at times disorienting narrative style with *Tracks* (1976), which takes place on a moving train where a soldier played by Dennis Hopper accompanies the coffin of a fallen soldier who died in action during the Vietnam War. The effects of the Vietnam War make it difficult for the soldier to comprehend reality. The film captures his confused mind and erratic behavior. The friendship between Henry Jaglom and Orson Welles was lifelong and the two men continually exchanged ideas about their movies.

Tuesday Weld was born Susan Ker Weld. After her father died, she supported her family as a child model and actress. The stress of working in Hollywood caused Weld to drink and she had a breakdown as a teenager. Weld began appearing in movies in the fifties and worked through the sixties in films including *Pretty Poison* (1968), directed by Noel Black, in which she plays Sue Ann Stepanek, a teenager who attracts the attention of a parolee from a mental institution, played by Anthony Perkins. She established herself in the seventies with *A Safe Place* and *Play It as It Lays* (1972), directed by Frank Perry and based on the book by Joan Didion. In it she plays a former model who becomes depressed and is institutionalized. In *Who'll Stop the Rain* (1978) directed by Karel Reisz, Tuesday Weld played a woman dealing with substance abuse.

Duel, directed by Steven Spielberg in 1971 as a TV movie, first aired on the ABC television network, then became a theatrical release overseas and appeared in limited theatrical release in the United States. It can be recognized as Spielberg's first film. In *Duel*, the chase between a large, menacing truck and a car is unique among chase scenes. Spielberg demonstrated his technical and mechanical skills in a film with sparse dialogue and practically wall-to-wall action. The truck driver, whom we never see, is apparently angry because the driver of the car passes him because the truck is driving very slowly. The film is a tour de force for Dennis Weaver, who plays the driver of the car. Frank Morriss's editing is relentless, the cinematography successfully follows the vehicles, no matter the circumstances. Spielberg understood how to orchestrate the action in cinematic terms. *Duel* is a thrill ride, a study in paranoia and fear, and an outstanding first feature.

THX 1138 is the first feature film directed by George Lucas. It developed from *Electronic Labyrinth THX 1138 4EB*, the fifteen-minute short about a future society in which computers track civilians' every move that Lucas made while attending USC. An American Zoetrope production backed by Francis Ford Coppola, the film moved forward to Lucas's specifications, but when producer Coppola presented it to the financiers at Warner Bros., the executives disliked the film and ordered Coppola to hand over the negative to their in-house editor, who cut four minutes. It ran ninety-five minutes when it was released in 1971. The film was a flop. The experience motivated Lucas to push for total control over his work. *THX 1138* is dark and dystopian in contrast to the upbeat hope generated and projected in Spielberg's *Close Encounters of the Third Kind* (1977).

George Lucas started with the career goal of being an experimental/personal filmmaker. He graduated from USC in 1967. After *THX 1138*, he made another personal film, *American Graffiti* (1973), inspired by his northern California youth, car culture, and rock 'n' roll.

In Clint Eastwood's 1971 directorial debut, *Play Misty for Me*, a psychological thriller set in Carmel, California, Eastwood plays radio disc jockey Dave Garver. A female caller, played to the hilt by Jessica Walter, repeatedly calls in and asks the DJ to play "Misty," the jazz classic written by pianist Errol Garner. Garver gets involved with the caller until she complicates his life by stalking him. Donna Mills plays his girlfriend who is tricked into rooming with the disturbed woman, which leads to a dramatic conclusion. Eastwood is effective as Garver and economical as a director, creating scenes with ease and confidence. His mentor Don Siegel has a cameo playing a bartender. The film was made under the banner of Eastwood's production company, Malpaso Productions.

Clint Eastwood's road to success was a long one with minor roles in film, work in television, notably on *Rawhide*, and then performances in distinctive Westerns in Europe. He appeared in nineteen films before the seventies. He was in almost twenty movies during the seventies, including *Kelly's Heroes* (directed by Brian G. Hutton, 1970), *Joe Kidd* (John Sturges, 1972), and *The Enforcer* (James Fargo, 1976), playing Inspector "Dirty" Harry Callahan for the third time. After beginning his directing career in 1971, he directed a total of seven films in the decade. These included *The Eiger Sanction* (1975), *The Gauntlet* (1977), and *Every Which Way but Loose* (1977). Eastwood often played the outsider, and as a director was known for making movies fast and cheap; he was an independent who relied on the studios to distribute his pictures. Audiences found him reliable and distinctive.

Shaft (1971), directed by Gordon Parks, is an important blaxploitation film that was distributed by a major studio, MGM, and grossed $12 million on a $500,000 budget. Extremely popular, it was received as if it was a mainstream film. In the lead, Richard Roundtree in his screen debut plays a private detective who is being hunted by the mob. Wide success lifted *Shaft* above others in the genre. It was an early blaxploitation film and had a distinctive score by Isaac Hayes, which won two Grammy awards. "Theme from Shaft" won an Academy Award for Best Song and became an iconic seventies sound: heavy on rhythmic, wah-wah pedal guitar and driving drumsticks on closed high-hat cymbals.

Gordon Parks was a multitalented, artistically gifted African American man. He was a self-taught photographer who, after myriad assignments, was given a staff position at the most prestigious picture magazine of his time, *Life* magazine. In 1963 he wrote a semiautobiographical novel, *The Learning Tree*. In 1969 Warner Bros. was behind him when he directed *The Learning Tree*, a film adaptation of his book about a teenager growing up in Kansas. Parks was a natural with actors, and as a writer understood visual storytelling, wrote the score, and was able to translate the words into cinematic images in a stylistic fashion. He is the first major black film director of the modern era.

After *Shaft*, Parks directed the sequel, *Shaft's Big Score!* (1972), which cost twice as much as the original, received mixed reviews, but earned a big box office return of $10 million. *The Supercops* was based on the true story of New York cops nicknamed Batman and Robin. *Thomasine and Bushrod* (1974) was intended as a black *Bonnie and Clyde*. *Leadbelly* (1976) was a biopic of the folk and blues singer Huddie William Ledbetter, played by Roger E. Mosley. Parks tells the story of the music legend and his troubles on chain gangs in the South during the thirties and forties.

Richard Roundtree, who played John Shaft in *Shaft, Shaft's Big Score!*, *Shaft in Africa* (1973), and Uncle John Shaft in *Shaft* (2000), is considered the first black action hero. In 1972 he won the Golden Globe Award for New Star of the Year as John Shaft. He played a CIA officer in *Embassy* (1972). In *Charley One-Eye* he played a Union army deserter under threat by a racist bounty hunter. In 1974 he was a member of the large cast in the disaster film *Earthquake*, directed by Mark Robson. In 1975 he played the title role in *Man Friday* opposite Peter O'Toole in a reversal of the Robinson Crusoe story. He continued to play action and dramatic roles throughout the decade.

Billy Jack was a phenomenon of seventies cinema. Billy Jack was played by Tom Laughlin, who wrote, produced, and starred in the film. Billy Jack is a half-breed American Navajo, Green Beret Vietnam War veteran, and a hapkido master who defends a hippie-themed Freedom School and its students from townspeople who don't understand the counterculture. The school was run by its director Jean Roberts, played by actress Delores Taylor, who developed the project with her husband, Laughlin. The character of Billy Jack had been gestating in Laughlin since 1954 and in 1967 he introduced him in *The Born Losers*. The filming of *Billy Jack* began in the fall of 1969 in Prescott, Arizona, but completion of the film didn't occur until 1971. American International Pictures pulled out of the project, halting filming. Later, 20th Century Fox backed the production and work on the film resumed. When the film was completed, Fox refused to distribute *Billy Jack*. Then Warner Bros. committed to distributing the film, but Laughlin found their plans inadequate and took the bold step of booking *Billy Jack* in theaters himself. When *Billy Jack* was finally in the marketplace, it was a major hit, eventually grossing $32.5 million on its $800,000 budget. When it was rereleased and carefully tracked by Laughlin, its earnings continued to rise astronomically. The Native American movement was well underway in the early seventies, as was interest in martial arts. The brilliance of *Billy Jack* was that it brought these together and convinced audiences that fighting violence with violence—the opposite of the sixties' nonviolent credo—appeared righteous insomuch as it resolved the problem and protected those unable to protect themselves. Audiences may have been drawn to the action in *Billy Jack*, the hero physically fighting off bad guys with martial arts rather than the school's nonviolent philosophy.

Billy Jack had three sequels directed by Laughlin. *The Trial of Billy Jack* (1974), *Billy Jack Goes to Washington* (1977), and *The Return of Billy Jack* (1986). In 1975 Laughlin directed *The Master Gunfighter*, in which he played Finley, an outnumbered gunman and swordsman who tries to stop local landowners from wiping out the Native American population. A complex man with a background unequaled during the seventies in the film industry, Tom Laughlin was an educator, lectured on Jungian psychology, ran for president of the United States, and spoke out on subjects concerning society and the making of movies.

Cisco Pike is a drama about a musician, played by Kris Kristofferson, who is desperate for funds and feels forced to enter the drug trade. Many films released during the seventies dealt with aspects of drug use and drug dealing. It was considered part of the culture and a draw for the box office. *Cisco Pike* was directed by B. L. Norton, who also cowrote the film. Gene Hackman, Karen Black, and Harry Dean Stanton were also in the cast.

Kris Kristofferson, singer, musician, songwriter, and actor, was a Rhodes Scholar at Oxford University. He entered the service and later moved to Nashville where he became an in-demand singer and songwriter. With his rugged good looks and deep, textured voice, Kristofferson began acting during the seventies. In 1971 he played a minstrel wrangler in *The Last Movie* (1971), in which he sings his legendary composition "Me and Bobby McGee." He made three films with director Sam Peckinpah: *Pat Garrett & Billy the Kid* (1973), *Bring Me the Head of Alfredo Garcia* (1974), and *Convoy* (1978). He played the other man in *Blume in Love* (1973), directed by Paul Mazursky, and the love interest in *Alice Doesn't Live Here Anymore*, directed by Martin Scorsese. He played a second ship officer in *The Sailor Who Fell from Grace with the Sea* (1976) based on a 1963 novel by the Japanese writer Yukio Mishima and directed by Lewis John Carlino. In *Vigilante Force*, directed by George Armitage (1976), Kristofferson played a Vietnam veteran who is part of a group of mercenaries who control oil field workers and eventually take over the town. In 1976 he performed opposite Barbra Streisand in a remake of *A Star Is Born*. Kristofferson, who wrote legendary songs including "Help Me Make It through the Night," played an aging star living life on the edge. *Semi-Tough*, directed by Michael Ritchie (1977), is a football comedy that parodies the transformational training known as EST, popular in the seventies and referred to as BEAT in the picture. A natural actor with an innate screen presence, Kris Kristofferson continued to work in music and film for the rest of his career.

Alfred Sweeney was the art director on *Cisco Pike*. Robert C. Jones edited *Cisco Pike* and several films for seventies icon Hal Ashby.

Vanishing Point is an enigmatic road movie directed by Richard C. Sarafian. *Vanishing Point* is a standout in the road movie genre. Although it is about a man in a car who travels long distances, it is more about his background and the purpose for his driving. Kowalski, played by Barry Newman, works for a car delivery service. His job is to drive a car to the person who purchased it. When he finishes a job in Denver, Colorado, he is eager to continue to his next assignment. Eventually he buys Benzedrine from his dealer and they bet that he can arrive in San Francisco days before the car delivery is due. *Vanishing Point* is structured with flashbacks that reveal Kowalski is a Medal of Honor Vietnam veteran, a former racecar and motorcycle driver, and was once a police officer. While he is speeding down the road, police try to stop him, and the chase becomes involved and complex. Kowalski is listening to his car radio on a station broadcasting from Goldfield, Nevada. Cleavon Little plays "Super Soul," a blind black disc jockey who is listening to the police frequency and encourages the outlaw to evade the police. At one point, Kowalski believes that Super Soul is deliberately trying to lead him into a police roadblock. The chase continues until the end of the film. There is some confusion and alternate interpretations of what occurs. When Kowalski finally does reach the roadblock, it is at his highest speed ever. Law enforcement has set up two large bulldozers to stop him. Kowalski is smiling as he crashes into them. There is a fiery explosion, firefighters move in to extinguish the flames, and the crowd that had gathered disperses.

There are many theories about *Vanishing Point*; one is that the whole movie is a post-death flashback. Barry Newman has gone on record saying that his character smiles because he believes he can drive through the bulldozers. He further stated that a glint of light between the two bulldozers proved there was always an escape in life. The director of photography was John Alonzo, highly ranked among seventies cinematographers.

Sweet Sweetback's Baadasssss Song is the only film of its kind in the seventies. It is an action film, a thriller, a personal film, a blaxploitation film, and an experimental film. The star and director, Melvin Van Peebles, was a self-taught filmmaker, erudite and expansive in his artistic vision. Van Peebles also was a producer on the film and worked with Earth, Wind, and Fire, who performed the music. Van Peebles edited the film's complex and at times rapid-paced structure. His director of photography, Bob Maxwell, had worked on B movies, pornography, and exploitation films in the sixties and seventies. The story followed a poor black man fleeing from white authority. Van Peebles turned down a three-picture deal at Columbia Pictures because he wanted to make the first film about the black power movement that emphasized empowerment. The cast and crew contained many amateurs. He worked nonunion and because that angered some members of the industry, Van Peebles had a gun on set. The film was filled with sex scenes and Van Peebles contracted gonorrhea. A confrontation loomed with the Hells Angels during the shooting of one scene for this volatile movie. *Sweet Sweetback's Baadasssss Song* was rated X and Van Peebles asserted that the rating was determined by an all-white jury during the advertising campaign.

Frank Zappa, guitarist, composer, and performer with the Mothers of Invention, directed *200 Motels*. It was an attempt to capture the insanity of a rock 'n' roll tour. It is the first feature film shot totally on videotape and transferred to 35mm film using a Technicolor film printer to create vivid visual effects onto the images.

Drive, He Said was Jack Nicholson's directorial debut. He also wrote the screenplay and produced the picture. Nicholson, a lifelong basketball fan, adapted this story about a college basketball player distracted by his affair with a professor's wife and a roommate who spouts political dogma and is going insane. Karen Black plays Olive, the professor's wife, and Bruce Dern is a standout in his role as a coach. Fellow writers and directors Robert Towne and Henry Jaglom were part of the cast. A BBS Production released by Columbia Pictures, *Drive, He Said* was based on the prizewinning first novel by Jeremy Larner.

Karen Black acted in more than twenty movies during the seventies. She is indelibly linked with the American New Wave and seventies cinema. She began her memorable career in 1966 with Coppola's *You Are a*

Big Boy Now as Amy Partlett, who has a crush on the main character, a former classmate. In 1970 she created a character who helped define an aspect of the seventies woman in *Five Easy Pieces*. Rayette is vulnerable and personable; she is a product of her working-class hometown upbringing and is loving but challenged in her relationship with Bobby Dupea. Played by Jack Nicholson, Dupea is superior intellectually and in status. In *Nashville* (1975) Black portrayed the glamorous country singer Connie White. Her singing is authentic, engaging, and genuine. Karen Black's wide range of roles was carried out with diversity, professionalism, and a firm understanding of the world in which she lived and worked.

Bill Butler, the director of photography for *Drive, He Said*, was just at the beginning of his career. In the seventies he achieved great renown shooting *Jaws* (1975), *Grease* (1978), and several *Rocky* sequels.

Four editors worked on the postproduction of *Drive, He Said*: Donn Cambern and Christopher Holms, who had just completed *Five Easy Pieces*; Pat Somerset, who worked on Frank Perry's *The Swimmer* (1968); and Robert L. Wolfe, who collaborated with Sam Peckinpah.

A New Leaf is Elaine May's directorial debut. She also wrote the screenplay. Her costar was Walter Matthau. He plays a man who is losing his inheritance, so he decides to marry rich. May plays a wealthy botany professor. Elaine May was methodical about details and contacted a botany professor at Columbia University in New York who wrote accurate lines for her about the profession. After ten months of editing, May continued to refuse to show Paramount Pictures the rough cut, so honcho Robert Evans took *A New Leaf* away from her and had his editor recut it. When they received it, the film ran 180 minutes. May had the negative under her bed as a bargaining chip, but it was reduced to 102 minutes anyway. Elaine May tried to remove her name from the credits and sued unsuccessfully. She set a pattern that would follow her on future projects: the film was $2.2 million over budget and production was forty days behind schedule.

In the 1950s Elaine May made a splash as an improvisational comedian teamed with Mike Nichols as Nichols and May. Next, she wrote and directed the film noir *Mikey and Nicky* (1976) with Peter Falk and John Cassavetes, which was crafted to look as if Cassavetes had written and directed it. Production was chaotic and the film went way over budget and way off schedule. She was fired by Paramount but retained the project by hiding reels of the film until they agreed to reengage her.

Zachariah is a surrealistic Western musical loosely based on Herman Hesse's *Siddhartha* directed by George Englund. Four members of the popular counterculture troupe the Firesign Theatre were in the film, which starred John Rubinstein and Don Johnson. Providing musical support were Doug Kershaw, the James Gang, Country Joe and the Fish, Elvin Jones, and the New York Rock Ensemble.

Michael Ritchie was an essential member of seventies cinema. His oeuvre was widespread. In 1972 he directed Robert Redford in *The Candidate*, about a packaged candidate running for governor of California. *Prime Cut* contains nudity and violence in its depiction of the corruption in the meatpacking industry; Gene Hackman and Lee Marvin give strong performances. *Smile* (1975) starred the usually intense Bruce Dern in a lighter role in a movie about a beauty pageant. In 1976 Ritchie directed *The Bad News Bears*, about a ragtag kids' baseball team and their less-than-sober coach played by Walter Matthau. *Semi-Tough* (1977) starred Kris Kristofferson and Burt Reynolds as pro football players in love with the same woman, portrayed by Jill Clayburgh. *An Almost Perfect Affair* (1979) was set at the Cannes Film Festival, where a filmmaker (Keith Carradine) has a love affair with a film producer's wife (Monica Vitti).

More than in any decade, cinema of the seventies echoed contemporary culture by presenting women and men who had complex and evolving personalities and lifestyles and were placed in situations involving relationships, spirituality, racial tension, and sexuality in genres, subgenres, and new storytelling forms.

In 1967 black activist H. Rap Brown said, "Violence is as American as cherry pie" (often revised as apple pie). For numerous social and political reasons, the United States has been known around the world as a violent country. In 1969 a game-changing Western was released—*The Wild Bunch* directed by Sam Peckinpah. The film shows graphic violence, often in slow-motion, alternated with speeds beyond standardization and intercut with action from multiple angles. *The Wild Bunch* opened the door to the darkest side of man's violent nature and employed bravado camerawork and Russian-inspired montage to create what Peckinpah called a ballet of death.

During the 1970s Sam Peckinpah directed nine feature films, three without excessive violence and six with over-the-top violence, including double rape, overkill of intruders, excessive gunplay, and decapitation. While Peckinpah was formulating his seventies films, the decade was filled with movies that featured a gun-wielding vigilante, a police detective brandishing a 44 Magnum used at will without regard for the law, a sheriff protecting his town with a big stick, an Asian with supreme martial arts skills, and the horror of a country music queen assassinated during a concert. *The Godfather* films reveal Sonny Corleone machine-gunned to a bloody pulp. Michael Corleone assassinates a mobster and a police captain, and Luca Brasi is brutally strangled in close-up, facing the viewers. Carlo, Connie Corleone's husband, experiences the same fate but in a car, as viewers witness his feet shattering the windshield as he is pulled back to his death.

Movies mirror life. Sometimes they capture it; sometimes they amplify it with dramatic license. During the seventies there were outcries against excessive screen violence. The question has been raised whether it was used to add to the box office till or if it was dramatically appropriate. The films of the seventies presented a wide spectrum of man's inhumanity.

4

1972

January 25: African American Congresswoman Shirley Chisholm becomes the first woman to announce her candidacy for president of the United States. . . . June 17: Five men were arrested for breaking into the Democratic National Committee offices in the Watergate Office Complex in Washington, D.C. Two young *Washington Post* journalists, Bob Woodward and Carl Bernstein, doggedly followed the story and learned of a conspiracy that eventually led to the resignation of President Richard M. Nixon on August 9. . . . July 21: Comedian George Carlin performs his "Seven Words You Can Never Say" routine in Milwaukee, Wisconsin, and was arrested for obscenity. The case went to the Supreme Court, which ruled what Carlin had said was indecent but not obscene. . . . November 8, 7:30 p.m. EST: Home Box Office (HBO) is founded and launched by Time Inc. with a broadcast of an NHL hockey game and the first motion picture it distributed and released theatrically, an adaptation of Ken Kesey's 1964 novel *Sometimes a Great Notion* (1971), directed by and starring Paul Newman.

Boxcar Bertha was Martin Scorsese's second feature film. Roger Corman was looking for another female gangster B movie after the success of *Bloody Mama* (1970). Corman, who was not all that involved in preproduction, hired Scorsese for the project, which was all set to go. Corman insisted his directors follow his formula precisely as to where violence, nudity and the possibility of nudity, and other provocative elements should appear in the narrative. Nevertheless, Scorsese managed to bring atmosphere and style to the picture. Barbara Hershey, in the lead role, is nude in scenes, a rarity in later Scorsese films. *Boxcar Bertha* ends with

Stacy Keach in *Fat City*. *Columbia Pictures/Photofest © Columbia Pictures*

the crucifixion of David Carradine's character, Big Bill Shelley, who, like Bertha, is a train robber now involved in the lives of railroad workers and met by violent opposition. This is the first major religious event in a Martin Scorsese picture. When he directed the controversial *The Last Temptation of Christ* in 1988, Scorsese would go back to the scene when Big Bill Shelley is victimized to use it as an exacting model of how Christ was crucified.

Barbara Hershey was active in the seventies, appearing in ten films. They include *The Baby Maker* (1970), the first feature by James Bridges. She plays the controversial role of Tish Gray, a young woman who agrees to have a baby for a middle-class couple. Also in that year she worked with Classical Hollywood great William Wyler in his last feature film, *The Liberation of L. B. Jones*, as Nella Mundine, the wife of a young lawyer. The title character was an African American funeral director. For a period at this time Hershey changed her stage name to Barbara Seagull as a tribute to a creature killed during work on a film. Hershey acquired a reputation as a drug addict, especially after publicly breastfeeding Free, her child with David Carradine. She denied using drugs and continued as one of the hardest-working actresses of the decade, eventually returning to the surname Hershey.

David Carradine was a member of an eminent family of actors. He was the firstborn of John Carradine, the legendary Hollywood actor who appeared in *Stagecoach* (1939), *The Grapes of Wrath* (1940), and *The Man Who Shot Liberty Valance* (1962). David had two brothers who were significant in seventies cinema, Keith Carradine, who had a critical part in *Nashville* (1975), and Robert Carradine, who played a Vietnam vet in *Coming Home* (1978). David Carradine acted in sixteen films during the seventies. In 1973 he was directed again by Martin Scorsese in the film-maker's breakthrough movie *Mean Streets*, in which he played a bar drunk who is assassinated by a young mobster played by brother Robert. He appeared in *You and Me* (1974) as a biker. The cast included his brothers Keith and Robert and Barbara Hershey, whom he meets on the road. *Death Race 2000* (1975) is a cult film directed by Paul Bartel and produced by Roger Corman that takes place in a dystopian future. Carradine plays Frankenstein, a racer in the transcontinental road race, a national entertainment event filled with violence and death. In 1976 Carradine played the role of his lifetime as Woody Guthrie in the biopic *Bound for Glory*, directed by Hal Ashby. An epic American film about the power of song and freedom, Carradine's musicianship, singing ability, and capacity for capturing the times and Guthrie's attitude made him perfectly cast as the man who wrote *This Land Is Your Land*. In 1977 Carradine costarred with Liv Ullman in *The Serpent's Egg*, directed by Swedish film great Ingmar Bergman and produced by Dino De Laurentiis. Carradine plays a Jewish man in postwar Germany struggling with alcoholism. *Circle of Iron* (1978), a fantasy/martial arts film, was set to star Bruce Lee, but he died suddenly (and suspiciously) before production began. Carradine was given the part, playing the Blind Man, the Monkey-man, Death, and Chang-Sha. Although Carradine had appeared in many movies, he was best remembered as Kwai Chang Caine in the ABC television network series *Kung Fu*, which ran from 1972 to 1975 and became a cult classic.

Director James Bridges made a series of eclectic films beginning in the seventies with his first film, *The Baby Maker* (1970). The film was attacked by some critics for its forced hipness, but Roger Ebert found it human and honest, especially during the natural childbirth sequence. *The Paper Chase* (1973) was a box office hit. The film observes a Harvard

Law School classroom and examines the educational process and the relationship between a traditional, strict professor played by John Houseman in an Oscar-winning performance and a first-year student played by Timothy Bottoms. *September 30, 1955* (1977) is a drama that takes place on the day that James Dean died in a car crash, a significant date for the young people in a small town in Arkansas. *The China Syndrome* (1979) was a controversial success, and its content, a nuclear plant rupture, was an exposé from current news headlines. Bridges realistically stages the drama and creates a movie both entertaining and politically effective.

By the time the seventies rolled around, Robert Mulligan had established himself as a fine director with his stellar credit, *To Kill a Mockingbird*, in 1962. In 1971 he directed *Summer of '42*, a coming-of-age film in which a young man falls in love with a woman whose husband is off to war. *The Other* (1972) is a psychological thriller with a complex plot based on the novel by Thomas Tryon.

Hollywood master cinematographer Robert Surtees, who shot *The Last Picture Show* at the end of an illustrious career, shot *The Summer of '42*. His son Bruce Surtees would photograph twenty films during the seventies including *Conquest of the Planet of the Ape*s (directed by J. Lee Thompson, 1972), *Lenny* (Bob Fosse, 1974), *The Shootist* (Don Siegel, 1976), and *Big Wednesday* (John Milius, 1978). He was also the director of photography on Clint Eastwood's directorial debut, *Play Misty for Me*. Production designer Albert Brenner, who designed forty-seven films during his long career, could physically envision both comedy and drama. Editor Carl Pingitore began editing television series in the mid-fifties and edited eight movies in the seventies including *Dirty Harry*.

Deliverance is an adaptation of a novel by Southern writer James Dickey who also wrote the screenplay. Director John Boorman approached the project head on. Photographed by Vilmos Zsigmond, *Deliverance* starred Jon Voight, Burt Reynolds, Ned Beatty, and Ronny Cox. The story involves four men on a canoe trip in a remote area of Georgia. Dealing with the river is formidable, but unimaginable peril is in store. There is a set piece where Ronny Cox plays guitar and a peculiar local boy plays virtuoso banjo on "Dueling Banjos." They trade riffs as the tune escalates and culminates in a lively crescendo. Another scene in *Deliverance* that is provocative, grim, and violent shows one of the men being sodomized by a local, who is then killed with a bow and arrow by Reynolds's character. *Deliverance* was recognized as an action drama

with deep emotional depth, inflammatory themes, and outstanding performances by the ensemble cast.

John Boorman is a British filmmaker who made a distinctive impact
on American seventies cinema. *Point Blank* (1967) with Lee Marvin was
an American neo-noir crime film filled with vicious violence in an ultra-
contemporary setting and a complex narrative structure that was ahead of
its time and had a strong influence on the American New Wave. Boorman
began the seventies with *Leo the Last* (1970), shot in London and Ireland
but released by United Artists, which featured Marcello Mastroianni and
Billie Whitelaw in a stylized examination of the wealthy class and political shifts. One of the most bizarre films of the era, *Zardoz* (1974), with
production in Ireland, takes place in 2293 in a postapocalyptic society, its
title and meaning a mystery until it is uncovered that Zardoz is code for
The Wizard of Oz, released by 20th Century Fox. Topping *Zardoz* is
Boorman's *Exorcist II: The Heretic* shot in America and distributed by
Warner Bros. The plot goes far afield from an ultramodern apartment,
treatment center, and a biofeedback machine to Africa and hordes of
locusts and is presented in a totally over-the-top fashion compared to the
original.

Burt Reynolds was a major superstar. His career was as complicated
as his image. The seventies was a fertile time and demonstrated the di-
mension of his talent. He made more than twenty movies during the
decade. In *Deliverance* (1972) he proved he was a charismatic dramatic
actor with a formidable physicality. *The Longest Yard* (1974), directed by
Robert Aldrich, is a sports comedy in which Reynolds's character Paul
"Wrecking" Crewe, is a former pro football player who goes to prison
after stealing his girlfriend's car then forms a team inside the prison
walls. *At Long Last Love* (1975), directed by Peter Bogdanovich, was a
mistaken attempt to make an old-fashioned Hollywood musical. After
another backward glance at Old Hollywood in *Nickelodeon* (1976), Reynolds hit gold with *Smokey and the Bandit* (1977), playing good ole boy
Bo "Bandit" Darville in an extended car chase with the police. The film
cost $4.3 million and grossed $300 million. The film gave Burt Reynolds
a new persona with which he seemed comfortable, and it carried him
through several years of his career.

Fat City is a boxing movie that avoids clichés and focuses on the
quality of life of the characters and the impact that their seedy world has
upon them. The film is a seventies movie that is much more than a genre

piece. It depicts the dark side of life and the hopelessness of the down-and-out boxer lead character played by Stacy Keach. Veteran director John Huston was a boxer as a young man, and he applied his personal insight into the lower depths of boxing life. This film concludes at a food counter, with Jeff Bridges playing a young fighter and Keach waiting for a cup of coffee. They are served by a very aged man, which prompts a discussion about age, sadness, and happiness. As Keach thinks about whether the man seems happy and whether he is happy, he turns around. The camera zooms into a tight close-up of his face, cuts to a table where men play cards in total silence and stillness, then pans to another table with a different group of card players, also silent and motionless. These images leave Keach more than stunned. The action returns to the counter and the two men start talking again. Huston captures how the mind perceives reality and impacts the audience's ability to read these unpredictable images in a manner that allows them to question their own perceptions.

Conrad Hall was born in Tahiti. His father was James Norman Hall, who cowrote *Mutiny on the Bounty*. He became one of the most inventive and creative cinematographers of the seventies known for desaturating color and using lens flares as design elements as he photographed. In the sixties he crafted the look of modern cinematography in *In Cold Blood* (1967) directed by Richard Brooks and *Cool Hand Luke* (1967) directed by Stuart Rosenberg, and he won the Academy Award for cinematography for *Butch Cassidy and the Sundance Kid* in 1969, directed by George Roy Hill, in which he overexposed the negative to soften the primary colors. After *Fat City* (1972), he shot *Electra Glide in Blue* (1973), directed by James William Guercio, emphasizing thorough use of compositional space by juxtaposing Robert Blake's five foot, four inch height with those around him. In *Smile* (1975), film about a beauty contest, Hall used candy colors, soft focus, and bright light. In *Day of the Locust*, directed by John Schlesinger (1975), Hall captured a devastating look at Old Hollywood, interpreting the condemnation expressed in Nathaniel West's novella. In *Marathon Man* (1976), also directed by Schlesinger, he used contrasting lighting styles to define the diverse characters and a handheld camera for the running scenes.

Production designer Richard Sylbert captures the grit and grimy atmosphere in *Fat City*. He was the twin brother of Paul Sylbert, also a prominent production designer in the seventies. Richard began as a designer in live television working on Shakespeare productions. He designed many important projects including *Baby Doll* (1956) and *Splendor in the Grass* (1961) for Elia Kazan, *The Manchurian Candidate* (1962) for John Frankenheimer, *Who's Afraid of Virginia Woolf?* and *The Graduate* (1967) for Mike Nichols, and *Rosemary's Baby* (1968) for Roman Polanski. During the seventies Richard Sylbert worked on numerous marquee projects. In 1970 he designed *Catch-22* for Mike Nichols, taking on Joseph Heller's magnum opus. *Carnal Knowledge* (1971) was stylized in hyperrealism to focus on the four main characters. *Chinatown* (1974), written by Robert Towne and directed by Roman Polanski, is one of the most stylish period films of the seventies, enhanced by visual metaphors built into the design to support the narrative. In 1975 Sylbert designed *Shampoo* for Hal Ashby and cowriter, star, and producer Warren Beatty, which included a hair salon—described by the designer as the garden of heavenly delights—to support the character's womanizing.

Fritz the Cat is based on cartoon characters created by a teenage Robert Crumb who self-published them in a magazine with his brother before he became an underground comic superstar. Animator Ralph Bakshi came upon a *Fritz the Cat* comic while browsing in the East Side Book Shop. Bakshi traveled to San Francisco to meet Crumb to obtain the rights for a movie. After a week living with Crumb and his wife, Dana, the rights were still not solidified. Finally, Dana realized she had power of attorney over the material and signed with Bakshi. Drug use, sex, and blue language were excessive. Bakshi embraced the counterculture, the new morality (or amorality), and sexual freedom of the times and rejected the joyful singing animals of Walt Disney. Because of an X rating, *Fritz the Cat*'s advertising was severely hampered by newspaper rules against advertising X pictures. Then the *New York Times* and *Rolling Stone* wrote favorably about it, and *Fritz the Cat* was even invited to the Cannes Film Festival. The cantankerous Crumb was invited to see the film. He was convinced that Bakshi was a repressed individual and believed this affected the film. He threatened to sue to remove his name from the film. Bakshi had bad things to say about Crumb's artistic ability, but none of this got in the way of the film's success.

The Godfather is a masterpiece of seventies cinema that has stood the test of time, maintaining its high status as a celebrated American film. It is a long work, about three hours, that transcends its principal content, which is organized crime. The characters, the Corleones, are an Italian mob, but the film reaches for larger themes by exploring the nature of the family within the family and their complex relationships to the world and each other. *The Godfather* is about power, loyalty, territoriality, violence, and the politics of crime. Francis Ford Coppola directed it not because of a knowledge of organized crime, but because of his Italian American cultural background, which helped him humanize the characters.

Coppola allows the story to unfold as it keeps the audience engaged with the characters and presents brutal violence with the power of grand opera. The cinematographer Gordon Willis creates tableaus painted with strong light and dark, known as chiaroscuro, and rich color. The cast of *The Godfather* is legendary, including Marlon Brando as Vito Corleone, the head of the family; Al Pacino as Michael Corleone, the youngest son who eventually becomes head of the family; Diane Keaton as Michael's wife Kay; and Robert Duvall as Tom Hagen, the family's lawyer and consigliere. In addition to the many major roles is the uniquely talented John Cazale, well respected by his peers. There are character parts, friends and foe, who fill out the colorful ensemble. *The Godfather* is a great film in the way that great films are judged: by their content, themes, and visual style. It surpasses the genre of the mafia movie and takes its place with other great American films that are more than the sum of their parts.

Francis Ford Coppola was the oldest of the American New Wave filmmakers, and in his position in the movement and his relationship to the others and their accomplishments, Coppola was the dean. Coppola earned a degree in theater arts from Hofstra College in 1960 and did graduate work in film at UCLA. He worked with Roger Corman in various capacities. After directing two soft-core films, *The Bellboy and the Playgirls* and *Tonight for Sure* (both 1962), and a few days on a horror film starring Boris Karloff for which he was uncredited, he directed his first feature, *Dementia 13* (1963). He then directed the old-fashioned musical *Finian's Rainbow* (1968), starring Petula Clark and Fred Astaire, but it showed little if any sign of the beginning of the New Wave. *The Rain People* (1969) was a personal movie for Coppola, a road movie of sorts about a pregnant woman looking to find freedom and to examine her life. Also in 1969, Coppola decided to avoid the studio system by co-founding American Zoetrope with George Lucas, a privately run production company for developing young filmmakers and new movies geared to audiences looking for progressive cinema. Coppola began the seventies by cowriting *Patton* (1970), which won the Academy Award for Best Original Screenplay. After *The Godfather*, Coppola returned to the small personal films he cherished with *The Conversation* (1974), about a surveillance expert whose life slowly comes apart when the craft of surveillance is turned on him. It became a cult movie that gained respect over the years. The success of *The Godfather* led to *The Godfather: Part II*, a rare sequel that many believe surpasses the original. Francis Ford Coppola closed out the seventies with *Apocalypse Now* (1979), a film about the Vietnam War, which almost destroyed his spirits and finances.

Talia Shire, Francis Ford Coppola's sister, played Connie in *The Godfather* and is an accomplished actress in her own right. She enjoyed a second round of stardom playing Adrian Pennino, Rocky Balboa's girlfriend then wife in many of the franchise sequels.

James Caan, who played the hotheaded Sonny, was in numerous films during the seventies including *Rabbit Run* directed by Jack Smight (1970), an adaptation of the novel by John Updike; *Slither* directed by Howard Zieff (1973); *Cinderella Liberty* directed by Mark Rydell (1973); *The Gambler* directed by Karel Reisz (1974); *Funny Lady* directed by Hebert Ross (1975); and *Rollerball* directed by Norman Jewison (1975). He also appeared in *A Bridge Too Far* (1977) and *Comes a Horseman* (1978) directed by Alan J. Pakula. Uncredited, he played a sailor in a fight scene in Scorsese's *New York, New York*.

Robert Duvall, who played consigliere Tom Hagen, was in twelve movies during the seventies including Coppola's *The Conversation* (1974), in which he portrays a powerful man who seems to be hiding a secret; Peckinpah's *Killer Elite*; *The Seven-Percent Solution* directed by Herbert Ross (1976); *Network* directed by Sidney Lumet (1976); Coppola's *Apocalypse Now* (1979) as the unflappable Lieutenant Colonel Kilmore, for which he won an Oscar for Best Supporting Actor; and *The Great Santini* (1979) as an ultra-strict father.

John Cazale, who played Fredo in the first two *Godfather* films, portrayed an assistant to the surveillance expert (Gene Hackman) in *The Conversation* directed by Coppola in 1974 and Sal, the doomed member of a failed bank holdup team in *Dog Day Afternoon* (1978) directed by Sidney Lumet. His last role was as Stan, a crass member of the working-class group of friends in *The Deer Hunter* directed by Michael Cimino. Cazale was dying of cancer during filming and continued working until his role was completed.

Character actor Al Lettieri played the dangerous mobster Sollozzo in *The Godfather* and a pathological criminal in Peckinpah's *The Getaway* (1972). He also appeared in the John Wayne cop movie *McQ* (1974) directed by John Sturges and with Charles Bronson in *Mr. Majestyk* (1974) directed by Richard Fleisher.

Actor Sterling Hayden is known for his work in two Stanley Kubrick films: the leader of a racetrack heist in *The Killing* (1956) and a maniacal brigadier general in *Dr. Strangelove* (1964). In *The Godfather* he plays Captain McCluskey, a crooked cop paid off by the mob who is hit along with Sollozzo by Michael Corleone. In 1973 he appeared in Robert Altman's *The Long Goodbye* and in 1979 he was in *Winter Kills* directed by William Richert.

John Marley plays Hollywood studio head Jack Woltz who finds a severed horse's head in his bed when he refuses the Don's request for a favor. Marley worked with John Cassavetes in *Faces* (1968) and appeared in *Love Story* (1970) directed by Arthur Hiller.

Richard Bright is in all three *Godfather* movies as Al Neri, who was an assistant doing whatever needed to be done for the Dons. He worked with Sam Peckinpah on *The Getaway* (1972), *Pat Garrett & Billy the Kid* (1973), and again in *Bring Me the Head of Alfredo Garcia* (1974). In 1976 he was in *Marathon Man* for director John Schlesinger.

Dean Tavoularis is a major production designer known for the totality of the environments he has created on films. He began working with Arthur Penn to design the seminal *Bonnie and Clyde* and on *Little Big Man* in 1970. Also in that year, he designed *Zabriskie Point*, directed by Michelangelo Antonioni, the Italian director's only film made in America. He collaborated with Francis Ford Coppola on the three *Godfather* films (1972, 1974, 1990), *The Conversation* (1974), and *Apocalypse Now* (1979). He also designed *The Brinks Job* in 1978 for William Friedkin.

Gordon Willis had the respect of all cinematographers of his generation. He believed most pictures were overlit, which led to his nickname, "the prince of darkness." His aesthetic was rigorous. Often his camera shot directly into a bright light and the characters in the foreground were dramatically modeled in shadow. He worked with extremely low light levels and frequently positioned his camera directly in front of the characters as opposed to employing angles. The *Godfather* movies reveal the painterly aspects of cinematography including Rembrandt lighting, a strong definition of chiaroscuro. In *All the President's Men* (1976), directed by Alan J. Pakula, Willis photographically re-created the *Washington Post* newsroom. His work with Woody Allen on *Annie Hall* (1978) and *Manhattan* (1979) provided the writer/director with photography that suited Allen's funny and serious identities. *Interiors* (1978) translated Ingmar Bergman into an austere American style.

During the editing of *The Godfather*, Coppola was concerned about the length of the picture. At one point he asked his two Hollywood veteran editors, two-time Oscar winner William Reynolds, *Love Is a Many Splendored Thing* (1955) and *Sound of Music* (1965), and Oscar winner Peter Zinner, *The Professionals* (1966) and *In Cold Blood* (1967), to remove scene after scene until Robert Evans, head of Paramount at the time, screened the material and said if it's good—and it was—it stays in.

Musicals provide an effective platform for presenting a powerful point of view about serious subjects. *Cabaret* is set in the Weimar Republic in Berlin as Adolf Hitler's Nazi party gains power. The film draws from several sources including the 1966 Broadway musical and Christopher Isherwood's *The Berlin Stories*, written in 1945. Songs are by John Kander and Fred Ebb, which were from the Broadway musical. The story centers on the Kit Kat Club, a decadent den fueled by sexual desire and raunchy fun. Liza Minnelli plays Sally Bowles, the lead performer whose romantic escapades and mesmerizing routines are part of the story. Joel Grey is the master of ceremonies who keeps the all-woman band, the raucous customers, and the dancers under control like a ringmaster. Director Bob Fosse handles the dancing with his signature choreography and tracks the rise of the Nazis by slowly adding them to the crowd until, by the end, it is clear that the uniformed soldiers of the Third Reich have taken over. During the year of *The Godfather*, *Cabaret* proved stiff competition. It won eight Oscars including a statue each for Fosse, Minnelli, and Grey. It was nominated for Best Picture but lost to Coppola's *The Godfather*. *Cabaret* is everything a musical can be; it is entertaining, slick, and well produced, with great musical and dance numbers, and it documents a time when the fate of the world was at stake.

In the 1970s filmmakers began to take on challenging contemporary novels with complex structures. *Slaughterhouse-Five* (1972) was skillfully adapted into a film that cinematically created an equivalent for the phenomenon experienced by the main character Billy Pilgrim, a prisoner of the Germans during the Allied bombing of Dresden in World War II. In Kurt Vonnegut's novel, Billy becomes "unstuck in time." He has no control over where he is, whether back in the war, in contemporary time in his home, or on the planet Tralfamadore. The key to the movie was finding moments and images for the transitions from one place to another, a collaboration among director George Roy Hill, cinematographer Miroslav Ondříček, and film editor Dede Allen. The result is a fine adaptation of a difficult book and a movie that is far from traditional.

After *Slaughterhouse-Five*, Hill had a major hit with *The Sting* (1973), starring Paul Newman and Robert Redford. This elaborate period caper movie was highly entertaining and a big box office success. *Slap Shot* (1977) was a raucous sports movie. George Roy Hill was a craftsman, not considered a film artist, but his films enlivened the decade by exploring different narratives with entertainment on his mind.

Dede Allen was the most significant film editor of her time. She brought the craft of editing into the modern era during the sixties and seventies. Allen's approach to editing was to concentrate solely on performance and story; everything else was taken out or vastly reduced. She is considered the master of compression, squeezing out anything that slowed down a shot or scene. She is best known for her revolutionary editing on *Bonnie and Clyde*, in which she moved away from traditional methods of progressing from one scene to another, eliminating or reducing the fade-to-black/fade-in-from-black editorial transition and bringing modernity to a period film. During the seventies Allen worked on the epic police drama *Serpico* (1973), coedited by Richard Marks and directed by Sidney Lumet, a true-life story in which the lead character, Frank Serpico, changed his lifestyle and the police department itself. *Dog Day Afternoon* (1975), a complex film involving a bank robbery, the crowd gathered outside, law enforcement, and a barbershop used as a communications headquarters. There are many characters, and Allen brings pace and clarity to the involved proceedings.

Czechoslovakian-born Miroslav Ondříček may have spoken little English when he shot *Slaughterhouse-Five*, but his images were eloquent and interpreted Kurt Vonnegut's contemporary literary masterpiece beautifully. Henry Bumstead, the film's veteran production designer affectionately known as "Bummy," had a long career and was deeply respected. He made numerous pictures with director Clint Eastwood.

Super Fly is a blaxploitation film directed by Gordon Parks Jr. about an African American pimp and drug dealer who is trying to quit the drug business. The soundtrack is iconic, written and produced by soul musician Curtis Mayfield. Like most blaxploitation films, *Super Fly* was produced by a large corporation, in this case Warner Bros., and had a white producer. The film was financed, in part, by the director's father, Gordon Parks, and the screenwriter Phillip Fenty. Reaction to the film was strong. The NAACP opposed blaxploitation films that exposed children to pimps and drug dealers. Post–civil rights figures saw the movie as a portrayal of how black men could rise in a white society. The NAACP, along with other organizations, wanted to block distribution of *Super Fly*. Some claimed it showed the failure of the civil rights movement to provide positive incentives to young black men, whereas the film's producers insisted the film showed the negatives of the drug life.

Gordon Parks Jr. followed *Super Fly* with *Three the Hard Way* (1974), in which a trio takes on a white neofascist group who wants to wipe out all African Americans. As with his first film, it is also a blaxploitation movie. *Thomasine & Bushrod* (1974) is a blaxploitation Western considered a counterpart to *Bonnie and Clyde* (1967). *Aaron Loves Angela* (1975) is a modern retelling of *Romeo and Juliet*. Irene Cara, who would become a star in *Fame* (1980), played Angela, and Kevin Hooks from *Sounder* played Aaron. Tragically, while on his way to Kenya to make a film, Gordon Parks Jr. and three others died after their small plane crashed after takeoff. Parks was forty-four years old.

In 1972 John Flynn directed *The Jerusalem File* about an American in Israel before the Six-Day War. In 1973 Flynn wrote and directed *The Outfit*. It is the story of a thief, Earl Macklin, played by Robert Duvall, who gets out of prison and learns his brother has been killed in a hit. *The Outfit* ends after the main characters, driving in a car, establish that they are the good guys since they took out the mob boss and his compound, thereby achieving revenge. The film ends in a freeze-frame on their triumphant faces. John Flynn closed out the seventies with the controversial *Rolling Thunder* (1978). Like *The Outfit*, it was extremely violent but went further with a gut-churning sequence written by Paul Schrader in which a man's hand is jammed into a sink's garbage disposal and ground to bits.

During the seventies, the editing transition known as a freeze-frame was a popular tool, especially when used to end a film. The seventies films were before the digital revolution, which changed the way movies were made. Then, movies were shot and edited on film. A freeze-frame is when a shot suddenly stops and freezes into a still image. It was prepared by the editor and created in a film laboratory. A freeze-frame that ends a film stops the action, allowing the viewer to contemplate the state of a character at that final point in time.

The contemporary history of the freeze-frame famously begins in a foreign black-and-white film *The 400 Blows* (1959) directed by French New Wave director François Truffaut. The movie concludes with a troubled boy jogging on a beach, who turns and moves toward the camera. There is an optical (laboratory zoom-in) and then a freeze-frame. The audience wonders what becomes of the boy as he stares at us in a haunting manner. In the 1969 Western *Butch Cassidy and the Sundance Kid*, directed by George Roy Hill, Paul Newman and Robert Redford find themselves holed up in a small town in Bolivia where an army waits to capture them. Eventually they draw their guns and charge outside. They run toward the camera, shooting at an unseen enemy, then the scene freezes. Off-camera, a voice signals a barrage of gunfire.

Rocky (1976), directed by John G. Avildsen and written and starring Sylvester Stallone, concludes with the dramatic and vicious fight between Apollo Creed and Rocky Balboa. The fight is gripping and brutal. Creed is the winner of the split decision, but Rocky has gone the distance—the fifteen rounds—which is the metaphor for this crowd-pleaser. Rocky's girlfriend Adrian (Talia Shire) enters during the last moments of the bout. With the fight over, Rocky sees Adrian and loudly shouts her name, and she returns the call. Bill Conti's legendary musical score bursts from the theater speakers. The cutting goes back and forth until finally Adrian enters the ring and they embrace in close-up, the freeze-frame displaying his exhaustion and deep love for this woman.

In *The Hills Have Eyes* (1977), directed by Wes Craven, a suburban family is hunted by a group of cannibals. In the end there is a long battle between a cannibal and a civilian. The civilian stabs the cannibal to death, a knife plunging into his body. Finally, he is dead and the image of the exhausted survivor freezes and turns to red, symbolizing the cannibal's blood. The demise of the cannibal and the brutality of the scene are necessary to end the clash between civilization and cannibals.

One of the most controversial and talked-about endings in a seventies movie is in Monte Hellman's *Two-Lane Blacktop*. The Driver, played by James Taylor, is about to begin a drag race. Inside the car he looks intense and determined. Reality begins to change with a sound: an echoed effect signals altered reality. The camera, now positioned behind him, captures his long hair bouncing gently up and down as the race begins. The image slows gradually, his hair bouncing more slowly, as does the view of the road in front of him, until everything comes to a full and complete stop. Suddenly, the image bursts into flames and is no more. It should be noted that all of this was done in the predigital era, so it was accomplished on film in a laboratory. During the seventies (and earlier), if a piece of celluloid film got stuck in the gate of a projector, it eventually burst into flame, burning until the screen went blank. This is what many viewers seeing *Two-Lane Blacktop* in first run thought had happened. At that time and since then, there have been many theories as to the meaning of this ending. Hellman has said little except that it came to him in a dream and that, looking back, it was an intellectual conceit. Was it that the filmmakers didn't know how to end this film? Is it a way of signaling to the audience that these characters have come to the end of their largely aimless journey? Hellman was an existentialist and this lack of finality sits within his philosophy. Whatever interpretation is chosen, this ending is an expansive use of the freeze-frame and one that evokes considerable thought.

Images was directed by Robert Altman. The film is stylish, photographed by Vilmos Zsigmond, with production design by Leon Erickson, who designed *McCabe & Mrs. Miller*. In *Images* the female lead, played by Susanna York, is going insane. Altman takes the viewer in and out of her point of view as her grip on reality continues to change. Her personal existence begins to unravel, and she confuses all the men in her life. Altman was a strong admirer of Ingmar Bergman, a director interested in the inner lives of women. Altman often tried to better understand the female psyche through the camera.

Bob Rafelson moved in an art-house direction for *The King of Marvin Gardens* and cast one of the principal characters against type. Jack Nicholson had established himself as a strong leading man, usually unpredictable, who played characters often connected to the counterculture and very masculine. In *Marvin Gardens* he plays David Staebler, host of an offbeat literary talk radio program in which he tells long stories that are strong on mood and less so on narrative. He is bespectacled, quiet, and reserved, totally the opposite of his brother Jason, played by Bruce Dern, a flamboyant braggadocio who convinces David to join his moneymaking scheme in Atlantic City. It is winter in a summer resort area, and the film has a depressed, grim quality occasionally broken by Dern's bluster. Ellen Burstyn is Sally, a former beauty queen and prostitute, who is Dern's girlfriend. Jessica, her stepdaughter, played by Julia Anne Robinson, seems to follow in Sally's footsteps. All the relationships deteriorate as the story progresses. The ending is sudden, violent, and shocking. *The King of Marvin Gardens* demonstrated Rafelson's ability to create movies that explored unknown directions. The film did poorly at the box office, which rejected the idea of an actor going against type and a director moving into uncharacteristic realms.

László Kovács was one of the seventies' busiest cinematographers, working with Bob Rafelson for the second time. Again, Rafelson's ex-wife Toby created the production design.

Bruce Dern is a fine actor who was in more than twenty movies during the seventies. Although he has a dramatic and comedic range, Dern often played deranged, off-balanced characters who were emotionally on the edge. Dern appeared in several biker movies such as *The Rebel Rousers* (1970), in which motorcycle riders participate in a drag race to "win" an architect's pregnant girlfriend. In *The Incredible 2-Headed Transplant* (1971), Dern plays a rich scientist experimenting with head transplants. In *Drive, He Said* (1971) Dern portrays a college basketball coach with inspired realism, incorporating appropriate emotions as he deals with his team. In *Silent Running* (1971), directed by special effects wizard Douglas Trumbull, Dern plays a future astronaut experimenting on reforesting in space. When the project is endangered, he commits murder to save the plants he has been growing. Bruce Dern worked with Alfred Hitchcock on *Family Plot*, in which he is the boyfriend of a fake psychic. *Coming Home* (1978), directed by Hal Ashby, is one of Dern's best performances as a soldier in Vietnam who experiences a marital crisis while on a tour of duty when his wife (Jane Fonda) has an affair with a paraplegic veteran portrayed by Jon Voight.

The Poseidon Adventure defined the disaster movie genre. The premise is simple, effective, and powerful. A ship packed with passengers is sailing to Greece on New Year's when horrendous ocean conditions turn the vessel upside down. The cast is filled with Oscar winners and actors easily recognizable to the audience, including Gene Hackman as the rebellious minister Reverend Scott, Ernest Borgnine as the impatient and volatile retired police officer Mike Rogo, and Shelley Winters as Belle Rosen, whose husband Manny, played by Jack Albertson, is a retired store owner. The Jewish couple is traveling to see their grandson in Israel.

Red Buttons as James Martin is a kind, gentle haberdasher who is shy around women. Chaos consumes the large dining room where a celebration is in progress. There are enormous fatalities and massive injuries. Martin quickly understands that the only way out is to move up, and the reverend organizes a small group willing to take the risk. A series of explosions break open part of the ship, and everyone who was waiting in the ballroom drowns. The reverend and his small group proceed upward. The cinematic genius behind walking up to the bottom of the damaged ship presents possibilities for production design and special effects. Every part of the ship that was upright before the accident is upside down, and the group must constantly deal with and understand this new logic. There is plenty of drama and personality reveals. Not everyone makes it, and the film ends with a major sacrifice. *The Poseidon Adventure* is the brainchild of producer Irwin Allen and his team. It even contains an Academy Award–winning musical number, "The Morning After," performed in the film by Carol Linley's character Nonnie Parry. The film won four Academy Awards including Best Visual Effects (as a special achievement award) and eight nominations including Best Art Direction. *The Poseidon Adventure* led the way for many more disaster pictures that explored people under extreme pressure dealing with life and death.

Sounder is a drama with an African American cast that is not a blaxploitation picture. It was directed by Martin Ritt, who devoted his career to social issues and the human condition. *Sounder* deals with sharecroppers during the Great Depression. Sounder is a dog. The dog is David Lee's (Kevin Hooks) pet and companion. *Sounder* was nominated for four Academy Awards: Best Picture; Best Actor for Paul Winfield as the father, Nathan; Best Actress for Cicely Tyson portraying the mother, Rebecca; and Best Screenplay based on material from another medium. Lonnie Elder III wrote the screenplay based on the young adult novel by William H. Armstrong. Skeptics, assuming the market for black films was strictly blaxploitation and action movies, felt that the film would do poorly at the box office, but *Sounder*—made for less than $1 million— earned $9 million in U.S. theatrical rentals and was the fifteenth highest-grossing film of 1972.

Cicely Tyson began acting in the fifties. *Sounder* gave her attention as a strong black woman and established her as a formidable actress. In 1976 Tyson joined Elizabeth Taylor, Jane Fonda, and Ava Gardner in the children's fantasy film *The Blue Bird*, directed by legendary Hollywood director George Cukor. Also in 1976 Cicely Tyson appeared in *The River Niger* as a member of a family trying to live in the Watts ghetto in Los Angeles, California. In *A Hero Ain't Nothin' but a Sandwich*, Tyson plays the mother of a teenager who is struggling after his father has left the family. In an early role with great pathos, she played a conflicted daughter of a prominent surgeon who is dying in *The Heart Is a Lonely Hunter* (1968) directed by Robert Ellis Miller.

Film director Martin Ritt began in the theater and was politically astute and liberal minded. He was surrounded by the Red Scare and pigeonholed as a communist. He denied the charges but was blacklisted by the television industry and could not work for many years. He returned to the theater, and when fear of communist infiltration in the industry lessened, he began to direct movies. Throughout his career he returned to themes of corruption, racism, and intimidation of the individual. In 1970 Ritt directed *The Molly McGuires*, which examines the exploitation of coal mine workers. Also in 1970 *The Great White Hope* was released about the great boxer Jack Johnson and his controversial marriage to a Caucasian woman. Martin Ritt directed *Conrack* (1974), which features Jon Voight as a white teacher of mostly poor black children in the South. *The Front* (1976) is a comedy that directly addresses the blacklist; Woody Allen plays a character who "fronts" for a blacklisted writer by selling the writer's script—a practice that actually occurred. *Norma Rae* (1979) was based on the true story of a worker in a cotton factory who is radicalized and becomes a labor unionizer. Sally Field won the Oscar for portraying the title role.

John Alonzo shot the seminal film *Chinatown* (1974). For *Sounder* he captured the period and the rural life of the characters. Production designer Walter Scott Herdon crafted several films for *Sounder*'s director Martin Ritt including *Conrack*.

The Visitors is a low-budget independent film, a bare-bones production directed by Hollywood filmmaker Elia Kazan, who was known for *On the Waterfront* (1954), *East of Eden* (1955), and *Splendor in the Grass* (1961). The screenplay was written by Christopher Kazan, son of the director, and shot in and around his Connecticut home. The film was photographed and edited by Nicholas T. Proferes, who did the same on *Wanda* for Barbra Loden, who had been married to Elia Kazan. Two Vietnam vets, Sergeant Mike Nickerson (Steven Railsback) and Tony Rodriguez (Chico Martinez), visit fellow soldier Bill Schmidt (James

Woods in his first screen role). It unfolds that Mike was responsible for killing a civilian and Bill testified against him, landing Mike in the stockade for two years. Mike and Tony are there for revenge. *The Visitors* is a volatile film that covers another aspect of Vietnam films in the seventies: uncontrolled rage among fellow soldiers who believe they have been wrongly accused.

Elia Kazan had a muscular directing style and was known for his success with talented and difficult actors, many of whom he discovered. During the blacklist era, he named names and many colleagues never forgave him. Kazan's last film was *The Last Tycoon* (1973), based on an unfinished novel by F. Scott Fitzgerald in which Robert De Niro plays Monroe Stahr, based on Hollywood wunderkind Irving Thalberg. This film fared poorly at the box office.

What's up Doc? was a huge hit for Peter Bogdanovich and one of the biggest films of the year. It is his tribute to the screwball comedy subgenre style. Bogdanovich was a solid admirer of the Hollywood Studio System great Howard Hawks, and this film is inspired by that director's classic *Bringing up Baby.* Ryan O'Neal plays Howard Bannister, a musicologist with a theory about ancient man, rocks, and the production of music. Barbra Streisand plays Judy Maxwell, a goofy, hippie-like woman who keeps getting in Howard's way. There are many subplots that deepen the planned illogic of the story. The film made the point that audiences still responded to old-fashioned comedies in the seventies while serious dramas and new forms were being released.

Ryan O'Neal made a name for himself as an actor on television playing Rodney Harrington on the ABC nighttime soap opera *Peyton Place.* When he transitioned into movies, he was immediately successful with *Love Story* (1970), a cinema soap opera in which a couple in love must face the wife's early death. In *Paper Moon* (1973), directed by Peter Bogdanovich, O'Neal and his daughter Tatum play con artists during the Great Depression. Tatum O'Neal won the Oscar for Best Supporting Actress, the youngest actress to receive the statuette at ten years old. In 1975 Ryan O'Neal played the title role in Stanley Kubrick's epic period film *Barry Lyndon.* In 1978 O'Neal worked with writer/director Walter Hill in the existential crime film *The Driver.*

Barbra Streisand entered the seventies as a major superstar in theater, film, and as a recording artist. In 1970 she appeared in *On a Clear Day You Can See Forever*, an adaptation of a 1965 stage production. It was directed by the legendary Hollywood director Vincente Minnelli. In *The Owl and the Pussycat*, also released in 1970, Streisand plays an uneducated actress-model and part-time prostitute. After *What's up, Doc?* Barbra Streisand appeared in *The Way We Were* (1973) with Robert Redford, directed by Sidney Pollack. It was a period piece about left-wing political fervor, disparate beliefs, and love. Streisand also sang the title song, which won an Oscar. In 1976 she starred with Kris Kristofferson in the third remake of *A Star Is Born*.

The Last House on the Left (1972) is Wes Craven's low-budget breakthrough horror film with a new viciousness. The story was inspired by Ingmar Bergman's *The Virgin Spring*. The film was produced by Sean S. Cunningham, who later directed *Friday the 13th* (1980), a key film in the slasher film subgenre of the horror movie. The grisly plot concerns two teenage girls who are tortured in the woods. It was a box office hit. Reviews chided the filmmakers for the use of violence against young women for exploitative purposes.

Wes Craven began as a professor of humanities at Clarkson College of Technology in Potsdam, New York. He bought a 16mm camera and began making short films. His friend Steve Chapin told him about a messenger job in a New York City production house where his brother, folk-rock star Harry Chapin, worked. Craven's first creative job in the film industry was as a sound editor. He stated that it was Harry Chapin, who worked in industrials (sponsored films made to highlight a company), who taught him the nuts and bolts of editing. In 1977 Craven directed an unsettling and disturbing movie, *The Hills Have Eyes*, in which a middle-class family is stranded in a Nevada desert where they are attacked by a band of cannibals. This cult classic has been interpreted as a commentary on morality and politics.

Slasher films usually involve a traumatic anniversary that activates a murderer to viciously kill individuals with bladed instruments. They are bloody and gruesome. Hitchcock's *Psycho* (1960), Tobe Hooper's *The Texas Chainsaw Massacre* (1974), and John Carpenter's *Halloween* (1978) are watersheds in this movement, which was intended to create a catharsis in the audience, casting off their sexual and violent feelings. Other slasher movies include *Silent Night, Bloody Night* directed by Theodore Gershuny (1972), *Black Christmas* (1974) directed by Bob Clark, and *Drive-in Massacre* (1976) directed by Stu Segal.

Night Call Nurses is the third film in the *Nurses* series by king of the B movies, Roger Corman, which began with *The Student Nurses* (1970). The plot centered around the adventures of each of the three night-call nurses played by Patty Byrne as Barbara, Alana Hamilton as Janis, and Mittie Lawrence as Sandra. Jonathan Kaplan was the director, recommended to Corman by Martin Scorsese, who had been his film teacher at New York University. Corman laid out the formula for the cycle: Dick Miller, who appeared in countless Corman films, had to be in the movie. There had to be a Bulova watch and a Jensen automobile in the picture. The three nurses in the film included a brunette, a blonde, and a nurse of color. The brunette would be involved in a kinky subplot, the nurse of color would be involved in a political subplot, and the blonde was in the comedy subplot. On nudity, Corman stated it was to be from the waist up, total nudity from behind, and no pubic hair. *Night Call Nurses* cost $75,000 and grossed $1 million.

Jonathan Kaplan made the award-winning short *Stanley* (1965). In 1973 Corman hired Kaplan again for *The Student Teachers*, inspired by the *Nurses* cycle, another series of films featuring young women and sexual hijinks. Corman's exploitation formula was applied. *The Slams* (1973) was a starring vehicle for NFL great Jim Brown, who plays a man caught by the police after a heist. Once in prison, many people want to know where the money is, and he must escape and retrieve it before the location where it is hidden is demolished. *Truck Turner* (1975) is a blaxploitation picture with Isaac Hayes, Yaphet Kotto, and Nichelle Nichols. The film was edited by Michael Kahn, who three years later would begin a forty-year relationship with Steven Spielberg. In 1975 Kaplan directed *White Line Fever*, an action film featuring Jan-Michael Vincent that focused on the complications encountered by a trucker. *Over the Edge* is a 1979 film in which a group of teenagers lives in an isolated planned community. Their rebellious behavior explodes when one of them is shot to death by a police officer. Cinematographer R. Michael Stringer has 157 credits that include just about every job there is in the camera department, mostly on B pictures.

Jan-Michael Vincent was a blond bad-boy type popular in the seventies in films including *White Line Fever* directed by Jonathan Kaplan (1975), *Vigilante Force* directed by George Armitage (1976), and *Big Wednesday* directed by John Milius (1978).

Harry Northup is a character actor who often worked with Martin Scorsese and Jonathan Demme in the seventies. He was unforgettable as Doughboy in *Taxi Driver* (1976), who tries to hustle Travis Bickle, played by Robert De Niro. He played Sargent Doberman in *Over the Edge* (1979), a defining film about the angst of youth. Other films Harry Northup appeared in include *Boxcar Bertha* (1972), *Mean Streets* (1973), *Alice Doesn't Live Here Anymore* (1974), and *Blue Collar* (1978).

Dick Miller was a character actor who was in 180 films, most produced by Roger Corman. Miller was a likable person who often played everyman. He most often appeared in one scene in a film. Some of the movies he performed in include *Not of This Earth* (1957), *A Bucket of Blood* (1959), *The Little Shop of Horrors* (1960), *Night Call Nurses* (1972), *Truck Turner* (1974), *Death Race 2000* (1975), *New York, New York* (1977), *Piranha* (1978), and *Rock 'n' Roll High School* (1979).

Painters Painting is a major documentary about artists and art movements from abstract expressionism to pop art. This feat is accomplished through conversations with artists in their studios. The painters include Willem de Kooning, Jasper Johns, Andy Warhol, Helen Frankenthaler, Hans Hoffman, Frank Stella, and Barnett Newman. This examination of the New York art scene from 1940 to 1970 was made by documentarian Emile de Antonio.

Emile de Antonio was an important political and counterculture documentary filmmaker. During the sixties, de Antonio made two films about Joseph McCarthy that exposed his demagogy. He also investigated the assassination of President John F. Kennedy on film in *Rush to Judgement* (1967). The controversial *In the Year of the Pig* (1969) took a hard look at the Vietnam War, which was still in progress. In 1971 he made *Millhouse: A White Comedy*, a scathing exposé of Richard Nixon. After *Painters Painting*, De Antonio, along with activist and cinematographer Haskell Wexler and film editor Mary Lampson, took the bold step of making *Underground* (1976), a documentary about the extremely radical Weather Underground, a militant faction of the Students for a Democratic Society. The filmmakers are seen in the film, but not the members of the group who were photographed behind or through a screen. After *Underground* was completed, the FBI subpoenaed the filmmakers to get all the footage they had shot to aid them in arresting the Weather Underground members. A community of actors and directors in Hollywood stood behind the filmmakers and eventually the subpoena was withdrawn based on free speech grounds. *Underground* (1976) tested the rights of the documentary filmmaker.

Play It as It Lays is an adaptation of the novel by Joan Didion. The director was Frank Perry and the screenplay was written by the successful husband-and-wife team, Joan Didion and John Gregory Dunne. Tuesday Weld, Adam Roarke, and Anthony Perkins play lost, disturbed characters in a story that shifts from a mental institution to flashbacks of early life to create a dim portrait of lives adrift.

Frank Perry started his feature film career with the independent film *David and Lisa*, a love story between two mentally ill young people released in 1962; it was controversial due to its openness about the subject. In 1968 Perry directed *The Swimmer*, in which Burt Lancaster plays Ned Merrill, a man who decides to swim home from one swimming pool to another, engaging with people all the way. The seventies began for Frank Perry with *Diary of a Mad Housewife* (1970), starring actress Carrie Snodgrass, with an adapted screenplay by his then-wife Eleanor Perry. In this film, the burgeoning women's movement is embraced with a feminist view of a woman's role in society. This breakthrough movie is a candid look at a troubled marriage.

Eleanor Perry was a powerful and influential screenwriter during the sixties and seventies. She was a feminist who spoke out against sexism and for women's rights and recognition in the industry. She began as a novelist and playwright and had a master's degree in psychiatric social work. She married director Frank Perry in 1960 and wrote scripts for his films including *Diary of a Mad Housewife*, *David and Lisa* (1961), *The Swimmer* (1968), and *Last Summer* (1969). They divorced in 1971 and she continued to speak out about the plight of women in film and to write screenplays such as *The Man Who Loved Cat Dancing* (1973), the story of the murder of a Native American woman, directed by Richard C. Sarafian. She continued writing until her death at sixty-six.

Jordan Cronenweth, the cinematographer on *Play It as It Lays*, has the distinction in film history of being the director of photography on Ridley Scott's *Blade Runner* (1982), a high example of the art. Production designer Pato Guzman designed *Bob & Carol & Ted & Alice* (1969), which explored the sexual revolution and at the same time served as a gateway to the 1970s. Editor Sidney Katz spent the sixties editing films, often for director Frank Perry.

Dirty Little Billy is a Western cowritten and directed by Stan Dragoti in his feature film debut. The film stars Michael J. Pollard—who appeared in *Bonnie and Clyde*—as Billy the Kid. The film breaks the long-standing myth of Billy the Kid, challenging who he was and his appearance. Compared to old Hollywood images, this portrait of him and the world around him is darker and more threatening.

The Heartbreak Kid is a dark romantic comedy written by Neil Simon and directed by Elaine May. The female lead, Lila, is performed by Jeanne Berlin, Elaine May's daughter, who marries Lenny Cantro, played by Charles Grodin. On their honeymoon, complications arise when Cantro meets the calculating Kelly Corcoran, played by Cybil Shepard. May explores Jewish identity and the dark but funny crevices in relationships. May's idiosyncratic style received much attention.

In 1966 Jack Valenti, former press liaison for the Kennedy and Johnson administrations, devised the Motion Picture Association of America's (MPAA) film rating system at the insistence of Universal Studios chief Lew Wasserman. It had four distinct ratings—G, M, R, and X—to help guide viewers about the content of films. At the time, the X rating was the most extreme rating, which was used to denote explicit sex and violence, but because it was not trademarked, the adult pornography film industry usurped the X, transforming it into XXX, and self-applying the unofficial rating.

Midnight Cowboy (1969) is about two misfits in New York, Jon Voight, who becomes a hustler, and Dustin Hoffman, a disabled, physically ill con man. They live together in squalor and desperation. The adult sexual content is graphic, and the film was rated X. *Midnight Cowboy* (1969) became the first X-rated major studio film to win the Academy Award for Best Picture, so rated for its highly charged sexual content. The Academy accepted the film as a tough, gritty, legitimate drama.

Stanley Kubrick's *A Clockwork Orange* (1971), an adaptation of the Anthony Burgess novel, is a violent and sexual film that makes the point that people can't change. The film received four Oscar nominations including Best Picture and Best Editing and also received the dreaded X rating. Eventually the system was revised to avoid mainstream mature films being incorrectly classified.

During the seventies, movies began to photograph actors and actresses totally naked straight on; this was coined full-frontal nudity. It was daring and used to enhance the reality of the story. Some of the most audacious examples include *American Gigolo* (1980). This Paul Schrader film features a male prostitute with the finesse of a model. In a career-making role, Richard Gere mesmerizes as Julian Kaye and has the audacity to perform several full-frontal sequences. In *Don't Look Now* (1973), Julie Christie and Donald Sutherland play husband and wife and engage in a graphic, protracted lovemaking scene, which was highly controversial at the time. In *Heaven's Gate* (1980), directed by Michael Cimino, Isabelle Huppert plays a madam in love with two men. There is logic in her appearing naked and displaying her body without inhibition as a madam. The result is a fair amount of screen time dedicated to nudity, including a lengthy scene in which she appears full-frontal at times.

In society, sex in the seventies had become more open, and movies began to reflect that freedom with honesty and without inhibition.

5

1973

February 27: Approximately two hundred Oglala Lakota Indians and followers of the American Indian movement took over the town of Wounded Knee, South Dakota, for seventy-one days while FBI agents, marshals, and law enforcement surrounded the area. . . . April 3: The first cell phone call was made by Motorola engineer Martin Cooper to rival Bell Laboratories at AT&T to tell them that Motorola had developed and built a portable handheld phone, which weighed two and a half pounds. . . . August 11: Sixteen-year-old Clive Campbell, known as DJ Kool, is credited with originating hip-hop music in Bronx, New York, when he hosted a "Back-to-School jam," making musical and cultural history.

American Graffiti was a semiautobiographical film directed by George Lucas based on his memories of driving around town all night in northern California in a tribal car ritual called "cruisin'." Teen guys drove their hot cars looking for girls. There were street races, antics, and pranks. The film, set during high school graduation in 1962, featured characters who were a cross section of American teenage prototypes, including the nerd, the girl next door, the slick hot-rodder, and the blonde bombshell. The cast was largely unknown, and many became stars after the film played across America. These included Ron Howard, Cindy Williams, Paul Le-Mat, Richard Dreyfuss, and Harrison Ford. Although two cameramen, Ron Eveslage and Jan S'Alquen, are credited with shooting *American Graffiti*, the director of photography behind the period look and the night-time cruisin' atmosphere was one of the most respected cameramen in the

Robert De Niro, Harvey Keitel, Lenny Scaletta, and George Memmoli in *Mean*
Streets. Warner Bros. Pictures/Photofest © Warner Bros. Pictures

business, Haskell Wexler. The nonstop rock 'n' roll records on the soundtrack became a song score that helped define the fifties and sixties. These
"golden oldies" were rerecorded so it sounded as if they were coming
from the interior of an upholstered vehicle on the car radio. *American
Graffiti* grossed $140 million on a $777,000 budget, an astounding financial feat for a personal film. The film was a big success. Audiences from
all over the country related to the lively action that occurred when the
characters drove the main drag of town. *American Graffiti* received a Best
Picture Oscar nomination. The film resonated in the early seventies, when
there was a nostalgia craze for the early sixties, partly because the new
decade of the seventies was less innocent and remembering the early
sixties lifted spirits. In 1979 Lucas sponsored a sequel to *American Graffiti*: *More American Graffiti*, directed by Bill L. Norton, which barely
made money. The film takes place on New Year's Eve 1964 to 1967 and
follows the characters as their lives progress.

Richard Dreyfuss began his film career with appearances in *The Valley of the Dolls* (1967) and *The Graduate* (1967), both uncredited. After

playing Curt Henderson, who spends much of *American Graffiti* deciding
whether he is going to fly east the next morning to attend college, he
played Baby Face Nelson in a standout performance in *Dillinger* (1973)
directed by John Milius. In *The Apprenticeship of Duddy Kravitz* (1974),
directed by Ted Kotcheff, Dreyfuss plays a poor kid growing up in Mon-
treal seeking the attention of his family that has been given to his older
brother. In 1975 Dreyfuss was in the controversial film *Inserts*, directed
by John Byrum, about actors who could not transition from silent films to
talkies and then turned to pornography. *Inserts* was originally rated X,
which changed to NC-17 in 1996. *Jaws* (1975) made Dreyfuss a major
star with his role as Matt Hooper, a marine biologist who goes on the
expedition to destroy a killer shark. In 1977 Richard Dreyfuss worked
with Spielberg again in the science fiction epic *Close Encounters of the
Third Kind* as Roy Neary, an electrical maintenance worker drawn to
UFOs. In 1977 Dreyfuss won the Oscar for Best Actor in the romantic
comedy *The Goodbye Girl*, directed by Herbert Ross. Dreyfuss played an
aspiring actor who subleases an apartment from a jilted dancer portrayed
by Marsha Mason, who has a ten-year-old daughter (Quinn Cummings);
they eventually fall in love. In 1978 Dreyfuss portrayed a private detective and former student activist in *The Big Fix*.

Paul LeMat made four appearances during the decade and his free-
flowing style linked him to the era. In 1975's *Aloha, Bobby and Rose*,
LeMat plays an automobile mechanic who races a 1968 Chevy Camaro.
In *Citizen's Band* (1977), renamed *Handle with Care*, LeMat plays a
young man who spends his time repairing CB radios. In 1979 he reprised
his role as John Milner in *More American Graffiti*.

Charles Martin Smith, who played the awkward nerd Terry the Toad
in *American Graffiti*, was also in *The Buddy Holly Story* (1978), directed
by Steve Rash, and reprised his role in *More American Graffiti*.

Cindy Williams, who played Laurie, Steve's (Ron Howard) girlfriend,
also appeared in *The Conversation*, directed by Francis Ford Coppola
(1974), and *More American Graffiti*.

Candy Clark, who played Debbie, also was in *The Man Who Fell to
Earth*, directed by Nicholas Roeg, opposite rock star/actor David Bowie
in 1976. In 1977 she played Electra in *Citizen's Band* and Camilla Stern-
wood in *The Big Sleep*, directed by Michael Winner and starring Robert
Mitchum. She reprised her role in *More American Graffiti*.

Superstar Harrison Ford, who played drag racer Bob Falfa, also appeared in *The Conversation* (1974) directed by Francis Ford Coppola; *Star Wars* as Han Solo (1977) directed by George Lucas; *Heroes* (1977) directed by Jeremy Kagan; *Apocalypse Now* directed by Coppola (1979); and *Force 10 from Navarone* directed by Guy Hamilton (1978).

Badlands is the impressive debut film by writer, producer, and director Terrence Malick. The story is inspired by the true-life murder spree of Charles Starkweather and his young girlfriend Caril Ann Fugate in 1958. Malick turned the dark crime story into an American visual tone poem and a portrait of a dangerous relationship. The film, featuring breakout performances by Martin Sheen and Sissy Spacek, was well reviewed, marking the beginning of Malick's directorial cinematic career.

Little is known about Terrence Malick. He is a literary filmmaker and a meticulous pictorialist who often tells stories via narration. Malick was one of the original fellows to study at the American Film Institute (AFI) conservatory. While there he directed *Lanton Mills*, a seventeen-minute film starring Warren Oates and Harry Dean Stanton about the plotting of a bank robbery by characters who appear to be from the nineteenth century but perhaps are not. Malick established contacts that led to writing gigs, including early drafts of *Dirty Harry* (1971), directed by Don Siegel, and *Drive, He Said* and *Pocket Money*, directed by Stuart Rosenberg and starring Paul Newman. After his screenplay *Deadhead Miles* was directed by Vernon Zimmerman but never released by Paramount Studios, Malick decided to direct his own films. After the acclaim of *Badlands*, Terrence Malick directed *Days of Heaven* (1978), a film some critics and scholars consider among the most beautifully photographed of all time. It depicts a love affair in the Texas Panhandle during the early twentieth century starring Richard Gere, Brooke Adams, and Sam Shepard. Malick started developing a film for Paramount titled *Q* about the origins of life on Earth. While in preproduction, he suddenly went to Paris and remained out of public view for years. He wrote several screenplays during this time including an adaptation of *The Moviegoer* by Walker Percy, a legendary and well-respected novel about a man who finds more meaning in movies than in everyday life. Malick would not complete another film until *The Thin Red Line* in 1998, a World War II drama based on the novel by James Jones. The twenty-year gap between movies found Malick even more obsessed with poetic imagery, such as the movement of the camera through blades of grass on the battlefield.

Sissy Spacek was born Mary Elizabeth Spacek in Quitman, Texas. She began a singing career but when record sales dwindled, she switched to acting. In 1972 she played a young woman sold into sexual slavery in *Prime Cut*, directed by Michael Ritchie. In 1973 she gained attention as Holly Sargis in *Badlands*. She proved her versatility in the challenging *Carrie* (1976), based on the Stephen King novel, in the title role of high school student Carrie White who is bullied terribly and gets revenge when her telekinetic powers go haywire. In 1977 she was in *Three Women*, a film director Robert Altman conceived in a dream. Her character Pinky experiences strange emotional shifts and eventually she is unable to recognize her own parents—if that is who they are. In the end the three women evolve into a new set of relationships. Operating in a dream reality, Spacek is believable throughout the film. In 1980 Spacek won the Oscar for Best Actress for her role as Loretta Lynn in *Coal Miner's Daughter*, directed by Michael Apted. She sang all the songs on camera and perfectly captured the country music superstar. Sissy Spacek is married to production designer Jack Fisk, who has worked with Terrence Malick and David Lynch. Jack Fisk has collaborated several times with Malick and does not approach a film in a traditional Hollywood manner. He creates total environments in which the sets appear to be interconnected.

The exquisitely shot *Badlands* credits three cameramen: Tak Fujimoto (*Beloved* [1998]), Steven Lardner (*The Buddy Holly Story* [1978]), and Brian Probyn (*The Revolutionary* [1970]).

Black Caesar is a blaxploitation film that stars Fred Williamson, Gloria Hendry, D'Urville Martin, and Julius Harris. It is a remake of a legendary gangster film—*Little Caesar* released in 1931 with Edward G. Robinson. This film, directed by Larry Cohen, takes place in Harlem, New York. Tommy Gibbs (Williamson) was assaulted as a kid by a police officer, which led him to a life of crime. Once of age, he joins the mafia and becomes the head of a syndicate in Harlem. He has a violent marriage, which sets forces against him. The musical score is by the legendary James Brown. A sequel, *Hell up in Harlem*, was released in late 1973. The original film had been conceived and tailored for entertainer Sammy Davis Jr., but financial problems made his appearance impossible.

Fred Williamson was a high-profile personality also known as the Hammer. Before his career in movies and television, Williamson played football in the NFL. He became a prolific performer on TV and in movies and appeared in more than 120 projects with more than thirty appearances in the seventies. He became a major star in the blaxploitation subgenre. He played Dr. Oliver "Spearchucker" Jones in Robert Altman's *M*A*S*H* (1970). After *Black Caesar* Williamson played in many blaxploitation films including *The Soul of Nigger Charley* (1973) in which his character tries to stop Southern soldiers from reigniting the Confederacy. In *That Man Bolt* (1973), he is Jefferson Bolt, who is told to transport a briefcase without knowing what is in it. In *Three the Hard Way* (1974), directed by Gordon Parks Jr., he played record producer Jimmy Lait opposite Jim Brown and martial artist Jim Kelly.

Blume in Love was directed by Paul Mazursky and starred George Segal, Susan Anspach, and Kris Kristofferson. Segal, as Blume, plays a divorce lawyer trying to get back with his ex-wife. The principal theme of *Blume in Love* is self-discovery and the complications of love and relationships in the 1970s.

George Segal was quite active as a film actor during the sixties. His seminal role was as Nick, one half of the couple invited to the home of George and Martha, played by Richard Burton and Elizabeth Taylor, for a night of nastiness and unpleasantries in *Who's Afraid of Virginia Woolf?* (1966), directed by Mike Nichols. In this adaptation of the explosive Edward Albee play, Segal's character is involved with sexual material, profane language, and actions that were considered verboten in the movies. He was critically acclaimed for his fine performance. In 1970 Segal was in *Loving*, directed by Irvin Kirshner, an examination of the difficulty of relationships, another look at the popular seventies theme. In 1970 Segal played a writer living with a part-time prostitute played by Barbra Streisand in *The Owl and the Pussycat*. He portrayed a strung-out drug addict in *Born to Win*, directed by Ivan Passer (1971), another theme that reflected life in the seventies. In 1974 Segal was directed by Robert Altman and costarred with Elliot Gould in *California Split*. They play degenerate gamblers who bet on practically anything that comes along. In *Fun with Dick and Jane* (1977), directed by Ted Kotcheff, Segal and Jane Fonda play a couple who turn to a life of crime when their income sources dry up. The comedy is a strong critique of the American suburban way of life.

Bruce Surtees, son of the legendary Hollywood cameraman Robert L. Surtees, shot *Blume in Love*. Pato Guzman also added a production design credit to his seventies career. The much-in-demand editor Donn Cambern continued to stretch his postproduction talents.

James William Guercio was an American music producer and songwriter. He is best known as the producer of the extremely successful rock band *Chicago*. In 1973 he made his directorial debut with the film *Electra Glide in Blue*. Full-page ads pictured him in a heroic pose and announced the introduction of a major new filmmaker. Guercio took a $1 salary so that he could hire master cinematographer Conrad Hall. The story follows a motorcycle policeman who patrols the highways of rural Arizona. The part is played by Robert Blake. Also in the cast is Billy "Green" Bush, Mitchell Ryan, Jeannine Riley, Royal Dano, and Elisha Cook, as well as members of *Chicago*, including singer Peter Cetera and guitarist Terry Kath. Before shooting, Hall made some camera tests showing desaturated, pastel color. Guercio was unhappy with the results and wanted the full, rich color as seen in his hero's, director John Ford's, films. Hall eventually moved away from the postcard color the director wanted and toward the more desaturated look he saw for the picture. Upon release, the *New York Times* considered the film amateurish. In retrospect, *Electra Glide in Blue* is considered a cult film, representative of seventies cinema with Hall's nuanced cinematography and Robert Blake's idiosyncratic acting.

Enter the Dragon was considered one of the greatest martial arts films of all time. It stars Bruce Lee, the best known and most respected actor in his field, in his last completed performance prior to his controversial death on July 20, 1973, at age thirty-two. Other cast members include John Saxon, Ahna Capri, Bob Wall, Shih Kien, and Jim Kelly. It is one of the first films to combine the martial arts genre with blaxploitation. The film was shot on location in Hong Kong with Warner Bros. completely behind the production. The film explored changes in Asian societies since World War II. *Enter the Dragon* is well shot in widescreen format. The fights are intricately choreographed and slow motion is applied to accentuate selected blows during a martial arts battle scene. The film was enormously popular, grossing $90 million on an $850,000 budget.

Bruce Lee was an actor and martial artist. He raised the bar in martial arts movies in terms of content, production, and fighting style, which led to mixed martial arts. His indomitable spirit, physical fitness, and approach to characters helped change how audiences perceived Asians onscreen. In 1972, after making many films in China and the United States,

Bruce Lee won a lead role that made him a major star in Asia. The Hong Kong film *Return of the Dragon* in 1972 starred Lee, who also directed the film. *Game of Death* (1978) was incomplete at the time of Bruce Lee's death. Using stand-ins and careful editing, it was released five years after Lee's death. In 1974 several episodes of *The Green Hornet*, originally aired in 1966 in which Lee played Kato, the Hornet's sidekick, were edited together and released as a feature film. *Game of Death* (1978) uses footage from earlier Bruce Lee films along with new footage. Although the release of these manipulated films took advantage of his sudden and tragic death for box office gain, it is also a sign of what a superstar Bruce Lee had become and how thoroughly he entertained moviegoers.

The novel *The Exorcist* by William Peter Blatty was a major bestseller in 1971. Director William Friedkin not only managed to put what seemed unimaginable on the screen, but he did so on a scale beyond that of any horror film to date. Friedkin created a blockbuster movie and a cultural phenomenon. In 1973, when the film was released, there were no computer-generated effects to bring the book's vivid and horrifying images to life. All the illusions—such as twelve-year-old Regan levitating and her head spinning 360 degrees while possessed by the devil—were created with film technology and practical effects. Friedkin's approach was to produce the movie on a superior scale rather than the inferior level historically used for horror films. The acting was first class with Ellen Burstyn, Jason Miller, Max von Sydow, and a remarkable transformation performed by Linda Blair as Regan. Movie theater lines extended around the block for showings of the film. *The Exorcist* proved that a film in the horror genre with such controversial content could redefine the event film and gain much attention while probing an aspect of religion usually kept secret.

Ellen Burstyn appeared in ten movies during the seventies. Her career had a late start but quickly accelerated as she created strong, multidimensional female characters. Among her memorable roles was Lois Farrow in *The Last Picture Show* (1971), directed by Peter Bogdanovich, the unfulfilled mother of Jacy, played by Cybil Shepard. In *The King of Marvin Gardens* (1972), she was an aging girlfriend locked in desperation and fantasy. In *The Exorcist* (1973) Burstyn played Chris MacNeil, an actress whose daughter Regan becomes possessed by the devil. Played aggressively with a range of emotions, Burstyn's performance is sharply verbal and constantly physical and won her an Oscar nomination for Best Actress.

Cinematographer Owen Roizman was nominated for an Academy Award for his iconoclastic work on the film. Several editors working on *The Exorcist* were either let go or could not take William Friedkin's constant screaming. Two who survived and are part of the film's chilling success were Norman Gay (*Honeysuckle Rose* [1980]) and Evan Lottman (*The Panic in Needle Park* [1971]).

Bill Gunn was known primarily as a playwright when in 1972 he was approached by the independent production company Kelly-Jordan Enterprises to make a black vampire film with a budget of $350,000. That August *Blacula* was released and became a box office success. There was now a market for a black vampire movie. Privately Gunn said he had no interest in making a black vampire film, but he accepted the project because he looked at vampirism as a metaphor for addiction. Gunn set out to make his first feature film. The inexperienced producers allowed him artistic control over the project, then called *Ganja & Hess*. The story concerns Dr. Hess Green, played by Duane Jones, an anthropologist researching an ancient African nation of humans who drink blood. One night after a violent confrontation, he drinks the blood of an assistant portrayed by Bill Gunn and becomes a vampire. Then Gunn's estranged wife Ganja, played by Marlene Clark, comes searching for her husband. She falls in love with Green and becomes a vampire. Eventually Green becomes disillusioned and goes back home and kills himself. Ganja continues her life as a vampire.

When *Ganja & Hess* was released, the producers were unhappy with the poor box office and did not like Gunn's approach to style and structure. They pulled the picture out of distribution and sold it to Heritage Enterprises, which replaced the score and drastically recut the film. It was then titled *Blood Couple*. Bill Gunn totally denounced this version. It was released on VHS under different titles. The original cut of the film survived, and Heritage Enterprises donated the film to the Museum of Modern Art. Critics have embraced *Ganja & Hess*, and it is considered an artistic achievement of high magnitude in black cinema. This unusual film is an independent movie in an experimental style that has been categorized at times as blaxploitation, though it bears little resemblance to that genre. Many shots are held for an extremely long time and draw the viewer in rather than quick cuts that advance the story. The cinematography features artful lighting and compositions that add to the mystery of the film. The score is inventive, and the sound is atmospheric.

James E. Hinton's résumé is short, with few credits as cinematographer, producer, and second unit director, but because of the unusual cult status of *Ganja & Hess*, he has more than an asterisk next to his name in film history. Editor Victor Kanefsky has several gory horror films on his ticket, but this one goes beyond the slasher genre into black studies, ancient studies, and blood as life.

Jesus Christ Superstar began as a recorded rock opera with music by Andrew Lloyd Webber and lyrics by Tim Rice released in 1970. Then a Broadway production was mounted in 1971. Norman Jewison directed the film version released in 1973. The movie used a different structure than the play. The picture begins as a group of performers travel by bus to a desert to enact the passion of Christ. There are many rousing musical numbers in the film. The movie ends with the performers, out of costume, getting back on the bus. Ted Neeley, who played Jesus, is not there, indicating that Christ has been crucified. There were negative comments about this interpretation during production, resulting in quite a few revisions that were made to avoid offending the devout. Although mixing rock 'n' roll with the Bible was considered blasphemous by some, others, including Pope Paul VI, believed that this modern rendition could bring young people into the church.

The Last Detail sports a memorable performance by Jack Nicholson, and his line, "I am the goddamn shore patrol!" has entered the vernacular. Nicholson and another patrol officer are en route escorting a naive young sailor to prison for a minor infraction. They are determined to afford him a good time before his jail term. The film was directed by Hal Ashby, based on a 1969 novel by Darryl Ponicsan, screenplay by Robert Towne. There was controversy at the script stage about the number of curses delivered by the sailors. Towne defended them as authentic for these characters, whereas the studio found them inappropriate and potentially bad for the box office. This carried back and forth into production and postproduction. In the end *The Last Detail* received an R rating for a record number of four-letter words. The film was a success with audiences who found it lively, funny, and poignant.

The Long Goodbye is an adaptation of Raymond Chandler's 1953 novel. The screenplay was by Leigh Brackett, who had cowritten the script for the author's *The Big Sleep* (1946), directed by Howard Hawks and starring Lauren Bacall and Humphrey Bogart. Robert Altman, the director of *The Long Goodbye*, moved the story to 1970s Hollywood and emphasized Chandler's Philip Marlowe as a man out of his time and place and living an old morality. A unique feature of the film is the music. Johnny Mercer and John Williams wrote a self-named song "The Long Goodbye," which occurs repeatedly throughout the film, an old practice in Classic Hollywood. The switch here, though, is that every time this song appears, it is in a different style including Muzak and a hippie chant. Elliot Gould, increasingly more visible in seventies cinema, played Marlowe. The film is surprising in its emotional shifts from partying, semi-naked hippie girls who are Marlowe's neighbors, to a gangster, Marty Augustine (played by director/actor Mark Rydell), who in a shocking, violent moment breaks a bottle on his girlfriend's face. Robert Altman with *The Long Goodbye* continued to develop his signature directorial style with naturalistic sound and a fluid application of the camera.

Elliot Gould appeared in more than twenty films during the seventies. Audiences related to him; he represented the spirit of supercool characters that viewers were attracted to and wanted to emulate. He looked trendy with his thick head of dark curly hair. His voice was low and casual, his demeanor unflappable. Gould was in several films in the sixties then went full-steam ahead in *Bob & Carol & Ted & Alice* (1969), Paul Mazursky's first feature, playing Ted, a member of the spouse-swapping quartet. He was full of wacky antics in *M*A*S*H* (1970). *The Long Goodbye* is one of his finest performances of the decade, and in *California Split* (1974), also directed by Robert Altman, he is one of two obsessed gamblers who sprint to the finish line. Elliot Gould's celebrity, screen presence, and smooth acting ability carried him from film to film beyond the seventies.

Lou Lombardo edited *The Long Goodbye*. He spent the seventies working with two controversial and influential film directors, Robert Altman and Sam Peckinpah, proving that editing is editing and that the same principles apply to the diverse material these two directors provided.

When Martin Scorsese showed John Cassavetes, his mentor and father of independent filmmaking, his film *Boxcar Bertha* (1972), Cassavetes made it clear in no uncertain terms that the young director should not make that kind of film again. He asked Scorsese if he had anything personal he wanted to make, which led to the evolution of *Mean Streets* (1973), Scorsese's homage to *I Vitelloni*, the Federico Fellini film of

1956. Both films feature young men living in small towns. Although it is
Scorsese's third feature film (*Who's That Knocking at My Door* [1967]
was first), *Mean Streets* is the first true Martin Scorsese feature film. It is
fully realized, develops a character (Charley) who represents him on
screen, contains a full song score that creates an aural mood, and comments on the narrative action. *Mean Streets* is a neo-noir, neorealistic
picture that reflects life in the community of New York's Little Italy,
where the director was raised. It is a crime film and one of self-discovery.
Mean Streets is a landmark film about everyone's neighborhood, anywhere. It was a starting point for one of the most noteworthy directors of
the seventies—Martin Scorsese.

Harvey Keitel is a daring actor who pushes the characters he plays and
his formidable acting abilities as far as possible. He works frequently in
independent films because he is allowed more freedom of expression than
in studio pictures. He has also advanced the making of low-budget pictures by lending his support. In the seventies alone Keitel worked with a
raft of directors including Martin Scorsese, Robert Altman, Ridley Scott,
James Toback, and Paul Schrader. Charley Cappa (Cappa is the maiden
name of Scorsese's mother Catherine) in *Mean Streets* is caught between
the world of the mafia through his uncle and his responsibility to straight-
en out his unmanageable friend, Johnny Boy, played in a full-tilt performance by Robert De Niro, and a forbidden relationship with Johnny
Boy's epileptic cousin Teresa. In 1978 Harvey Keitel appeared in *Fingers*
as Jimmy Fingers, a man split between his mania for music and running
down debts for his loan shark father, played by Michael V. Gazzo. It is a
harrowing and realistic portrayal.

Intense, hyperdetailed, and totally immersed into his characters are
just some of the ways to describe Robert De Niro's work as an actor.
When Johnny Boy blows up a mailbox in the opening of *Mean Streets*,
De Niro has already defined his character as a very loose cannon. In *The
Godfather: Part II* (1974), he not only plays Don Corleone as a young
man, but he is *also* playing Marlon Brando playing Don Corleone. For
Taxi Driver De Niro drove a cab for research and created a character,
Travis Bickle, from the volatile script by Paul Schrader in collaboration
with Scorsese. Bickle was lonely, angry, and obsessed with the rescue of
a teenage prostitute. The result of De Niro's work is a scary, violent, and
self-obsessed man who comes close to assassinating a presidential candidate.

In the musical *New York, New York* (1977), working again with Scorsese, De Niro's character Jimmy Doyle manages to grate on everyone's nerves and systematically destroy his marriage to Francine Evans played by Liza Minnelli. *The Deer Hunter* (1978), directed by Michael Cimino, is an epic film about three men who begin their journey at home, are in Vietnam during the Vietnam War, and return home again. Mike Vronsky, played by De Niro, goes back to Vietnam to rescue his friend Nick, portrayed by Christopher Walken. De Niro's vocal and physical actions during the controversial Russian roulette sequence reach a dynamic so intense that the audience is emotionally stretched to the limit, waiting for release, and when it comes, it is overwhelming.

Martin Scorsese attended New York University, where he studied film and made several shorts for which he received positive attention and revealed his talent. After much effort and revision, Scorsese made his first feature *Who's That Knocking at My Door* in 1967, which in many ways was a sketch for his signature movie *Mean Streets*. After *Boxcar Bertha* and *Mean Streets*, Scorsese directed a documentary *Italianamerican* (1974), which focused on the director's parents, revealing much about their early days and their neighborhood in Little Italy, New York. In 1978 Scorsese directed *The Last Waltz*, considered one of the finest rock documentaries ever made. The project developed when the Band announced that they were ending their long run. The rock concert/documentary with feature film elements, especially in the elaborate set, included performances by Bob Dylan, Neil Young, Joni Mitchell, Van Morrison, Ringo Starr, and Eric Clapton.

Scorsese's films are like a personal compendium of film history as he quotes and references specific shots in specific movies while shaping his own distinctive cinematic style. His nervous energy is expressed in the movement of the camera and the rhythm of the editing by longtime editor Thelma Schoonmaker. A film historian/film director, Martin Scorsese's love of American and world cinema is exponential—watching his movies makes audiences embrace filmmaking itself while engaged with the movie on the screen.

The social drama is not a new genre in the movies, but motion picture code restrictions made it difficult to fully express and explore the morality of societal issues. Sidney Lumet was consumed with the ethics of law enforcement in New York City. Justice, fairness, and acts of conscience permeate many of his films. The social drama explored the torment of an individual's struggle with right and wrong.

Serpico is based on Frank Serpico's career as a police officer, an honest New York policeman brought down by the pervasive corruption around him. With Al Pacino in the title role, *Serpico* was shot in New York City with a large cast of more than twenty character actors, bit parts, and extras. *Serpico* is realistic and full of action and emotion. As the corruption builds in the police department, Serpico undergoes lifestyle changes as his belief in honesty in policing grows.

Sidney Lumet has never been considered an auteur or a member of the American New Wave, but he left an impressive résumé of work addressing a preoccupation with criminal justice. Lumet was a New York director. He kept his budgets low and schedules tight and short so that he could quickly move on to the next picture. As a boy, he began as an actor and later directed live television. His first film, *12 Angry Men* (1957), established Lumet as a strong director of drama with themes of justice and individual responsibility in full sight. He made strong films in the sixties, especially with moral dramas such as *A View from the Bridge* (1962), *The Pawnbroker* (1964), and *Fail Safe* (1964).

Sidney Lumet began the seventies with *King: A Filmed Record . . . Montgomery to Memphis* (1970), the only documentary he directed during his entire career. The film utilizes stock footage and follows Dr. King's fight for civil rights. There is a long list of celebrity narrators including Paul Newman, Harry Belafonte, Charlton Heston, Ruby Dee, and others. After *Serpico* (1973), Lumet directed a large cast in a period Agatha Christie mystery *Murder on the Orient Express* (1974). In 1975 came *Dog Day Afternoon*, one of Lumet's finest accomplishments, which included a flawless performance by Al Pacino in this true-life drama about a man who robs a bank to finance a sex reassignment operation for his male lover. For *Network* (1976), Lumet worked with an acerbic Paddy Chayefsky screenplay, which was a scathing attack on television and the news media, launching into the vernacular the line "I'm mad as hell and I'm not going to take this anymore!" Lumet also had a penchant for the theater and adapted several plays to the screen including the drama *Equus* (1977) about a boy undergoing psychiatric treatment for blinding horses. Sidney Lumet continued a steady output of films until 2007.

Woody Allen is one of the most prolific American filmmakers with a continual output of films. He began as a television writer and stand-up comedian. In the sixties he directed and starred in *Take the Money and Run* (1969), a mockumentary concerning an inept bank robber, Virgil Starkwell, played by Allen. Allen starred in and directed *Bananas* (1971) playing Felding Mellish, a bumbling New Yorker dumped by his activist girlfriend who becomes involved in a Latin American revolution. *Everything You Always Wanted to Know about Sex (But Were Afraid to Ask)* (1973) was loosely based on the bestselling book by Dr. David Reuben. In a run of short segments, Allen pokes fun at sex and sexual attitudes. It was an enormous box office hit. *Sleeper* (1973) is a science fiction parody in which Allen plays Miles Monroe, a man who is cryogenically frozen and defrosted two hundred years later in a police state. Diane Keaton costarred as Luna Schlosser, a socialite who falls in love with him while he is disguised as a robot. By now Allen had a well-established screen character as a neurotic, darkly comic figure who is inept and anti-intellectual. His early films, though funny, were not shot or designed well. *Love and Death* (1975) is a satire of Russian literature. Set in the Napoleonic era, Allen and Diane Keaton play Boris and Sonja who have mock serious philosophical debates. In *The Front* (1976), Woody Allen is the lead character in a film he didn't write or direct. *The Front* is about the blacklist era, when other writers were asked to pose for those who were blacklisted. It is directed by Martin Ritt and written by Walter Bernstein (two men affected during that period). Later in the seventies Woody Allen would make an artistic leap from a filmmaker who made funny films that were less-than-inspired aesthetically to an auteur who merged content with style and purpose.

Brian De Palma is often left off the list of American New Wave film directors, which angers and distresses him. On the surface, he certainly does fit in. The sticking point may be that he is primarily a horror/thriller director, and his adoration of Alfred Hitchcock is more than evident. De Palma quotes Hitchcock often and his attraction to *Psycho* (1960) is overboard, but in fairness he has incorporated lessons learned into an original and effective style. One element that separates De Palma from others is his oft-used application of split-screen technique to give the viewer multiple views of a narrative action.

De Palma's *Hi Mom!* (1970) features an early appearance by Robert De Niro. In it he plays a character who wants to be an adult filmmaker and films his neighbors through their windows. Peeping Toms are a recurring theme in De Palma's movies. The film is also known for the "be black, baby" sequence in which a black radical group shows Caucasians what it is like to be black. *Dionysus in '69* (1970) is a film record of the Performance Group's stage work. *Get to Know Your Rabbit* (1972) is a comedy that brought De Palma to Hollywood. Tommy Smothers of the famous Smothers Brothers act was the star of an offbeat story of a corporate executive who has enough of his rat race existence and goes on the road as a traveling magician. Smothers did not have confidence in the director and was hostile to the production. In postproduction the film was taken away from De Palma and recut. The experience kept De Palma away from the studios for some time. *Sisters* (1972) is a horror film about conjoined twins. As is often the case with De Palma, there are many references to Hitchcock films, and the Hitchcock's composer Bernard Hermann conducts the music (uncredited). *Phantom of the Paradise* (1974) is De Palma's rock 'n' roll version of *The Phantom of the Opera*. *Obsession* (1974) is a psychological thriller shot in high style by Vilmos Zsigmond about a man (Cliff Robertson) whose wife and daughter are kidnapped. Later he finds a look-alike of her, echoing Hitchcock's *Vertigo*. *Carrie* (1976) is an adaptation of the Stephen King book in which a girl who is constantly bullied has powers no one knows about until it is too late. The film received a big box office and has become a pop culture hit. *The Fury* (1978) had two big stars, John Cassavetes and Kirk Douglas, and dealt with mental powers. In 1980 De Palma was teaching at his alma mater, Sarah Lawrence, when he devised an autobiographical film called *Home Movie*, which he directed. His students served as the crew and all the support positions. Brian De Palma continued to have a vigorous career through the 1980s and beyond.

With *Butch Cassidy and the Sundance Kid* (1969), directed by George Roy Hill and costarring Paul Newman and Robert Redford, Hollywood learned that buddy films were gold at the box office. The formula is two male, usually contrasting, characters who embark on an adventure. *The Sting* (1973) was supported by the same team: Hill, Newman, and Redford. The two actors, who became lifelong friends, had an undeniable chemistry and audiences enjoyed watching their antics. *The Sting* is an elaborate plot to con a mob boss played by Robert Shaw. The film took place in the thirties and featured a large supporting cast, which included Ray Walston, Charles Durning, Eileen Brennan, and Jack Kehoe. The music was a clever idea; Marvin Hamlish adapted Scott Joplin's rags, which were correct for the period and gave the action a lively atmosphere.

The Sting was nominated for ten Academy Awards and won seven. The film was a box office smash, a real crowd-pleaser. *The Sting* is in the Old Hollywood tradition, confirming there was still some interest in traditional film entertainment.

George Roy Hill was a talented director who made entertainment films. *Slaughterhouse-Five* (1972) was an exception, a science fiction film with an involved narrative via the Kurt Vonnegut novel. *Slap Shot* (1977) follows a minor league hockey team and is bawdy and raw in its language and lively in action. *A Little Romance* (1979) follows the romance of a thirteen-year-old boy and girl after they meet in Paris. The teens were played by Diane Lane and Thelonious Bernard in their film debuts. *A Little Romance* also featured Sir Laurence Olivier.

Paul Newman was a major movie star of considerable talent. He was versatile but strongly remembered for roles considered antiheroes, a character type with a rebellious nature. Best known are Newman's portrayal of Hud in *Hud* (1963), directed by Martin Ritt, and *Cool Hand Luke* (1963), directed by Stuart Rosenberg, which changed the nature of a dramatic male film lead. In *WUSA* (1970), also directed by Stuart Rosenberg, Newman plays a man who gets a job at a right-wing radio station but doesn't believe in its philosophy. In 1972 he appeared in *Pocket Money* as Jim Kane, an indebted cowboy who gets involved in nefarious dealings. In *The Life and Times of Judge Roy Bean* (1972), written by John Milius and directed by John Huston, Newman plays the title role of an outlaw who becomes a judge who rules above the law. After *The Sting*, Newman played an architect in the disaster film *The Towering Inferno*, directed by John Guillemin. In 1976 Newman starred in the revisionist Western *Buffalo Bill and the Indians or Sitting Bull's History Lesson* directed by Robert Altman. After *Slap Shot*, Newman worked again with Altman in *Quintet* (1979), a postapocalyptic science fiction film, the story taking place during a new ice age.

Newman was also a fine director. In 1970 he directed an adaptation of Ken Kesey's novel *Sometimes a Great Notion*, a drama that takes place in a logging town located in Oregon. *The Effect of Gamma Rays on Man-in-the-Moon Marigolds* (1972) was based on a Pulitzer Prize–winning play by Paul Zindel. Throughout his career, Paul Newman was a political activist who acted, produced, and directed movies revealing a committed movie star. From time to time he collaborated with his equally talented wife, Joanne Woodward.

Robert Shaw was a dangerous actor with his strong, low voice and broad physicality; he often looked as if he could strike at any moment and other actors in a scene appeared to fear him. He acted on the stage as well as on film and was a novelist and playwright. After appearing in *The Sting*, Shaw was the leader of a dangerous group of men threatening to blow up a New York City subway full of people in *The Taking of Pelham One Two Three* (1973). In 1975 Shaw played his most memorable role as Quint the fisherman in *Jaws* (1975).

Eileen Brennan was an active character actress, versatile and funny. She worked well with an ensemble and steadily in the seventies. Director Peter Bogdanovich cast her in three of his pictures, *The Last Picture Show* (1971), *Daisy Miller* (1974), and *At Long Last Love* (1975). She worked with director Jerry Schatzberg in *Scarecrow* (1973). In *The Sting* she played Billie, the only woman who could stand up to the tough guys around her. In *Murder by Death* (1976, directed by Robert Moore), Brennan was part of a large comedy ensemble in this whodunit spoof. In *The Cheap Detective* (1978, also directed by Moore), she worked in the style of Humphrey Bogart films.

Robert Redford is a movie star, director, and founder of the Sundance Institute. Redford is a well-trained and experienced film actor with signature tousled blond hair. To some he seems like a matinee idol, to others a man's man. Redford has worked in front and behind the camera as a director and is a force mentoring young filmmakers and giving them a place and the tools to develop their skills.

In *Little Fauss and Big Halsy* (1970), by Sidney J. Furie, Redford plays a motorcycle racer. In *Jeremiah Johnson*, directed by Sydney Pollack, he plays a mountain man, a film that expresses Redford's pro-environment feelings. In *The Candidate* (1972) Redford portrays Bill McKay, a senatorial candidate crafted and molded by his handlers, which emphasized the lack of substance in politics at that time. After *The Sting* Redford paired with Barbra Streisand in *The Way We Were* (1973, directed by Pollack). She is Katie Morosky, a political radical, and he is Hubbell Gardiner who has no political bent. He played Jay Gatsby in an adaptation of F. Scott Fitzgerald's *The Great Gatsby* (1974, directed by Jack Clayton, screenplay by Coppola). In 1975 Redford appeared in *Three Days of the Condor* (1975, directed by Pollack) as a CIA researcher who tries to figure out who killed all of his coworkers while he was out to lunch. In *All the President's Men* (1976, directed by Alan J. Pakula) he plays Bob Woodward, who along with fellow journalist Carl Bernstein, played by Dustin Hoffman, exposed the Watergate scandal, which led to Richard Nixon's resignation as president. Redford's directing career began in 1980 with the Academy Award–winning *Ordinary People*.

Walking Tall is based on the life of Sheriff Buford Pusser. In this extraordinarily successful film, Pusser was played by Joe Don Baker, a highly experienced actor in television and movies. The director was Phil Karlson, who started directing in 1942 and was known for crime films, film noir, and Westerns. His style was hard and tough. The story follows Pusser as he is seriously injured in a corrupt gambling and prostitution establishment. The dishonest sheriff annoys him and Pusser wins a court case against him. He campaigns against the corrupt sheriff and wins the job. His weapon against the bad guys in town is a four-foot hickory stick. The main interest in the picture is when Buford uses his stick to deliver justice. Audiences related to the carry-a-big-stick philosophy and the visuals were strong and direct. *Walking Tall* was produced for $500,000, and it grossed a phenomenal $23 million domestically.

Clint Eastwood is a unique talent in film. He became a movie star in Westerns in Europe. He began directing in 1971, and for six decades has been acting and behind the camera. As an actor during the seventies, he worked with his mentor, director Don Siegel, on *Two Mules for Sister Sara* (1970), a Western costarring Shirley MacLaine, who plays a prostitute initially disguised as a nun. The story is about her interaction with Hogan, a former Civil War soldier played by Eastwood. Siegel and Eastwood came together again on *The Beguiled*, in which a Union soldier is wounded and tended to by Southern women who have romantic flings with him. Again with Siegel in 1971, Eastwood plays Harry Callahan, a cop with a magnum who seeks his own justice in *Dirty Harry*. Also with Siegel, Eastwood starred in *Escape from Alcatraz* (1979). Eastwood also appeared in several of the films he directed. He made his directorial debut with *Play Misty for Me* (1971), in which he stars as a disc jockey who cannot rid himself of an obsessed female fan. He directed Westerns during this time, a genre with which he was familiar. One was *High Plains Drifter* (1973), in which Eastwood plays a mysterious gunman who, like Harry Callahan, takes justice into his own hands. In 1973 Eastwood moved in a different direction with *Breezy* (1973), about a significantly older man, played by Hollywood veteran William Holden, in a romantic relationship with a teenage girl. In 1978 Clint Eastwood appeared in the box office bonanza *Every Which Way but Loose* (1978), directed by James Fargo, in which he played a brawler with a pet orangutan. Clint Eastwood continued to direct films on a regular basis. His style is all his own, with influence from Don Siegel and Sergio Leone from his spaghetti Western days. Clint Eastwood worked right through the American New Wave; although he was never a part of it, he always obtained a sizable piece of the general audience.

Mark Rydell was first trained in music and as a young man aspired to be an orchestra composer. His interests shifted to acting and he studied at the Neighborhood Playhouse School of the Theatre in New York City. His most notable role in feature films was as Marty Augustine, a vicious Jewish mob boss in Robert Altman's *The Long Goodbye* (1973). Rydell started his directing career with *The Reivers* (1969), adapted from the book by William Faulkner. He entered the seventies with *The Cowboys* (1970), a Western starring John Wayne as a rancher who is forced to have schoolboys work a drive. *Cinderella Liberty* (1973) tells the story of a sailor, played by James Caan, who becomes romantically involved with a prostitute, portrayed by Marsha Mason, and acts as a surrogate father to her ten-year-old mixed-race son. In *Harry and Walter Go to New York* (1976), two struggling vaudevillians, played by Caan and Elliot Gould, plan to pull off the greatest heist ever but find opposition in the best bank robber of all time (Michael Caine) and a crusading female journalist (Diane Keaton). *The Rose* (1979) is partially based on the life of rock legend Janis Joplin, the story of a self-destructive rock star coping poorly with constant demands. In the lead, Bette Midler gives a tour-de-force performance as an actress and vocalist.

The Mack, directed by Michael Campus, is a rise-and-fall movie, one that some say is more than blaxploitation. Goldie, played by Max Julien, comes home from a five-year stretch in prison with plans to gain power as a pimp. His brother Olinga, played by Roger E. Mosley, is a black nationalist trying to save the community from drugs and violence. Slim, played by Richard Pryor, assists Goldie. The script for *The Mack* was written on prison toilet paper. Goldie is based on a real person, Frank Ward, a pimp whom the director Michael Campus met. Ward appeared in the film in exchange for his guidance and protection. He recruited real street people for the film. The Black Panthers were also in Ward's territory and disrupted the shooting. A deal was made with Huey Newton and Bobby Seale, two of the Panthers' hierarchy who then provided extras. Frank

Ward was shot and killed while *The Mack* was in production, which caused the cast and crew to relocate for safety.

Larry Cohen was a B-movie master who worked in the horror, science fiction, and blaxploitation genres. His films were low budget and highly imaginative. He was a screenwriter, producer, and director—an auteur who looked for the unusual everywhere. In his 1972 directorial debut, Cohen directed *Bone*, a black comedy that starred Yaphet Kotto in the title role as a man who menaces a couple he takes hostage. In 1973 he directed the blaxploitation film *Black Caesar*, in which screenwriter Cohen deconstructed the Edward G. Robinson classic *Little Caesar* (1931) into the popular blaxploitation genre. That movie was so successful that Cohen made a sequel, *Hell up in Harlem* (1973). In 1974 Larry Cohen turned to horror with the startling film *It's Alive*. The story concerns a couple and their infant child, who turns out to be a mutant monster that kills when frightened. The score was composed by Hitchcock regular Bernard Hermann, and the puppet effects were developed by makeup master Rick Baker. *God Told Me To* (1976) is a science fiction horror film that, like many of Cohen's films, also contains a police procedural element. The storyline concerns a cult leader whose members feel that he is psychically ordering them to kill. *The Private Lives of Edgar J. Hoover* (1977) is a biographical film about the man who founded and ruled the FBI, starring Hollywood great Broderick Crawford as Hoover. *It Lives Again* (1978) is a sequel to *It's Alive*.

6

1974

February 4: Nineteen-year-old newspaper heiress Patricia Hearst kidnapped from her apartment in Berkeley, California. The Symbionese Liberation Army takes responsibility. . . . October 29: World championship boxing match between champion George Foreman and challenger Mohammed Ali in Zaire. Ali positioned himself on the ropes with Foreman slamming him with body punches. Eventually Foreman had little left and in the eighth round with a series of punches Ali took out the champ. Later he called this strategy the rope-a-dope. . . . August 9: Richard Nixon resigns as president of the United States.

Only two feature films dedicated solely to the story of Watergate have been released as of 2020. *All the President's Men* (1976), directed by Alan J. Pakula, was released two years after Nixon resigned and on the exact day the historic event occurred. The film starred Robert Redford and Dustin Hoffman as *Washington Post* reporters Bob Woodward and Carl Bernstein, who broke the story and saw it through to the end. Jason Robards played Ben Bradlee, executive editor of the *Washington Post*, and Hal Holbrook portrayed "Deep Throat," the source who helped bring the president down. The ensemble captures the real-life counterparts, and the tension and drama increase as the film progresses. Production designer George Jenkins reproduced the *Washington Post* newsroom with exactitude, director of photography Gordon Willis captured the brightness of the workspace contrasted with the mysterious and ominous darkness of the night, offices, and homes where the investigation lived and the noir-like encounters between Woodward and Deep Throat. Film editor Robert

Faye Dunaway and Jack Nicholson in *Chinatown*. *Paramount Pictures/Photofest* ©
Paramount Pictures

L. Wolfe, who worked with Sam Peckinpah three times, paces the film
with complex intercutting that joins the seriousness of the story with the
entertainment of a police procedural, making the drama compelling, in-
formative, and detailed. Audiences knew the story because of the swift-
ness of the film's release and the book by Woodward and Bernstein, and
the filmmakers kept the narrative fresh. The film was a huge success with
a $10.6 million return on a low $1.5 million budget. In *Mark Felt: The
Man Who Brought Down the White House* (2017), directed by Peter
Landesman, Liam Neesom plays Mark Felt, the real Deep Throat, an FBI
agent who was at the heart of the story.

The journey of *Alice Doesn't Live Here Anymore* began during the
filming of *The Exorcist*, when Warner Bros. executives knew they
wanted to work with Ellen Burstyn again. The women's movement was
developing in strength. Burstyn wanted to be in a new kind of movie that
portrayed women trying to change and gain more control over their lives.
She got in touch with Francis Ford Coppola and asked him if he knew any
young and exciting film directors. He recommended that she see Martin

Scorsese's *Mean Streets*. She loved the picture and Scorsese and Burstyn became collaborators.

The story concerns Alice Hyatt, whose husband is killed in a car accident. She and her precocious son Tommy pack up their house and set out for her childhood hometown of Monterey, California, so she can become a singer, a goal she put behind her when she married. Finances dictate they stop in Phoenix, Arizona, where Alice gets work singing in a down-market bar. She becomes involved with a younger man played by Harvey Keitel, but the relationship turns abusive. In fear, she and Tommy leave town and Alice gets a job as a waitress in Mel's Diner in Tucson. There she becomes romantically involved with one of the regulars, rancher David, portrayed by Kris Kristofferson. Jodie Foster plays Audrey, a tomboy forced to fend for herself who becomes Tommy's pal. Later, Alice and David decide to live together in Tucson with Alice free to pursue her goals.

Scorsese understood he was taking on what Classical Hollywood called a woman's picture and devised strategies to structure the story visually. He worked in imagery from *The Wizard of Oz* (1939), made the early part of the film into a road movie, added a rock song score as he did in *Mean Streets*, and made extensive use of a handheld camera. This fresh approach to a woman's story received good reviews and strong box office returns.

Kent Wakeford was the director of photography for *Alice Doesn't Live Here Anymore*. After *Mean Streets*, the two men felt comfortable with the use of long takes and the moving camera. Toby Carr Rafelson was the production designer. Because Scorsese was on new ground making a woman's picture, he surrounded himself with as many strong women as possible, including editor Marcia Lucas.

In 1967 Mel Brooks directed *The Producers*. The hilarious comedy in which the two main characters search for the worst play ever written eventually yields *Springtime for Hitler: A Gay Romp with Adolf and Eva at Berchtesgaden*. They sell excess shares by wining and dining unwitting, aging ladies so that when the play fails, they can pocket the money. In the seventies Brooks first adapted a 1928 Russian novel *The Twelve Chairs*, by Ilf and Petrov, released in 1970. Then Brooks moved on to parodies, first *Blazing Saddles* (1974), which poked fun at the Western. One of the director's targets was racism, which he attacked by casting a black sheriff for the town. The humor is low and gross, with an infamous bean-eating sequence in which flatulence causes riotous laughter by the audience. Brooks also included anachronisms in the old West time frame, such as showcasing Count Basie and his orchestra. The film was an enormous hit, earning $119.6 million on a $2.6 million budget. In 1974 Brooks took on a Universal Studios classic with *Young Frankenstein.* Brooks used the framework of the Frankenstein story and loaded it with his style of degenerate comedy and exaggeration. In 1976 Brooks directed *Silent Movie*, a film that is without spoken dialogue (except for one surprise: when mime Marcel Marceau speaks) and an appropriate plot line for the story of Mel Funn, played by Brooks as a down-on-his-luck film director. In 1977 Brooks directed an Alfred Hitchcock spoof, *High Anxiety*, which includes comic vignettes from *The Birds*, *Spellbound*, and *Vertigo*. At the end of the decade Brooks created Brooksfilms with David Lynch's *Eraserhead* (1980) as its first project.

Bring Me the Head of Alfredo Garcia (1974), directed by Sam Peckinpah, concerns the hunt for the head of an individual who brought shame to a powerful family. The film is brutal, garish, outrageous, and a cinematic theater of the absurd: Warren Oates transports a man's severed head wrapped in a sack and kept fresh and moist with a bottle of tequila.

Chinatown (1974) is an iconic seventies neo-noir written by Robert Towne and directed by Roman Polanski, a director born in Poland who became a Hollywood hitmaker with *Rosemary's Baby* in 1968. The casting chemistry could not be better on *Chinatown*, especially with the leads in a romantic joust: Jack Nicholson as private detective J. J. Gettes and Evelyn Mulwray portrayed by Faye Dunaway. The charismatic and dangerous villain Noah Cross was played by actor/writer/director John Huston. The narrative was inspired by the California water wars in the twenties and involves many levels of plot and psychological intrigue. The handsome production was designed by Richard Sylbert and photographed by John Alonzo, with a haunting musical score by Jerry Goldsmith. There were many differences between Towne's original script and Polanski's film, such as the tragic ending the director insisted upon and the fact that the original script never had a scene in Chinatown. Judging the screenplay as a work of art, experts consider Robert Towne's screenplay one of the best of the art and trade. Towne's screenplays—and numerous instances when he was called in as script doctor, such as on *The Godfather*—made him a major artist and player in American seventies cinema.

The role of the film composer is to create music in the spirit of the narrative, character, and atmosphere of a motion picture. Jerry Goldsmith, who scored more than forty movies in the seventies alone, did that and more. He had the gift for finding the heart of a film and then interpreting it with a full orchestra or whatever instrumentation was needed. During the decade he worked with Robert Aldrich, Howard Hawks, John Milius, Sam Peckinpah, Ridley Scott, and Robert Wise on films that include *Patton* (1970), *The Other* (1972), *Papillon* (1973), *Logan's Run* (1976), *The Omen* (1976), *Twilight's Last Gleaming* (1977), and *The Swarm* (1978). Goldsmith's training was in television, where he worked on live broadcasts for prestigious programs such as *Playhouse 90* and the iconic *The Twilight Zone.*

Faye Dunaway is a meticulous and detailed actress. She considers her hair and makeup an intricate aspect of her performance and spends many hours before and sometimes during a scene adjusting these elements. She starred in *Bonnie and Clyde* (1967) directed by Arthur Penn and again with him in *Little Big Man* (1970), along with Dustin Hoffman on the revisionist Western, which has antiestablishment overtones concerning the military. In *Puzzle of a Downfall Child* (1970), directed by Jerry Schatzberg, Dunaway is extremely believable and compelling as a top model who suffers a mental breakdown. In 1975 she worked with Robert Redford in *Three Days of the Condor*, a political thriller directed by Sydney Pollack, an examination of the deep underpinnings of the CIA. In 1976 she played Diana Christensen, an assertive, driven television programming executive in *Network*, directed by Sydney Lumet. She won an Oscar for that performance.

Cockfighter was a highly anticipated Monte Hellman film. Roger Corman financed the low-budget project. Warren Oates starred as a mute cockfighter. The intrigue of a forbidden subculture gave promise to another *Two-Lane Blacktop*. Behind the camera was Cuban cinematographer Néstor Almendros, who worked in France on *My Night at Maud's* (1969), directed by Éric Rohmer, and *The Wild Child* (1970), directed by François Truffaut, and shot *Days of Heaven* (1978) for Terrence Malick. The film gained notoriety for using of real animals in the cockfighting sequences. *Cockfighter* had difficulty finding an audience. Corman, whose New World Pictures distributed the film, had the picture recut and rereleased under the title *Born to Kill*, but it still failed at the box office. Corman claims it is the only film he put out during the seventies that did not make money. Because of the high expectations, its failure in the marketplace hurt Monte Hellman's reputation.

After the massive box office success of *The Godfather*, Francis Ford Coppola wanted to make a smaller, personal film. Coppola developed an idea that combined Antonioni's *Blow Up* (1967), a film about photo enlargements that ultimately reveal a mystery, and the world of audio surveillance. *The Conversation* (1974) featured the character Harry Caul, played against type by Gene Hackman. Caul gets an assignment to tape two subjects in an open park. The intricate details of the task are shown. As he is putting together the tape, Harry hears something that suggests someone's life may be in danger. While hunting for the truth, his professional veneer peels away as he starts to come apart. The film ends with Harry Caul as a victim of surveillance, convinced his apartment is bugged as he literally tears it apart, desperately searching for microphones.

Walter Murch was the supervising editor for *The Conversation* and the sound designer. He decided that some of the out-of-range mike sounds would be digital, because of Harry's status in the industry, but no digital sound was available, so Murch created it. Murch is also credited as having created sound montages. What he accomplished here and on many movies in the seventies and beyond would be called sound design. Because the film was nonunion, there was concern about using a credit that might cause problems. Murch felt comfortable with the credit "sound montage" because it squarely defined what he did on the picture. Looking back on *The Conversation*, it is clear Murch's work is an early example of sound design, a credit that in future decades became a distinctive part of the filmmaking process. Sound design is akin to production design, wherein the sets and locations are designed to support the narrative and characters of a film. Sound design uses all the elements of sound in the toolbox—sound effects, atmospheric tones, background voices, landscape washes, Foley effects (sound effects created for a picture), echo, and modulating volume—to create aural support for the narrative, characters, and directorial vision of the film. Walter Murch is a pioneer and giant in the field of contemporary sound design. Editor Richard Chew cut three documentaries before *The Conversation*, which became his first feature film.

Orson Welles introduced Peter Bogdanovich to the Henry James novel *Daisy Miller*. The picture starred Cybil Shepard and was shot in Europe. It was a handsome production with Ferdinando Scarfiotti, who often collaborated with Bernardo Bertolucci, as production designer. In the end *Daisy Miller* didn't make money at the box office. Bogdanovich's ability to pick projects was going off kilter.

With crime rates rising in large American cities, the time was right for a vigilante movie. In *Death Wish* (1974), directed by Michael Winner, Charles Bronson plays Paul, a gentle, peaceful architect with a loving wife and daughter. Bronson seems miscast in the early scenes but is perfect when he acts out violently against street criminals in search of the thugs who killed his wife and raped his daughter. The police make it a priority to find this vigilante who is taking the law into his own hands. Winner made two critical additions to the story. He added a scene at the beginning with Paul and his wife on vacation to show how much they loved each other, which emphasizes the tragedy. The original script did not call for a scene that actually showed the attack on the wife and daughter by the three crazed thugs, and this was also added to help the audience understand what motivated Paul's rampage as a vigilante and accept his street justice. *Death Wish* had a $3.7 million budget and raked in around $20 million. Most critics condemned the film's morally offensive message, but because of the societal environment, audiences responded well to the movie.

Following his service in World War II and numerous odd jobs and acting training in a group located in Philadelphia, Charles Bronson began his career in Hollywood in the early fifties. After roles in the United States and Europe, he played the role of the vengeful vigilante in *Death Wish* (1974) and became an iconic legend. Charles Bronson starred or appeared in twenty-one movies during the seventies including *Red Sun* (1971), directed by Terrence Young, and *The Valachi Papers* (1972) and *Hard Times* (1975), both directed by Walter Hill.

The reason most sequels don't work is because the filmmakers' primary objective is to cash in on the success of the first film rather than to continue the story in an innovative or interesting manner. Francis Ford Coppola and Mario Puzo continued the saga on *The Godfather: Part II*, which ranks among the finest motion picture sequels. It was released two years after *The Godfather* with the encouragement of Paramount Studios due to the tremendous success of the original. *The Godfather: Part II* had the same director, the same look, and all the main cast. New characters logically fit into the trajectory of the story. The second film starts where the first ended. Michael is the head of the family and he functions in a more political and businesslike world. The look is consistent, and the characters behave according to what life has dealt them. Adding to the success was the inclusion of Don Corleone's backstory of how he came to America. He is portrayed as a young man in a spectacular Oscar-winning performance by Robert De Niro. The reception for *The Godfather: Part II* was every bit as positive as the original. It is often stated that the second film may be even more intriguing because of its investigation into mafia politics.

To a generation of television viewers, Art Carney was Ed Norton on *The Honeymooners*, the unforgettable series created by Jackie Gleason. Carney appeared in a few movies before being cast in the starring role of Harry Coombes, an elderly widower in the popular *Harry & Tonto* (1974), a road movie in which Harry travels with his cat, Tonto, directed by Paul Mazursky. Against tough competition Art Carney won the Oscar for Best Actor. The role and the win opened Carney's film career for the rest of the decade. In 1975 he appeared in *W. W. and the Dixie Dancekings* as a Bible-thumping ex-lawman who hunts down Burt Reynolds's character. In 1977 he had a featured role along with Lily Tomlin in *The Late Show*, directed by Robert Benton and produced by Robert Altman. In 1979 Carney appeared with George Burns and Lee Strasberg in *Going in Style*, directed by Martin Brest, about three older gentlemen who decide to become robbers.

Production designer Ted Haworth, who designed *Harry & Tonto*, began his craft working in the Hollywood studio industry on the original *Invasion of the Body Snatchers* (1956), directed by Don Siegel.

Hearts & Minds is a controversial documentary about U.S. military involvement in Vietnam directed by Peter Davis. In the film General William Westmoreland, commander of American military operations in Vietnam from 1964 to 1968 and U.S. Army chief of staff from 1968 to 1972, told Davis that life for Orientals was cheap; in another take he said he expressed himself inaccurately. Daniel Ellsberg, who released the Pentagon Papers, originally stated that he supported the war. One of the interview subjects put forth a legal challenge, saying the film did not represent him well and he wasn't given the chance to see the documentary in advance. Columbia Pictures refused to release the film, forcing the producers to buy back the rights. Warner Bros. released the movie. *Hearts & Minds* was nominated and won the Oscar for Best Documentary. Davis and producer Bert Schneider took the stage. Davis remarked that it was ironic to win an award for a film about a war that was still raging. Schneider presented a telegraph wire he was asked to read from the Vietnamese people about the Paris Peace talks, which thanked the United States for what it had done for peace. Later in the broadcast, Frank Sinatra, one of the hosts of the show along with Bob Hope, told the audience the Academy was not responsible for political remarks made by winners, indicating its displeasure with the statement by Schneider. Reaction to *Hearts & Minds* was mixed: some felt it reflected the true war situation, others claimed it was not a documentary but propaganda, and still others said it was both. In the end the film reflected the fractured status of the country. Even when the war was over, its effects lasted in most hearts and minds.

Lenny stars Dustin Hoffman in a biopic of the controversial comedian Lenny Bruce, who pushed the limits of free speech in his use of language considered unacceptable by authorities. The film was directed by Bob Fosse and shot in black and white by Bruce Surtees. The screenplay by Julian Barry, structured in flashbacks and flash-forwards during Lenny Bruce's nightclub routines, demonstrated the connection between his life and the content of his jokes and stories. The script was shot as written, but in postproduction Fosse and editor Alan Heim continued to fracture movements in time and in the real-time routines. A day before they showed the film to United Artists, Fosse and Heim realized that the ending was not working. They determined that they needed to work in Bruce's death. They removed quite a bit of previously edited material and the abrupt conclusion succeeded, true to the suddenness of Lenny Bruce's death due to a drug overdose. With Dustin Hoffman's compelling performance and the cinematic elements providing timescape and mindscape, *Lenny* captures the chaos of a comic and social critic legend.

In the early days of American film, movies were photographed in black and white. Even when color entered the industry, there still were a considerable number of black-and-white releases. By the seventies, color dominated and directors who had an artistic purpose for shooting in black and white had to push to work in the original medium. Peter Bogdanovich worked in black and white on *The Last Picture Show* (1971) and *Paper Moon* (1973) because of his adoration of Old Hollywood and his desire to make films that mirrored that era. Bob Fosse imagined *Lenny* in black and white because he wanted a documentary realism for the true story that captured the dark world of his subject. Woody Allen envisioned *Manhat-*

tan (1979) in black and white because he thought of the great city of his childhood in gleaming black and white. Factors for the diminished use of black and white were audience considerations: a younger audience less familiar with the style and the increasing number of cameramen who could not light and shoot in this medium.

Dustin Hoffman has always been a versatile character actor who will try anything when exploring a part. As an unknown he broke into the motion picture scene with *The Graduate* (1967), proving that leading actors did not have to look like matinee idols. Hoffman, who was a well-trained and experienced theater actor, established that a screen performer could honestly play an everyman. In 1970 he was directed by Arthur Penn in *Little Big Man*, a role with epic reach that involved aging him to a 121-year-old man. In *Straw Dogs* (1971) Hoffman portrayed a quiet mathematician who is tested when a group of local men want to enter his house against his will. The transformation is startling and proves director Sam Peckinpah's belief in the territorial imperative theory. In 1973 Hoffman was paired with Steve McQueen in *Papillion*, characters imprisoned during the 1930s under harsh conditions on Devil's Island. For the role of Louis Dega, Hoffman created a curious character both physically and vocally. After *Lenny* in 1974, Hoffman appeared in *All the President's Men* (1976) as Carl Bernstein. In *Marathon Man* (1976), directed by John Schlesinger, Hoffman played a young man whose brother pulls him into a dangerous political situation. *Kramer vs. Kramer* (1979), directed by Robert Benton, was another challenge for Hoffman. This was not a character part in the traditional sense. Hoffman is an advertising man whose wife, played by Meryl Streep, suddenly leaves him and their young son, then later starts a custody battle to get her son back. Hoffman won the Oscar for Best Actor for his performance.

Bob Fosse was a talented and complicated stage and film artist. Although he choreographed and directed countless stage musicals, Fosse was a substantial film director who explored the underbelly of show business. Fosse actualized the human figure in dance as a series of angles moving against each other. Federico Fellini was one of his directing heroes and Fosse's choices reflected this in much of his stage and film work. In 1972 Bob Fosse directed *Cabaret* with great success. It was a musical with social commentary about Germany's decadence during the rise of the Nazi party. The show has an extensive book; Fosse was skilled with the dialogue scenes as well as the musical ones. The production was handsome and well photographed by the superb cinematographer Geoffrey Unsworth, who photographed *2001: A Space Odyssey* for director Stanley Kubrick. At the Oscars, it was the year of *The Godfather*, but *Cabaret* won eight Academy Awards including Best Director, Cinematography, and Editing and Production Design. In 1979 Fosse created his masterpiece *All That Jazz*, an autobiographical film that the director refused to acknowledge had any relationship to his life. In many ways it was Fosse's American *8½* (1963). *All That Jazz* is an original musical in which the connections between "book" scenes and musical ones are often organic to the story. The story is realistic, but the cinema style is not. Alan Heim's editing won the Academy Award because it gave the film rhythm, velocity, and pace. It is the pinnacle of the art of editing. *All That Jazz* remains fresh because it moves at the pace of a long-form music video.

The Parallax View (1974) is a political thriller, the second in Alan J. Pakula's "paranoia trilogy," the first was *Klute* (1971) and the third *All the President's Men* (1976). Warren Beatty plays a journalist investigating a political assassination who learns that a nefarious corporation creates professional assassins. The film is stylish and modern with an ominous look developed by cinematographer Gordon Willis with production design by Gordon Jenkins. Well into the picture when Beatty infiltrates the company, he takes a test to gauge whether he is a good candidate to become a political assassin. The lights dim, a montage of still images, both black and white and color, begins accompanied by music. The images are in sections identified by black cards with white lettering. The sequence runs approximately five minutes. All the images are full frame and the musical accompaniment plays at full volume. The connections between still image and word are initially wholesome but later become dark and combine the personality of an assassin with more violent and sexual pictures. The categories on the cards repeat themselves; they include "love," "mother," "father," "me," "home," "country," "god," and "enemy." By around midpoint, the music no longer has pure American themes but is distorted. A rock guitar is introduced, and this later shifts back to the purer, patriotic, heroic music. The editing is deft and effective. This film is a political thriller, and Willis and Jenkins more than contribute to shocking the audience members who are on the edge of their seats. The film was edited by John W. Wheeler. For the test montage, the credits state that Don Record was the consultant designer with research by De Forrest research company.

The Sugarland Express starred Goldie Hawn, Ben Johnson, William Atherton, and Michael Sacks and was based on a true event in which a husband and wife try to outrun the law after removing their son from child protective services. Some critics thought there was too much emphasis on police cars and crashes; others found Spielberg to be an engaging entertainer, one critic comparing him to Classical Hollywood auteur Howard Hawks.

Tobe Hooper, director of *Texas Chainsaw Massacre*, developed the idea for this cutting-edge and controversial film during the early 1970s when he was working as a documentary cameraman. He started with the mood and loneliness of the woods. One inspiration for the film was graphic coverage of violence on local news outlets. He also based aspects of the plot on the real-life crimes of serial murderer Ed Gein, who inspired *Psycho* and other films. The murder weapon in the film's title came to Hooper when he was in a busy hardware store and saw a chainsaw; he imagined it as a means of getting ahead in the line.

The Texas Chainsaw Massacre is a splatter film, a subgenre of the horror film; others from the seventies include *The Wizard of Gore* (1970), directed by Herschell Gordon Lewis, and *Dawn of the Dead* (1978), directed by George A. Romero. Splatter films began in the seventies and came of age in the 1980s and 1990s. This extremely violent film was shot on 16mm film. Real parts of diseased cattle were used on the floor of the farmhouse, where a lot of gore takes place. In some cases, real blood was used instead of stage blood. The staging method posed danger for the actors due to their proximity to a sledgehammer and a chainsaw, two weapons in operation during shooting. They were used by Leatherface, played by Gunnar Hansen, on his victims. *The Texas Chainsaw Massacre* initially was rated X; after some cutting, it was rated R. The film was released as a horror movie in which the filmmakers dared the audience to watch it. Critics and a large portion of viewers were shocked and unprepared for this difficult and brutal film. Audiences did not know what to do with their emotions as they watched people massacred. In 1974 it was not totally clear that this film was a new kind of horror film, a subgenre that continued to expand after this bold movie, which never held back, was released.

When Clint Eastwood read and committed to the script for *Thunderbolt and Lightfoot*, a crime/comedy/road movie, he liked it so much he passed on directing it himself and asked the writer to direct it, thus launching Michael Cimino's directorial career. During production, Clint Eastwood, who didn't like too many takes for efficiency and budgetary reasons, kept Cimino from going off the plan. Ironically, later in the seventies, Cimino would go in an entirely different direction with *The Deer Hunter*, but here he proved to be a disciplined director with handsome results: a film with pace and style.

The Towering Inferno is a large-scale disaster movie about a skyscraper that catches fire. It was a coproduction between two major studios, 20th Century Fox and Warner Bros. The screenplay, by Stirling Silliphant, was based on two novels: *The Tower* by Richard Martin Stone and *The Glass Inferno* by Thomas N. Scortia and Frank M. Robinson. The all-star cast included Steve McQueen, Paul Newman, William Holden, Faye Dunaway, Fred Astaire, and others. The film was extremely successful at the box office, and at the Academy Awards it was nominated for six Oscars including Best Supporting Actor (Fred Astaire), art direction, score, sound, and picture and won for Best Original Song, Editing, and Cinematography. The special effects were extensive and involved a scale model of the building. The fire effects were real—this was an era before computer-generated imagery—and the results were frightfully realistic. For the shots with a helicopter flying above skyscraper, a miniature was created, which was believable and effective. Water tanks were blown up to spray enormous amounts of water on the burning building. This is a disaster movie featuring large-scale productions on an even grander scale than earlier films.

The genesis of *A Woman under the Influence* occurred when actress Gena Rowlands told her husband, actor/director John Cassavetes, that she wanted to appear in a play about issues contemporary women face. Cassavetes wrote the piece, which was so emotionally demanding that Rowlands felt she couldn't perform it on stage eight times a week. He adapted it into a film script but had no success in financing it, because no one wanted to deal with subject matter about a disturbed middle-aged lady with a husband and three children. When he could not get studio financing, Cassavetes mortgaged their home and borrowed from family and friends. One friend was actor Peter Falk, who was enjoying success on the *Columbo* series. Falk so believed in the project that he invested $500,000 in it.

Cassavetes was the first "filmmaker in residence" at the American Film Institute and was able to gather a crew of professionals and students as his crew for what became *A Woman under the Influence*. After completion Cassavetes couldn't find a distributor, so the film became the first independent movie to be distributed by convincing individual theaters across the country to show the picture. It was also run on college campuses with Cassavetes and Falk in the audience. Successful at film festivals, the movie received many strongly positive reviews. Rowlands was nominated for an Academy Award for Best Actress and Cassavetes for Best Director. Gena Rowlands won a Golden Globe for her performance, giving one of the most harrowing, emotional, genuine performances by an American actress of her time. Cassavetes is at his most disciplined, working in color in a realistic style that captures all the raw emotions and joy of his characters. *A Woman under the Influence* is one of the director's finest accomplishments as a film director.

Gena Rowlands began acting on stage and in television in the early fifties. She and her husband collaborated countless times; Rowlands was clearly a muse for his creativity. In 1971 Rowlands costarred with Seymour Cassel (a constant figure on and behind the camera in Cassavetes's films) in *Minnie and Moskowitz*, an emotionally complex relationship movie about a one-sided love. After *A Woman under the Influence* in 1977, Gena Rowlands was directed by John Cassavetes in *Opening Night*, in which she plays an actress who leaves the theater one night when a young female fan runs toward her in the street and is killed by an oncoming car. The actress is haunted and unable to return to her normal life as an actress. Both John Cassavetes and Gena Rowlands appeared in the thriller *Two-Minute Warning* (1976), directed by Larry Peerce, with Cassavetes playing a SWAT team leader and Rowlands as half of an argumentative middle-aged couple as a sniper threatens violence in a stadium packed for a football championship. In 1978 Rowlands was directed by William Friedkin in *The Brink's Job* about the famous robbery in Boston in 1950.

Jonathan Demme started in the seventies as a Roger Corman acolyte on low-budget movies. It was there he developed his quirky style of filmmaking. After two years writing and producing, Demme made his directorial debut in 1974 with *Caged Heat*, a women-in-prison genre picture. The film was made for Corman's New World Pictures. In 1975 he made *Crazy Mama*, starring Cloris Leachman, in which three women engage in a crime spree when their business is repossessed. *Fighting Mad* (1976) is about a farmer, Tom Hunter, played by Peter Fonda, who fights landowners attempting to evict him illegally. In 1977 Demme made *Citizen's Band*, later retitled *Handle with Care*, featuring Paul LeMat and Candy Clark—another film that reflected the country's CB craze. *Last Embrace* (1979) is a thriller in the Hitchcock mode distributed by United Artists that featured Roy Scheider and Janet Margolin. After the seventies Demme would have two breakthrough hits with *The Silence of the Lambs* (1991), exploring the mind and actions of serial killers, and *Philadelphia* (1993), investigating the social complications of the AIDS crisis. These successes demonstrated that his seventies films were a training ground for a more polished style able to reach a wider audience than the exploitation films of the seventies.

Joseph Walsh was an actor who couldn't get parts, so he decided to write about his gambling addiction. He had a friendship with Steven Spielberg, who was just beginning his career. They worked together on a script called *Slide* for nine months and had a deal to finalize the film at MGM with Walsh as producer and Steve McQueen as star. The studio began making demands about the movie's length and wanted it to take place at a casino in Vegas that MGM owned. After a corporate shake-up, MGM wanted the film to feature Dean Martin and have a mafia theme. Walsh was now told he would not be the producer. They took the project to Universal, where they had an agreement with Richard Zanuck and David Brown, who then hired Spielberg to direct *The Sugarland Express*. The result was that Walsh and his film were out. Walsh's agent sent the script to Robert Altman, who was excited about it but took his usual liberties. The product became *California Split*, one of the earliest films to employ an experimental eight-track sound system, which had separate recording channels and allowed Altman to create realistic overlapping dialogue. Altman added actual members from Synanon, the addiction treatment facility, as extras, and the legendary Amarillo Slim participated in a poker game for authenticity. Robert Altman (a compulsive gambler himself) may have been the only director to get away with making a film about two guys, played by Elliot Gould and George Segal, gambling on everything in sight, in and out of proper venues.

John Waters is a multitalented film artist who has a charming and civilized manner. His films are anything but and are categorized as transgressive cult films. There is a distinction between his early tasteless movies about repulsive people done in a low-rent fashion and his more polished later films that are more satiric than gross-out with better production values. Waters was a Baltimore, Maryland, filmmaker who had his own stock company and valued crew members. Before the seventies Waters made four films, all low-life vehicles with deranged activities. In 1970 Waters made the nine-minute film *The Diane Linkletter Story*, which relates the story of the daughter of popular TV host Art Linkletter. Diane committed suicide while on LSD. Waters said the story was improvised and accidental and distanced himself from the controversy. The film was not released until 1990. Waters often worked every aspect of his films, including cinematography and editing. *Multiple Maniacs* (1970) is about a show that contains every perversion imaginable. *Pink Flamingos* (1972) is one of the most outrageous and offensive films made in the era, starring Divine, one of Waters's superstars in drag. It is a study in bad taste with an ending in which Divine feasts on her dog's feces. *Female Trouble* (1974) is dedicated to an active member of the Manson family. *Desperate Living* (1977) is a film that focuses on deviant sex with a large female cast. Waters, a perfect gentleman with good manners but dark interests, liked to study serial killers. His films featured actors who switched gender roles and were the antithesis of old and new Hollywood actors. Waters could be considered an extension of the Andy Warhol philosophy of filmmaking but with a storytelling style that crossed over from cult to audiences looking for a dangerous but funny night at the movies.

Foxy Brown is a blaxploitation film written and directed by Jack Hill and starring Pam Grier. The original release by American International Pictures was a double-bill with *Truck Turner*. The narrative is a revenge story: Foxy Brown's boyfriend is killed by a drug syndicate. There is violence in the film and a lot of sexual attitude. There is a degree of stereotyping and exploitation, which was part of the genre. Still, the film was embraced by some women and feminists who felt empowered seeing a strong black woman overcome odds and dangerous situations.

Pam Grier is an accomplished actress well known to film audiences and was considered a star. She starred in many blaxploitation films during the seventies. In *The Big Doll House* (1971), directed by Jack Hill, Grier plays a lesbian cellmate joining other prisoners in a plan to break out of prison. *Cool Breeze* (1972, directed by Barry Pollack) was a predominately black remake of *The Asphalt Jungle*. *The Big Bird Cage* (1972), directed by Jack Hill, is a non-sequel follow-up to *The Big Doll House*. Grier plays Blossom, a bad girl. *Black Mama White Mama* (1973), directed by Eddie Romero, is another woman-in-prison movie like *The Defiant Ones* (1958). Grier is shackled to a white female prisoner played by Margaret Markov, an original story cowritten by Jonathan Demme and Joseph Viola. *Coffy* (1973) is written and directed by Jack Hill. Grier plays the title role, a female vigilante. *The Arena* (1974), directed by Steve Carter, is a gladiator exploitation film with slaves who must fight for their lives in an arena, not unlike *Spartacus* (1960) and *Gladiator* (2000). *Friday Foster* (1975), directed by Arthur Marks, is a blaxploitation film that became Pam Grier's last movie with American International Pictures. *Drum* (1976), a United Artists release directed by Steve Carver, is a sequel to *Mandingo* (1975). *Greased Lighting* (1977) is directed by Michael Schultz, one of the rare African American directors working in the field; it is a biopic of the first African American NASCAR winner. In 1997 as a tribute to blaxploitation films, Quentin Tarantino wrote and directed *Jackie Brown*, starring Pam Grier, who received a Golden Globe nomination for her performance in the title role.

Michael Schultz is an African American film director who worked extensively in series television. During the seventies, he was best known for directing the features *Cooley High* (1975), a coming-of-age film; *Car Wash* (1976), at times a profane and often hilarious comedy about a multiracial group of workers, with a large cast that includes Richard Pryor; and *Which Way Is Up?* (1977), featuring Pryor in a remake of Lina Wertmuller's *The Seduction of Mimi*.

Gone in 60 Seconds (1974) is an action film written, produced, directed, and starring H. B. "Toby" Hailicki concerning a group of car thieves and the forty-eight cars they must steal in just days. Ninety-three cars were damaged or destroyed during a forty-minute car chase sequence. In total, 127 cars were totaled during the making of the film. For this independent film Hailicki performed his own stunt work. He bought police cars and fire trucks at city auction for around $200 each. With no official script, dialogue and action were improvised by his friends and family who appeared in the movie. Editing was problematic because no one knew where any shot would go. There were real and near-accidents during shooting, and the extras often were real people going about their business, not knowing they were in a movie.

Road Movie is an aptly titled road movie directed by Joseph Strick who has a curious résumé that includes *The Savage Eye* (1960), a film utilizing fictional and documentary material; a cinematic adaptation of the James Joyce literary masterwork *Ulysses* (1967); and the documentary *Interviews with Mai Lai Veterans* (1971). *Road Movie* was distributed by Grove Press, known for its edgy book publishing list more than movies. Like other seventies films that were not particularly targeted toward a general or wide audience, *Road Movie* played in New York City for one week then seemed to disappear. Two independent truck drivers, played by Robert Drivas and Barry Bostwick, are struggling against union regulations when they come upon Janice, a prostitute played to the hilt by Regina Baff, who offers her services to them free of charge if they take her to New York. They take her to New York without taking her up on her offer, which launches Janice into a tirade about her miserable life and eventually leads to their demise. Strick had been a trucker, which gave the film authenticity. Judith Rascoe, a young female writer without any film credits whatsoever who was teaching writing at Yale, brought a female perspective and tough view of life on the road to the project. *Road Movie* is part of a genre that helped define the seventies.

Seizure is also a little-known movie from the seventies and the directorial debut of Oliver Stone. The story, with a screenplay by Stone, concerns a horror writer who sees his frightening nightmare come to life during a weekend. He and his friends are killed by three villains: the queen of evil, a dwarf, and a scarred-face strongman. *Seizure* had an extremely limited release in 1974, playing only in the Times Square area in New York City. Also in the seventies, Oliver Stone wrote the screenplay for *Midnight Express* (1978), directed by Alan Parker, based on the 1977 nonfiction book by Billy Hayes, who was sent to prison in Turkey for smuggling hashish. Oliver Stone won the Academy Award for Best Screenplay Based on Material from Another Medium.

7

1975

April 4: Microsoft created by Bill Gates and Paul Allen and will come to dominate the home computer and software markets, putting computers in the hands of consumers and impacting communication, art, science, literature, and much more. April: because of the women's movement, the First Women's Bank in New York was founded to give women equal opportunities in banking.

Low-budget films created by independent production companies and distributed by a major studio were part of the seventies. Their reception was sometimes unanticipated. One such example is *Aloha, Bobby and Rose* (1975), directed by Floyd Mutrux, who began his career as an uncredited writer on *Two-Lane Blacktop*. *Aloha, Bobby and Rose*'s theme was youth on the run from the law. It featured Paul LeMat, Dianne Hull, Robert Carradine, and Edward James Olmos. It received disastrous reviews, but on a $600,000 budget, it grossed $35 million domestically, especially surprising for a film about which few viewers claimed to be aware.

The American musical of the Classical Hollywood era was either based on a hit Broadway show or written for the screen. It was one of the key reasons the average moviegoer went to the hometown movie theater. This genre, in vivid Technicolor, with big-screen locations and colorful sets, was spectacular and put the audience in seats. Over the decades, these filmed musicals featuring fine Hollywood talent fell out of favor. They had little appeal to sixties youth and almost nothing to offer the seventies generation.

Roy Scheider and Richard Dreyfuss in *Jaws*. *Universal Pictures/Photofest* © *Universal Pictures*

The seventies decade saw the musical struggling to stay in the game and attempting to reinvent itself. The definitive 1937 drama *Lost Horizon*, directed by Classic Hollywood great Frank Capra, was remade into a musical in 1973, produced by the high-profile Hollywood figure Ross Hunter. It starred Liv Ullman of Ingmar Bergman renown. Despite this, the production was a monumental failure.

Peter Bogdanovich sought to reinvigorate the musical with *At Long Last Love* using the songs of Cole Porter in which the singing would be recorded live. Bogdanovich was motivated and inspired by musicals of the past and the great singers of the studio era. The director had the art direction capture what he called black and white in color. The costumes, sets, and props were either black or white. Flesh tones and sky and grass colors were natural, but the rest of the film had a bizarre combination of old and new, adding up to a surreal, dreamlike version of a Hollywood musical. Originally Bogdanovich, an experienced actor, was going to appear in the cast, but eventually he decided against it. Ryan O'Neal was in the cast and dropped out. Elliot Gould had musical theater experience and was in the cast, but he also dropped out. Then, according to Bogdanovich, he was talked into hiring the popular Burt Reynolds, who couldn't sing or dance that well—a criticism that also could be applied to the rest of the cast, with Shepard having a bit of an edge in singing but not in the dance department. Bogdanovich felt no one understood what he was trying to do; he wasn't even sure himself. The film's budget was $5.14 million and it grossed $2.5 million, along with bad reviews. It was a major flop for the once hot director. *At Long Last Love* has been called the biggest musical bomb of the seventies. Many felt director Peter Bogdanovich was arrogant with his retro attitude and too often cast his then-girlfriend Cybil Shepard, who had limited acting skills, in his pictures.

MGM struck a brilliant idea to keep the Classical Hollywood musical alive. In their vaults, they had pristine prints of some of the greatest movie musicals ever made. They asked Fred Astaire, Gene Kelly, Liza Minelli, and others to introduce these clips featuring wonders of Hollywood mastery with glorious singing and dancing. Called *That's Entertainment!* it was released in 1974 and was followed in 1976 by *That's Entertainment, Part II* and spinoffs in later decades. The genius of this idea was that these compilations were released in the finest movie theaters remaining in America; more notably, they got the older crowd out of their living rooms and into theaters. Money was made because the studios owned the clips and the cost was de minimis for the introduction shoots—the talent, a camera, some lights, and a live mike. They had little influence on new American musicals in the seventies, but they were a history lesson about Classical Hollywood.

There were successful new musicals in the seventies. *The Rocky Horror Picture Show* eventually crossed the line between a projected movie and a live stage cast populated by members of the audience. *The Rocky Horror Picture Show* was based on the 1973 stage production of the same name. It starred Susan Sarandon, Tim Curry, and Barry Bostwick. It is a parody of science fiction and horror B movies from the 1930s through the 1960s. The narrative includes a young couple whose car breaks down near a castle. Inside, people are dressed in strange costumes. The head of the house is Frank-N-Furter, a mad scientist who is an alien transvestite constructing a muscle man in a lab. The movie was pure camp and the audience participation made for role-playing that generated its musical excitement.

Pete Townsend's rock opera masterpiece, originally released on vinyl by the Who in 1969 and transformed into a movie helmed by Ken Russell in 1975, featured major rock stars such as Elton John and was structured like a series of music videos (yet to arrive on MTV) to illustrate the landmark achievement by a highly popular group.

Barry Lyndon is one of the most impressive period films ever made. It was directed by Stanley Kubrick and adapted from *The Luck of Barry Lyndon* by William Makepeace Thackeray. There was some surprise and bewilderment about the casting of Ryan O'Neal as Barry. At first it seemed that Kubrick cast the actor solely for his movie star good looks. O'Neal had a reputation of appearing in projects that weren't as substantial as *Barry Lyndon*. Kubrick understood he needed a name to sell his films, but he also understood that O'Neal could play the cad within Lyndon's character. Kubrick used a zoom lens to dissect a composition and related the images to classical paintings, which influenced and were also part of the images. The director also wanted to film by candlelight. He found a lens that could do this and had it permanently installed into his camera, rendering it unable to do anything else. Real clothes from the era were found and adjusted for contemporary bodies. Countless paintings were used as research to dress the complex, large sets. The score utilized classical music and Irish folk music. *Barry Lyndon* is a feast for the eyes that captures the past and reveals that human nature has not really changed much.

Kubrick's exceptional cameraman John Alcott shot *Barry Lyndon*. Ken Adam, who designed the best of the early Bond films and *Dr. Strangelove*, meticulously designed it. The greatness of *Barry Lyndon* lays in its detail and the affinity for its time. Kubrick identified with Barry Lyndon, the rogue who is the lead character. It fit in with his oeuvre of misanthropes like Alex DeLarge in the menacing and celebrated *A Clockwork Orange* (1971). *Barry Lyndon* was that magical time machine filmmakers dream of that can send them back to a bygone era and allow them to film the reality of that time.

With the New Wave decade of American filmmaking coming to the halfway point, it had been defined primarily with personal films that reflected the director and the darker aspects of U.S. life. Although some of these films made money at the box office, many did not. General entertainment films still existed and there were attempts at big outcomes, but New Wave was largely an introspective cinema, its creators abstractly linked to each other in spirit and committed to a new, artistic approach to the American film. From this conceptual model emerged what would be called the blockbuster.

On June 20, 1975, the third feature film directed by Steven Spielberg was released. *Jaws* was adapted from the bestseller by Peter Benchley. The story takes place in a beach community where a man-eating shark shows up and devours a citizen. Three men, including a sheriff, a scientist, and a Melvillian fisherman, set out on the deep sea to capture it.

Jaws is the first blockbuster of the seventies New Wave contemporary era. With a $9 million budget, it grossed $470.7 million. It became a pop culture icon. Word of mouth and publicity brought in audiences in droves all over the country. Although there are distinct characters and a human narrative, the primary draw of *Jaws* is the battle between man and shark. The film is cleverly crafted and directed.

The blockbuster form—an entertainment film designed to capture the attention of a wide audience and make a lot of money starting on the day of its release, a Friday for big weekend business—was the new goal of all the studios. Box office receipts were always meaningful but now there was a new standard. The American New Wave would never be the same after the box office gross bar was raised. Audiences reacted enthusiastically to this new phenomenon. Some critics and scholars deemed that the New Wave was over. But the personal film and all that the American film could be was not over—it simply readjusted.

If Steven Spielberg had not created the blockbuster with *Jaws*, someone else would have with some other film. From their inception, the movies have been about entertainment and big box office. What made the seventies so special was that art as well as commerce was important for the filmmakers and even the studios. When the studios saw that *Jaws* rolled in big money, the focus on art in films diminished. There was nothing personal about this film, the style was straightforward modern American filmmaking, with only the emotion necessary to support the story and characters. It was comparable to the reaction of the studios after *Easy Rider*'s low-budget windfall: they were willing to give any kid with long hair a picture. Now they analyzed *Jaws*, its story and screenplay, and tried to make lightning strike again, looking for what could be the next blockbuster. Box office was swiftly catching up to cinematic art.

The Day of the Locust is considered the most virulent attack on the Old Hollywood Studio System yet filmed. The source was the novel *The Day of the Locust* by Nathaniel West, who had worked as a screenwriter for Columbia Pictures and saw how badly some people were treated during the early days of moviemaking. Directed by John Schlesinger, shot by Conrad Hall, designed by Richard Macdonald, and edited by Jim Clark, it is visually expressionistic—a metaphor for the system falling apart. *The Day of the Locust* was not a success, but it is a film that could have been made only in the seventies with its excesses and total commitment to the vision of Nathaniel West.

British director John Schlesinger began directing movies in 1962 with the kitchen sink drama *A Kind of Loving*. Schlesinger ended that decade with his first film shot in the United States, *Midnight Cowboy* (1969), a gritty movie about two down-and-out misfits in New York City. Because of its content the film was rated X but still won the Best Picture Oscar. It is another movie that heavily influenced the seventies by taking on the grim lives of these two men. In 1971 Schlesinger directed *Sunday Bloody Sunday*, a landmark film that portrayed homosexuality in a nonjudgmental manner and showed a man-to-man kiss on-screen, which was a breakthrough. After *Day of the Locust* Schlesinger directed the political thriller *Marathon Man* (1976) about a vicious clandestine Nazi. It contains a dental torture scene that had audiences squirming in their theater seats.

Dog Day Afternoon was directed by Sidney Lumet and starred Al Pacino and John Cazale. It is based on the true story of a man who robbed a bank to finance a sex reassignment operation for his boyfriend. Once the bank robbers are revealed to the police, they arrive in force as does the FBI and a large crowd of locals watching the proceedings. At this point, esteemed film editor Dede Allen intercut footage of what happens in the bank, the police negotiator outside on the street, the barbershop now used as a communication base to reach Sonny (Pacino) inside the bank, and the crowds outside. Lumet was a director who provided little coverage; therefore, Dede Allen needed the option to cut to those locations to keep the movie "alive."

John Cazale started his career as a serious theater actor. His life changed when Francis Ford Coppola cast him as Fredo Corleone, the middle brother in his legendary 1972 film *The Godfather*. Cazale was part of a strong ensemble cast and immediately established himself as the not-too-bright brother who was passed over in the hierarchy of the family, scrapping to find his way in the power grid. In *The Conversation* (1974), again working with Coppola, he played Stan, a dim-witted electronics assistant who tried desperately to gain the respect of his first-class boss, portrayed by Gene Hackman. Also in 1974 Cazale reprised his role as Fredo in *The Godfather: Part II*, now a desperate man willing to sell out his own family for respect and power. In *Dog Day Afternoon* Cazale portrays Sal, identified as a Vietnam veteran who is assigned to guard Sonny with a rifle in the bank. He looks uncomfortable and frightened during this caper, which ends tragically for him. *The Deer Hunter* in 1978 was Cazale's last film before he died of lung cancer in 1977; he was seriously ill during production. Cazale plays Stanley, an acerbic member of a group of longtime working-class friends, who, on the night before his three buddies leave for Vietnam, go hunting and carp at each other. Cazale was respected for his superb acting abilities and delivered a courageous final performance.

Joan Micklin Silver is a key figure as a female feature film director of the modern era. She entered film directing by making two shorts, *The Immigrant Experience: The Long Long Journey* (1972) and *The Case of the Elevator Duck* (1974). In 1975 she wrote and directed the landmark independent film *Hester Street*, which details the lives of Jewish immigrants in New York at the turn of the century. It is a period film, and much of the dialogue is spoken in Yiddish with subtitles. Carol Kane was nominated for an Academy Award for her lead role in the film. In 1977 Silver directed *Between the Lines*, a film about a group of people who work for an alternative newspaper in Boston called the *Backbay Mainline*. The lively cast includes Jeff Goldblum, Lindsay Crouse, Joe Morton, and Marilu Henner. Both pictures were produced by her husband, Raphael D. Silver. In 1979 she directed *Head over Heels*, based on the novel *Chilly Scenes of Winter* by Anne Beattie. This release was not very successful. In 1982 it was rereleased with the last scene deleted and renamed *Chilly Scenes of Winter* to match the book title.

Carol Kane studied theater as a young person. She was quite active as an actress in film during the seventies. In *Carnal Knowledge* (1971) Kane played the eighteen-year-old girlfriend of the middle-aged Jack Nicholson character. In *The Last Detail* (1973) she plays a prostitute. After *Hester Street* Kane played one of the bank clerks held hostage in *Dog Day Afternoon*. She was also in *Annie Hall* (1977). In *Valentino* (1977), directed by Ken Russell, she plays one of the women in Rudolph Valentino's life. *The Mafu Cage* (1978) costars Carol Kane and Lee Grant as incestuous sisters in the psychological thriller directed by Karen Arthur.

Milestones is a three-hour-and-eighteen-minute film directed by Robert Kramer and John Douglas and written by Kramer. It was crafted to appear as if it were a cinema verité/direct cinema documentary, though it was not. More than fifty people cross-talk about their lifestyles as part of the American left during the period following the Vietnam War and about radical solutions to social problems of the sixties and seventies.

With the enormous output Robert Altman created during the seventies, *Nashville* is Altman's masterpiece and a film that defines the decade and the country at a point in time. There are twenty-four characters in *Nashville* whose lives intersect. *Nashville* takes place over five days. The intertwining of these various lives becomes complicated and involved. The film concludes with a concert for a presidential candidate from the Replacement Party when a shocking event occurs that mirrors the violence of U.S. society during the period. The cast includes Ronee Blakley as Barbara Jean, a fragile country superstar considered the sweetheart of Nashville. Henry Gibson plays Haven Hamilton, a powerful Nashville performer with political ambitions. Barbara Harris plays Winifred, an aspiring singer-songwriter. Michael Murphy is John Triplette, a political consultant, and Keith Carradine plays ladies' man Tom Frank, working to succeed as a solo artist. Lily Tomlin plays Linnea Reese, a gospel singer who has two deaf children. She has a one-night stand with Keith Carradine's character. Numerous other characters round out the enormous cast.

The story was written by Joan Tewkesbury. Altman sent Tewkesbury to Nashville to study the area and the mechanics of the city. A lot of what she discovered is evident in the script. *Nashville* was released a year before the bicentennial, when the country was getting ready for America's big birthday, so it was easy to see Music City as a microcosm of the country at large. *Nashville* is the great American movie because it defines our country at a critical time in its history during a major anniversary. It brilliantly uses country music to reflect America. It is a big, unwieldly movie with many characters, storylines, and music. On the surface, *Nashville* (1976) was a film celebrating country music: an American movie that embraced American morals and beliefs, but Robert Altman's film is a parody of the country music scene and of America itself. This film is at the zenith of Altman's crowded personal résumé. Altman was a restless man with a lot to say. Sometimes he said it well, and at other times no one wanted to listen to him. With *Nashville* Robert Altman made a film for the ages.

Ken Kesey worked as an orderly at a mental hospital in Menlo Park, California, and used his observations and experiences to write the novel *One Flew over the Cuckoo's Nest*, published in 1962. The book is narrated by Chief Bromden, and the principal character is Randle McMurphy, who is transferred from a work farm to a mental institution. Nurse Ratched runs the ward and is McMurphy's adversary. A theatrical adaptation of the novel written by Dale Wasserman played on Broadway with Kirk Douglas appearing as McMurphy. Later Douglas tried to get the play made into a movie, but he wasn't successful, so he gave the project to his son Michael to give it a try. Michael Douglas was totally successful in producing the film version of *One Flew over the Cuckoo's Nest*. Jack Nicholson played McMurphy, Louise Fletcher portrayed Nurse Ratched, Will Sampson portrayed Chief Bromden, and Brad Dourif was Billy Bibitt. One of the strengths of the movie is the ensemble cast depicting the other inmates. Once McMurphy enters the hospital, he takes control of the men and these interactions result in much drama and comedy. Paul Sylbert, twin brother of production designer Richard Sylbert, designed the film. In his work in cinema production design, Paul Sylbert drew from poetry, music, painting, and philosophy to create metaphors to define the essence of a film. During the seventies he worked on many projects including *Bad Company* (1972) directed by Robert Benton. After *One Flew over the Cuckoo's Nest*, he won an Oscar for his production design of *Heaven Can Wait* (1978), directed by Warren Beatty and Buck Henry. In 1979 he designed *Hardcore* for Paul Schrader and *Kramer vs. Kramer*, directed by Robert Benton. *One Flew over the Cuckoo's Nest* won five Academy Awards including one for Nicholson, Best Actress for Louise Fletcher, and Best Director, Best Adapted Screenplay, and Best Picture for Miloš Forman.

In 1975 Nicholson played a documentary filmmaker in the Sahara Desert in *The Passenger* (1975), directed by European maestro Michelangelo Antonioni. The actor's performance in a different low-key style minus some of his signature gestures and movements underscores Jack Nicholson's extensive dramatic range.

Miloš Forman was a Czechoslovakian film director who became a naturalized U.S. citizen in 1977. His 1967 film *Fireman's Ball* was banned in Czechoslovakia when officials determined it was a satire critical of the political system. *Taking Off* (1971) was Forman's first film in the United States. It is the story of a suburban couple whose daughter runs away from home. The parents join with other parents of runaways to learn about youth culture. After *One Flew over the Cuckoo's Nest*, Miloš Forman directed an adaptation of the musical *Hair* (1979).

Writer/director John Milius was attracted to the material that became *The Wind and the Lion*. Milius was immersed in military history and he echoed classic adventure films and stories, some from the British magazine *Boy's Own* and the stories of Rudyard Kipling. *The Wind and the Lion* is a good tale interwoven with real characters such as President Theodore Roosevelt. The film featured Sean Connery, Candice Bergen, John Huston, and Brian Keith. In 1972 Milius wrote *The Life and Times of Judge Roy Bean*, a tall-tale Western directed by John Huston and starring Paul Newman. In 1972 he wrote *Jeremiah Johnson*, directed by Sidney Pollack, with Robert Redford as a mountain man. In 1973 he cowrote, with Michael Cimino, *Magnum Force*, a Dirty Harry movie directed by Ted Post. In 1973 Milius wrote and directed his debut film, *Dillinger*, a well-made and well-told film about the legendary gangster, which starred Warren Oates. After *The Wind and the Lion*, Milius directed and cowrote *Big Wednesday* (1978), a surfing epic. In 1979 Milius cowrote, with Francis Ford Coppola, *Apocalypse Now*, which they based on *Heart of Darkness* by Joseph Conrad. Milius was with this project from the outset, when George Lucas hoped to direct it in Vietnam. In 1979 *1941* was released, directed by Steven Spielberg. Milius was one of the contributors to the story, which was a total flop, an unfunny comedy about World War II.

Cooley High is a coming-of-age comedy about high school seniors and their friends directed by Michael Schultz. The story is initially light-hearted and then turns tragic. The film was a big box office success, grossing $13 million on a $750,000 budget. The screenwriter Eric Monte based the story on his own experiences. The writer had grown up in the housing projects and wanted to dispel the notion that they were dreary, because in his case they weren't. There were many Motown songs on the soundtrack, which also brought in audiences. The film was distributed by American International Pictures.

Michael Schultz is an African American film director with extensive credits in television and on stage. In 1972 Schultz directed *Together for Days*, an independent blaxploitation film about a mixed-race relationship.

It featured Samuel L. Jackson's debut performance. After *Cooley High*, Schultz directed *Car Wash* (1976), about the ins and out of a raucous and profane car-cleaning establishment. *Greased Lightning* (1977) is a biopic about a black racecar driver starring Richard Pryor. *Which Way Is Up?* (1977) is a remake of the Italian comedy *The Seduction of Mimi*, directed by Lina Wertmuller (1972), in which the talented actor/comedian plays three different roles. *Sgt. Pepper's Lonely Hearts Club Band* (1978) is a musical with multiple performers playing Beatles songs. *Scavenger's Hunt* (1979) sports a large cast playing the time-tested game in which participants must find specific items in order to win.

Death Race 2000 is a science fiction sports film produced by Roger Corman and directed by Paul Bartel starring David Carradine. This film takes place in the future where a death race is a kind of entertainment. The film was distributed by New World Pictures. The film was low budget and made a profit.

Paul Bartel was an actor and film director who liked to work independently and foster on-the-edge content. In 1972 Bartel directed *Private Parts*, a psychological thriller with horror and black comedy seen through the eyes of an underground filmmaker. In 1976 he directed *Cannonball*, a film inspired by a man who ran an illegal road race cross-continent. Bartel acted in other directors' movies between his directing assignments. He was the epitome of an independent filmmaker.

Howard Zieff started in advertising commercials. In 1973 he directed the feature film *Slither*, which is about a con man, played by James Caan, and his wife who search for embezzled money. They are followed by undesirables. In 1975 Zieff directed *Hearts of the West*, in which a fan of the West, played by Jeff Bridges, travels there and becomes the star of a cowboy movie.

Shampoo, directed by Hal Ashby, produced and starring Warren Beatty, written by Robert Towne, and costarring Julie Christie, Goldie Hawn, Lee Grant, and Jack Warden was a popular film that proved audiences were interested in social satire while being entertained. The budget for the film, with music by Paul Simon and cinematography by László Kovács, was $4 million and it grossed $60 million, an example of what star and auteur power could do for a film in the seventies. *Shampoo* has been construed as a modern-day *Rules of the Game* (1939), the French masterpiece by Jean Renoir, an examination of the morality of the wealthy and privileged. *Shampoo* features Beatty as George Roundy, a Beverly Hills hairdresser who is a ladies' man juggling numerous affairs and trysts. He wants to move up in life and open his own shop. He finds the potential financing through a powerful man, with whom he has something in common—the man's wife is also Roundy's mistress.

As producer and star, Beatty had much to do with the making of this film, which takes place on the eve of the 1968 elections that led to the presidency of Richard Nixon. Ashby and his team, which included production designer Richard Sylbert, gave this effective social satire a polished look and lively pace.

F for Fake is a nonfiction film that is both a documentary and an essay picture. Directed by Orson Welles, it is focused on fakery, primarily the notorious forger Elmry de Hory, who was considered the best at copying the modern painting masters. There are numerous subtopics in *F for Fake*. Clifford Irving wrote a book on Elmry called *Fake!* and was himself part of a scandalous scam claiming that the reclusive Howard Hughes dictated his autobiography to the writer. When Hughes denied its authenticity, Irving went to prison for seventeen months. Also portrayed as a faker is Welles himself as a magician, a filmmaker, and the man behind the infamous *War of the Worlds* radio broadcast, which gave listeners the impression that alien beings were invading. Welles's female companion Oja Kodar frames the film with a story about posing nude for Pablo Picasso. Whether the story is true or not remains unresolved. The picture is edited in a brisk and at times elusive manner that plays with the audience's ability to determine what is real in the film. Welles, mellifluous master narrator, makes *F for Fake* entertaining and bewildering as it investigates and eludes the truth.

From 1955 to 1972 Welles directed but did not complete the film *Don Quixote*, the classic by Miguel de Cervantes. From 1968 to 1971 Welles worked on a short film, *One Man Band*, with sketches taking place around Europe. His most legendary unfinished project was finally completed after Welles's death by friends and associates. It was his last feature film. In 1970 he began directing *The Other Side of the Wind*, starring John Huston as a film director trying to complete his last film. During production, the project ran afoul of the Iranian government, which held it in a vault for decades. Eventually, through negotiations, the film was released. Welles died in 1985 and others—including many members of the American New Wave and seventies cinema who idolized him—completed the film, which was released on Netflix in 2018. Ironically, Welles was vocal about his dislike for the films of the New Wave and criticized the movement savagely at times in his final movie. His influence on the movement can be seen throughout the decade.

8

1976

April 1: Steve Jobs and Steve Wozniak create Apple computer. The design and functionality of their product would revolutionize the computer industry and the world of professional and home computing. . . . June 28: U.S. Air Force first admitted women. Even though women were still restricted from physical combat, they were educated in the military via the curriculum. . . . July 27: During a Legionnaires convention at the Bellevue-Stratford Hotel in Philadelphia, Pennsylvania, attendees were unknowingly exposed to bacteria that caused 182 people to become ill and twenty-nine deaths. This became known as Legionnaires' disease.

A big birthday party for the United States of America was long in the planning. The country was two hundred years old and this nationwide project was simply called the Bicentennial. Events of every sort were designated and readied. The movies were not a particularly big part of the celebrations, but there were some motion pictures directly connected to the Bicentennial, some metaphorically or symbolically. Not all were released in 1976 but addressed a wider celebration.

Christopher Columbus was a central figure in America's story. There were two competing movies about the controversial father/discoverer of America. There was *Christopher Columbus: The Discovery* produced by Alexander Salkind and Ilya Salkind. At the same time there was the Ridley Scott production *1492: Conquest of Paradise*. The Salkind production was stagnant and lacked drama and life. The Ridley Scott film was an epic with culture, pomp and circumstance, and history.

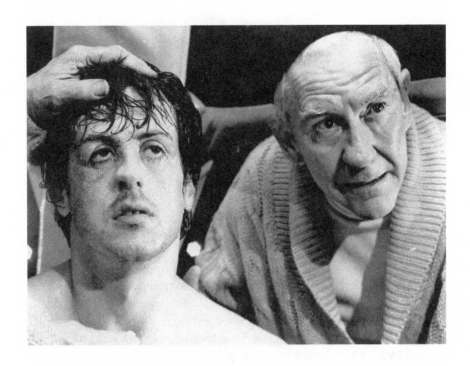

Sylvester Stallone and Burgess Meredith in *Rocky. Paramount Pictures/Photofest* ©
Paramount Pictures

Legendary screenwriter, actor, and director John Huston was commissioned to direct a twenty-eight-minute docudrama produced for the U.S. Parks Department on the Bicentennial. *Independence* was intended to give visitors an overview of the political events in Philadelphia between 1774 and 1800. Actors played George Washington, Thomas Jefferson, and Benjamin Franklin. The cast included Pat Hingle, Anne Jackson, William Atherton, and E. G. Marshall as the narrator.

Taxi Driver, also released during the Bicentennial year, was Martin Scorsese's disturbing film written by Paul Schrader. A presidential contender is the subject of an assassination attempt by the central character, Travis Bickle, played with chilling nuances and contradictions by Robert De Niro. *Taxi Driver* is the dark side, the underbelly of the Bicentennial—a rotting America without morals.

The principal Bicentennial film released in 1976 was a boxing movie written and starring a virtual unknown, Sylvester Stallone. *Rocky* took place in Philadelphia, the founding seat of the nation, and celebrated the individual and the underdog. The colors of the American flag are evident, and the dreams of love and success in the country are on display. This simplistic drama touched a chord with American audiences, and *Rocky* won the Oscar for Best Picture and began a successful long-running franchise with seven sequels.

In *Assault on Precinct 13*, which took place in South Central Los Angeles, a gang steals a cache of weapons and is hunted down by LAPD officers who kill several of them, prompting the gang to wreak revenge on the police. This independent thriller was written, directed, scored, and edited by John Carpenter. The models for this film were *Rio Bravo* (1959), a classic Western directed by Howard Hawks, a Hollywood Studio System–era filmmaker who Carpenter admired, and Hawks's 1951 version of *The Thing*, which inspired Carpenter's 1982 version. *Assault on Precinct 13* has an onslaught of gun violence and a constant barrage of firing bullets. An effective synthesizer score written and co-performed by Carpenter creates tension equal to the narrative pressure on the screen. Before its release, the rating board threatened to give *Assault on Precinct 13* an X rating because of a scene in which a gang member brutally guns down a little girl at an ice cream truck. The killing is shown in explicit detail. Carpenter gave the board the impression he would cut the offending scene, but when it was released the violent murder of the little girl was still there.

The Blank Generation is a documentary depicting the birth of punk, captured behind the scenes by Amos Poe and Ivan Král, with clips of Iggy Pop, Blondie, the Ramones, and Talking Heads. Inspired by the French New Wave, Amos Poe was one of the first punk filmmakers. He was on the forefront of the No Wave filmmakers, a movement that featured stripped-down guerrilla filmmaking. His films included *Night Lunch* (1975), about a psychotic sax player who lures people to their death with his music, and *Unmade Beds* (1976), about a young man who fantasizes that he's a gangster in Paris during the New Wave. It features Deborah Harry of Blondie.

Ivan Král was a Czech-born filmmaker and a multitalented musician. He moved to the United States in 1966 as a refugee, and because his home country banned rock music, Král began a Super 8mm diary and started filming rock concerts. Some of his clips found their way into his 1975 amateur film *Night Lunch*. He also filmed the bands and bandmates at the Chelsea Hotel and other places they could be found.

Bound for Glory is a biopic of folk singing legend Woody Guthrie. The epic film was directed by Hal Ashby and the source material upon which it was based steered the movie toward a realism that was more fable. The film was loosely adapted by Robert Getchell from Woody Guthrie's partly fictionalized 1943 autobiography *Bound for Glory*. Casting for the lead role included Dustin Hoffman and Jack Nicholson, who both turned down the offer. Richard Dreyfuss was considered. Singer Tim Buckley was about to be offered the part but died of a drug overdose. Hal Ashby interviewed actor David Carradine, who could play guitar and sing, but turned him down because he was too tall (Guthrie was five seven; Carradine six one). Eventually Ashby reconsidered because Carradine had the right rural look, the proper musicianship, and a to-hell-with-you attitude, which suited Guthrie. On set this proved right, when one day Carradine saw a group of union marchers and joined them, setting back production for several hours. *Bound for Glory* is an American epic that captures Guthrie's music and spirit. Historically biopics haven't always been true to the life depicted—screenwriters alter characters and actions and even create a composite from multiple real people—and although the film takes liberties, Guthrie's essence is fully realized.

Cinematographer Garrett Brown had been working on an invention that would allow a motion picture camera to be handheld and move totally smoothly without bumps. In the scene where Guthrie walks through a group of migrants, Brown and his Steadicam followed Carradine seamlessly, transporting audiences into America's past.

Carrie was Stephen King's fourth novel but the first to be published. It began as a short story for a men's magazine. King had been criticized for not being able to write female characters; he conceived an idea about a girl who had telekinesis, wrote three pages, decided he hated them, and threw them out. His wife Tabitha found these pages and convinced her husband to turn it into a novel; she offered her help for the female point of view.

Carrie White is a sixteen-year-old girl who keeps to herself. Her religious fanatic mother is abusive, distorting morals and confusing the girl. In a high school shower scene, Carrie menstruates for the first time and is taunted and bullied by her classmates. A female coach tries to help Carrie. She is then elected prom queen as an elaborate prank by a group of wicked kids. As she is being crowned, a bucket of pig's blood suspended above her head is yanked by a rope, and the scarlet liquid pours all over

Carrie's head, face, and prom dress. Carrie goes into a psychotic fit and violently attacks practically everything in sight.

Brian De Palma could not have been a better choice for director of a cinematic adaptation of *Carrie*. The film is considered a classic contemporary horror film. John Travolta plays a lowlife bad boy. The lead role was played by Sissy Spacek. Brian De Palma redefined himself as a pure horror director who pulled out all the stops and made the audience scream.

Sissy Spacek is an atypical movie actress in that she has a pale, almost frail physicality. She has an enormous range for playing unusual and distinctive characters. *Prime Cut* (1972) is a film that shows the brutal side of men, auctioning off naked women as if they were pigs. Spacek plays Poppy who is trapped in this situation. In 1973 Spacek plays the girlfriend of an out-of-control young man on a murder spree in Terrence Malick's directorial debut, *Badlands*. After *Carrie* (1976) Spacek was part of the ensemble in Alan Rudolph's *Welcome to L.A.* (1976). In 1977 Sissy Spacek portrayed a complex personality-changing character in Robert Altman's dreamlike *Three Women*.

Ron Howard began as a child actor in feature films and television. His appearance as Steve Bolander in *American Graffiti* ultimately led to a steady part on the hit television series *Happy Days*. He eventually became an A-list feature film director, which began when he and his father Rance Howard wrote the comedy *Tis the Season*, with half the money raised in Australia. He met with Roger Corman and agreed to star in the film if Corman would co-finance the movie. Corman didn't like the script but told the young actor if he would star in *Eat My Dust!* (1976), a movie about a stolen stock car, Corman would let Howard develop a second film in which he could direct and star. This became *Grand Theft Auto* (1977). Charles Griffith directed *Eat My Dust!* for four weeks, but Howard's scenes were shot in ten days. The original title *Eat My Dust!* was suggested by Griffith only as a joke, but the New World Pictures marketing department was ecstatic about it.

In *The Killing of a Chinese Bookie*, directed by John Cassavetes, Ben Gazzara plays Cosmo Vitelli, owner of a strip club—more a contemporary burlesque venue—on Hollywood's Sunset Strip. Cosmo is a degenerate gambler who loses $23,000 in a poker game run by mobsters. He doesn't have the money, so he is forced to do a hit for them of a Chinese mobster. Cosmos is shot and sees the blood dripping from his body as the show in his club begins once again. The film was released and was a failure. Gazzara disliked the initial version, which was 135 minutes, and told Cassavetes it was too long. The film was reedited by the director, both shortened and reordered. There were different edits of some scenes and a few sequences unique to the shorter 108-minute version. Most of the editing removed dance sequences. The film was then rereleased. It is now considered one of Cassavetes's most unique and unusual films with a magnificent performance by the celebrated Ben Gazzara.

Marlon Brando, considered one of the greatest American actors of his time, continued in the 1970s to seek out challenging parts in unorthodox films. In 1971 Brando played Peter Quint in *The Nightcomers*, directed by Michael Winner, which is a prequel to Henry James's *The Turn of the Screw*. In 1972 Brando played the central role of mafia chieftain Don Corleone in the three-hour epic *The Godfather* directed by Francis Ford Coppola. In this classic film Brando transformed himself with total physicality into an aging crime boss and a family man who spoke with wisdom and cunning. Brando, who had won an Academy Award for an early performance in *On the Waterfront* (1954), won his second Oscar for Best Actor but did not accept the award, instead asking a Native American woman, Sacheen Littlefeather, to accept it on his behalf. He politicized the occasion to protest the way Native Americans had been portrayed in Hollywood movies. In 1972 Brando appeared in the controversial *Last Tango in Paris*, directed by Bernardo Bertolucci, in which his morose character engages in anonymous sexual encounters with a young woman. The film was highly erotic and shocking and was given an X rating. In 1976 Brando was directed by Arthur Penn in *The Missouri Breaks*, an offbeat Western that costarred Jack Nicholson. In 1978 Brando appeared in *Superman* for a big paycheck—$3.7 million and 11.75 percent of box office profits—to play Superman's father Jor-El. In 1979 Marlon Brando worked with Coppola again as Colonel Kurtz in the director's Vietnam epic *Apocalypse Now*. The actor arrived unprepared and had put on too much weight to play the part as planned. He appears only at the end of the long film, making quite an impression with his shaved head. Because of his size, he was shot mainly in shadow, which brings mystery to his character and drama to the film's conclusion.

Arthur Penn was an accomplished theater and film director who believed that a film should be multilayered in its narrative and reflect its times. His work in the sixties and seventies was informed by politics and the counterculture, which gave a contemporary context to the genres and stories he selected. This was most evident in the landmark *Bonnie and Clyde*, a gangster film that took place during the Great Depression and followed a notorious real-life couple who robbed banks and killed people. The film spoke loudly to the youth culture when it was released in 1967, during the Vietnam era. What made this approach interesting and a bit troublesome was that these messages were not on the surface and required the viewer to be informed. In 1970 Penn directed *Little Big Man*, a revisionist Western based on a novel by Thomas Berger. *Night Moves* (1975) is a neo-noir film addressing the post-1968, post-Watergate era. In 1976 Penn teamed Jack Nicholson and Marlon Brando in *The Missouri Breaks*, a tough, epic Western, but the narrative was convoluted, and the superstars were not able to save it.

In 1974 a live suicide took place at a local Florida television station when a troubled, depressed anchorwoman shot herself while viewers watched in horror. Two years later Paddy Chayefsky wrote the screenplay *Network* and told an interviewer he used that incident to demonstrate that television would do anything for ratings. Writing a book about the film, cultural journalist Dave Itzkoff concluded that Americans exposed to Vietnam and Watergate wanted angry, divisive newspeople. Sidney Lumet, the director of *Network*, stated that the character Howard Beale, played by Peter Finch, was not based on anyone.

Obsession is another Brian De Palma film that found the director working in a Hitchcockian mode. The original screenplay for *Obsession* by Paul Schrader was strongly inspired by *Vertigo*, in the sense that a woman reemerges in the story after her disappearance. Both Schrader and De Palma embraced the *Vertigo* structural concept, but De Palma felt it was necessary to do a heavy rewrite on the Schrader screenplay. The film may be De Palma's most handsome production thanks to the lush cinematography contributed by Vilmos Zsigmond, allowing the look of the film to surpass a purely Hitchcockian imitation. In *Obsession* Brian De Palma successfully fused his own vision with his deep admiration for Alfred Hitchcock. For years Brian De Palma resisted all inferences that he was copying Hitchcock; in fact, he was paying homage to him and reinventing the master for a new, younger audience by employing his own visual and narrative style.

The boxing film genre has a long history in American cinema. A substantial number of the films deal with organized crime's influence on the sport and the toll on the boxer in the ring. Generally, it is not a positive genre but, in the seventies, it seemed to one young man that it was an opportunity to celebrate the underdog. Sylvester Stallone wrote his original screenplay *Rocky* in only three days. He had watched a championship match between Muhammad Ali and Chuck Wepner, known as the Bayonne Bleeder who lasted until the fifteenth round, when Ali knocked him down. The referee counted to seven and with nine seconds left in the contest called it a technical knockout. Years later Wepner sued, contending Stallone had used his story. Stallone denied the influence of Wepner on *Rocky*, and in the end, Stallone's total characterization of Rocky Balboa, his likable pugilist, was all his own. United Artists liked Stallone's script as a vehicle for a star such as Robert Redford, James Caan, Ryan O'Neal, or Burt Reynolds. Stallone wanted to play Balboa himself and told the studio it was a package deal: the script and him in the lead role. Eventually it worked, one of the great movie gambits in which everyone was a winner. *Rocky* has a no-frills look and a story with heightened realism, romance, and boxing action that holds up with the best of them. The soaring musical score by Bill Conti drives the emotional engine of the film. The film is low budget with production flaws, but no one cares when watching the spectacular fight finale and realizing *Rocky* is not really about boxing, but about Rocky's love for Adrian. At the Oscars *Rocky* won for Best Picture, Best Director (John G. Avildsen), and Best Editing (Richard Halsey and Scott Conrad). With a $1 million budget, the gross for *Rocky* was $225 million. As of 2018, the *Rocky* franchise totals seven sequels. Sylvester Stallone portrays Rocky Balboa in every film. Stallone wrote the screenplay for the first six sequels and directed four of the films. Rooting for the underdog and watching Rocky grow old has pleased the audience.

Sylvester Stallone began his career with small parts in movies including *Downhill Racer* (1969). His first starring role was in the softcore picture *The Party at Kitty and Stud's* (1970). Then he had brief appearances in *Bananas* (1971), directed by Woody Allen, *The Lords of Flatbush* (1974), and *Death Race 2000*. *Rocky* changed everything for Sylvester Stallone. The movie made him an instant superstar and created opportunities including film directing. In 1978 Sylvester Stallone starred in *F.I.S.T.*, directed by Norman Jewison, playing a union leader based on Teamsters boss Jimmy Hoffa. He was also one of the screenwriters. Again in 1978 Stallone wrote and directed *Paradise Alley*, which tracks three brothers who get involved in professional wrestling. In 1979 Stallone wrote and directed the first sequel to *Rocky*, in which Rocky Balboa becomes a champion by defeating Apollo Creed.

The Omen is a supernatural horror film starring Lee Remick and Gregory Peck. Richard Donner was the director. Since *The Exorcist* in 1973 audiences were drawn to films about the devil and the power to do evil in the guise of a human, in this case a boy. The narrative follows Damien, who under rather mysterious circumstances becomes the son of a U.S. ambassador and his wife. Violent acts begin to occur because of the boy's devilish abilities. *The Omen* became a box office phenomenon. Although the film is not as elaborately well-crafted as *The Exorcist*, it touched the same nerve by entering the world of supreme evil. The film filled movie theater seats in droves. The budget was $2.8 million, and the take was $60.8 million.

A Star Is Born had been made as a drama twice by 1976. The third version was set in the heart of the music business. The producers were Jon Peters and Barbra Streisand. First choice for the male lead was Elvis Presley, who was looking to revive his film career and interested in the project, but his manager the legendary Colonel Tom Parker wanted too much money for his client's services and didn't want Elvis portrayed as a failed entertainer as the role demanded. Marlon Brando was given consideration. Neil Diamond declined because of his demanding concert tour. Then the part went to Kris Kristofferson. Streisand's stardom and remarkable vocal abilities anchored the production with the Oscar-winning song "Evergreen" and her unique chemistry with Kristofferson. Streisand's *A Star Is Born* was a timely idea that reflected the era and transcended the two earlier films.

Barbra Streisand is a multiple award-winning recording artist considered one of the finest voices of her time. She began as a motion picture actress in two popular musicals, *Funny Girl* (1968), directed by William Wyler, for which she won an Academy Award for Best Actress, and *Hello, Dolly!* (1969), directed by Gene Kelly. Streisand began the seventies with *On a Clear Day You Can See Forever* (1970), another Broadway adaptation, directed by Hollywood Golden Age director Vincente Minnelli. The film has a fantasy element in which Streisand's character has multiple lives. Also in 1970 Streisand played a part-time prostitute in the comedy *The Owl and the Pussycat*. In 1972 Peter Bogdanovich directed Streisand in a contemporary screwball comedy *What's up Doc?* that proved audiences still liked older movie forms. *The Way We Were* (1973), directed by Sidney Pollack, costarred Streisand and Robert Redford as a woman and a man with wildly different personalities and personal philosophies who find themselves in love. Streisand sang the theme song, which won the Oscar for Best Song. Streisand appeared with Ryan O'Neal again after their coupling in *What's up Doc?* in *The Main Event* (1979), in which a woman finds she has inherited financial control of a boxer who is currently out of the ring. In the eighties Barbra Streisand began another aspect of her show business career as a film director, exerting another level of control for the talented artist.

In *Stay Hungry*, directed by Bob Rafelson, Jeff Bridges plays an idle, young Southern man from a rich family who unwittingly becomes involved with a group of criminals in a real estate enterprise. He eventually becomes interested in a local bodybuilding gym, part of the real estate deal. There he meets and falls in love with the receptionist played by Sally Field. The film concludes with one of the funniest oddball chase scenes. While trying to escape from the bad guys, the young man is aided by a large group of bodybuilders who position themselves in strategic areas and distract onlookers and the baddies by showing off their large muscles and attempting to outdo each other in a pose-off, wearing only colorful briefs. Bob Rafelson proved his versatility with this comedy, a full 180 degrees from the more solemn *The King of Marvin Gardens* released in 1972.

Sally Field played the romantic interest in *Stay Hungry*. She also appeared in *Heroes* directed by Jeremy Paul Kagan (1977), in which she plays a woman who eventually goes on a road trip across the United States with a Vietnam veteran with post-traumatic stress disorder (PTSD) played by Henry Winkler. In 1979 she was in *Beyond the Poseidon Adventure*, the sequel to the disaster film blockbuster, as a character who is part of an expedition to claim cargo rights.

World champion bodybuilder Arnold Schwarzenegger portrays a man training in the gym who hopes to win the Mr. Universe title and plays the fiddle in a local musical group. He also was a gangster in Robert Altman's *The Long Goodbye* (1973) before propelling to stardom in action movies as one of the biggest film draws in the world.

R. G. Armstrong plays the headstrong and sometimes violent owner of the gym in *Stay Hungry*. He appeared in *The Ballad of Cable Hogue*

(1970) and *Pat Garrett & Billy the Kid* (1973), both directed by Sam Peckinpah.

Before Robert Englund portrayed the villainous killer Freddy Kruger in the *Nightmare on Elm Street* franchise, he appeared in the surfer epic *Big Wednesday*, directed by John Milius (1978), and *Bloodbrothers* (1978), an adaptation of the Richard Price novel starring Richard Gere and directed by Robert Mulligan. In *Stay Hungry* he played an employee in the gym.

Taxi Driver (1976) is one of the seminal films of the seventies. Robert De Niro's performance as Travis Bickle depicts psychosis and the dark side of New York (and the country) during the mid-seventies. The story—as with several seventies films including *Close Encounters of the Third Kind* (1977), *Star Wars* (1977), and *Hardcore* (1979)—was directly influenced by John Ford's 1956 film *The Searchers*. Director Martin Scorsese and Paul Schrader were a perfect match for *Taxi Driver*, with Scorsese capturing a dream state he described as the process of watching a movie with a biblical fervor—in this case Travis Bickle's fixation that a wave will wash the filth off the streets of New York.

Scorsese's vision for the film was unrelenting and uncompromising. When *Taxi Driver* was in a director's cut, it was shown to the Motion Picture Association of America (MPAA) for a rating. The board concluded that *Taxi Driver* was dangerously violent, especially the bloody shoot-out during the climax. Scorsese did not return to the editing room to trim back the violence; instead he went to the lab and had Chemtone process applied to the offensive scene, which produced a brown/red wash over the entire image. Although this satisfied the MPAA, it produced a grimy, rusty, dried blood veneer that made the sequence even more effective in presenting the onslaught of gunplay and bloodletting. *Taxi Driver* highlighted a breed of American males in their early twenties and thirties who, like Travis Bickle, had many bad ideas that existed at the time because of their despair and loneliness. *Taxi Driver* could have been made only in the seventies as an outgrowth of the American New Wave. Scorsese was willing to delve into the dark heart of America.

Character actor Harry Northup has appeared in almost forty films. He worked multiple times with Martin Scorsese and Jonathan Demme among other filmmakers. He was there when the American New Wave formed and was part of its development. One of his most significant roles was Doughboy in *Taxi Driver*, another taxi driver who is constantly trying to hustle Travis to buy useless articles. An actor in American tradition, Harry Northup is a filmmaker who makes a specific contribution to each movie. *Boxcar Bertha* is a 1972 female gangster film directed by Martin Scorsese in which Northup plays Deputy Sheriff Harvey Hall. In 1973 he played a disillusioned soldier just returned from Vietnam in Scorsese's seminal *Mean Streets*. In 1974 he played a bartender in *Alice Doesn't Live Here Anymore*, with Ellen Burstyn in the title role, directed by Martin Scorsese. In 1975 Northup was in *Crazy Mama*, directed by Jonathan Demme, the follow-up to *Big Bad Mama* (1974), playing an FBI agent. After *Taxi Driver* Northup appeared in Scorsese's *New York, New York*, playing a character named Alabama. In 1977 Northup played Chief Goon in *Which Way Is Up?* starring Richard Pryor. In 1978 Harry Northup was in Paul Schrader's directorial debut, *Blue Collar*. In 1979 he played Sergeant Doberman, a law enforcement figure who is dreaded by the local teenagers in *Over the Edge*, directed by Jonathan Kaplan.

The Searchers was directed by John Ford and released in 1956. The Western featured John Wayne, whose character Ethan Edwards learns of a slaughter at his brother's home and the abduction of his eight-year-old niece. After a years-long search, he finds his niece, now living as a Native American, who wants to stay where she is. After a struggle he brings her home. The film is raw with emotion concerning race hatred and obsession. No other film has influenced the American New Wave as much as *The Searchers*. The list of directors includes George Lucas, John Milius, Martin Scorsese, Paul Schrader, and Steven Spielberg. The nature of the search and rescue influenced *Taxi Driver, Close Encounters of the Third Kind*, and *Star Wars*.

Tracks is an earlier experimental film about Vietnam. It takes place on a train with episodes largely inside the head of a soldier, Sergeant Jack Falen, played by Dennis Hopper. He has the solemn duty of escorting the coffin of a fallen comrade to its final destination. *Tracks* is an antiwar film that never shows a battle or the war. The impact Vietnam has had on Jack is communicated by his behavior. He is borderline psychotic and hallucinates about people and actions aboard the train. His experiences in Vietnam have left him in an extreme state of confusion and delusion. Henry Jaglom directed a brave film revealing a raw and authentic portrayal of a Vietnam vet with PTSD. The film is shot aboard a moving train, and the camera is mainly handheld. Jack has a box that plays old crooner recordings. This signifies that Jack lives in the past and the music contrasts periods in American musical history. More and more the songs address World War II and the country's attitude about that war. Jack feels people on the train can help him, especially a beautiful college student played by Tarryn Power, the daughter of Tyrone Power. The constant movement of the train is hypnotic. The theme of heading home is a central metaphor in *Tracks*. In the end, Jack totally loses his grip on reality and Hopper, who was a trained method actor, unleashes a frightening reality at the conclusion of what has been a long, despairing journey.

Henry Jaglom was a significant figure in the American New Wave. He directed two films in the seventies, *A Safe Place* and *Tracks*, both of which explore new cinematic avenues. Jaglom began training with Lee Strasberg at the Actor's Studio in New York and then, under contract with Columbia Pictures, worked on TV series such as *Gidget* and *The Flying Nun*. He received his counterculture credentials as part of the cast in *Psych-Out* (1968), directed by Richard Rush, a psychedelic film about hippies; in Jack Nicholson's directorial debut, *Drive He Said* (1971); and in Dennis Hopper's masterpiece/debacle *The Last Movie* (1971). He worked on the editing for the landmark pre–New Wave film *Easy Rider*. He was a lifelong friend and confidante of Orson Welles, a solid independent filmmaker, and someone who embraced the avant-garde/experimental film world. *Tracks* was barely seen in any venues. Jaglom would take it anywhere he could and talk about the making of this unusual Vietnam film. After the screenings, he talked for hours to anyone who wanted to discuss making movies.

In *God Told Me To*, written and directed by Larry Cohen, a series of mass shootings occur in New York City. When the various shooters are apprehended and asked why they committed the heinous acts, their answer is that a direct message from God told them to randomly kill innocent people. Cohen used guerrilla-style filmmaking to stage the murders and other outdoor scenes. The scenes contain large crowds, teams of police officers, frantic bystanders, and the victims. The impact of the active handheld cameras and staged realism is a believability and sense of out-of-control panic. The acting throughout the film, especially the lead performance by Tony LoBianco, is professional, spontaneous, and filled with personality quirks. Comedian/performance artist Andy Kaufman makes a brief appearance as a policeman who begins to shoot people randomly during the St. Patrick's Day Parade. *God Told Me To* is dedicated to film composer Bernard Herrmann, who had created the music for

Cohen's *It's Alive* and was scheduled to do the music for *God Told Me To* but died around fifteen hours after screening the director's cut and discussing the music with Cohen. This film is violent and has some nudity. A visual is shown repeatedly of a vagina-like structure in the body of an otherworldly character. It appears to be sculptural and intended to address the film's mystery behind all the mayhem. *God Told Me To* presents a complex narrative with a perplexing conclusion, a film that appears to be a police procedural, a horror film, science fiction, and a psychological thriller. Cohen and *God Told Me To* require the viewer to continue processing to try to understand the film's larger issues. Larry Cohen was a B-movie master who made blaxploitation, horror, science fiction, and hybrid genres.

Hollywood Boulevard was the result of a bet between Roger Corman and directors Allan Arkush and Joe Dante regarding who could make the cheapest film ever for New World Pictures. *Hollywood Boulevard* is about a young actress who comes to Los Angeles and gets involved in the motion picture business. Corman gave them $60,000 and ten shooting days. They shot on short ends, film stock left over from other productions. In order to pull off this feat, clips from other New World Pictures titles were cut into the story. Among the films used are *Battle Beyond the Sun* (1962), *The Hot Box* (1972), *Caged Heat* (1974), and *Death Race 2000* (1975). Also inserted were a series of in-jokes that referenced other New World Pictures films such as Dick Miller playing Walter Paisley, the character that the actor played in *A Bucket of Blood* (1959).

Allan Arkush worked at New World Pictures for Roger Corman, starting in the trailer department, where he edited countless spots. In 1978 Arkush codirected *Deathsport* with Nicholas Niciphor about a future world where battles are constant. It starred David Carradine and *Playboy* playmate Claudia Jennings. In 1979 Arkush directed *Rock 'n' Roll High School*, a facility where the students are distracted because of the music. Punk legends the Ramones and their music are in the film.

Like Allan Arkush, Joe Dante started in the trailer department for New World Pictures for boss Roger Corman. After *Hollywood Boulevard*, which Dante codirected and edited, he directed and edited *Piranha* (1978), a successful low-budget horror film inspired by *Jaws*, in which an infestation of deadly piranha threatens beachgoers. Next Dante codirected (without credit) *Rock 'n' Roll High School* with Allan Arkush.

On the surface, *Mikey and Nicky* (1976), a gritty crime drama starring Peter Falk and John Cassavetes, looks as if Cassavetes directed it, but he did not—Elaine May did. The film was plagued with problems. The original $1.8 million budget ballooned to nearly $4.3 million. May shot 1.4 million feet of film. She had three cameras running almost constantly to catch any nuance the actors might impart. May hid several reels of exposed film from Paramount to control postproduction. Paramount was angry with May and placed the film in only a few theaters. In 1978 Julian Schlossberg, who had been at Paramount and then formed his own company, Castle Hill Productions, purchased the film from the studio.

Alan Rudolph was a protégé of Robert Altman. He was assistant director on *The Long Goodbye* and *Nashville.* In 1972 Rudolph wrote and directed the horror film *Premonition.* In the film, red flowers cause drug-using college students to have premonitions of their own deaths. In 1974 Rudolph directed *Nightmare Circus* under the pseudonym Gerald Cormier, cowritten by Rudolph and Roman Valenti. Three showgirls are stranded when their car breaks down. They are picked up by a man who drives them to his place, keeps them in chains, and forces them to perform circus tricks. His father lives next door, too close to a nuclear plant, which makes him a homicidal mutant. Rudolph wrote and directed *Welcome to L.A.* (1976), which profiles the decadent upper class in the seventies. It was positively received by the critics who crowned him a new auteur. *Remember My Name* (1978), written and directed by Rudolph, is an update on the woman's picture genre, in which a woman's life is thrown into chaos when her husband's first wife is released from prison and wants him back.

9

1977

January 23: The miniseries adaptation of Alex Haley's 1976 novel *Roots* aired on the ABC television network and gained a faithful and record-breaking audience who watched episode after episode, following the story of African slave Kunta Kinte and his descendants. The show featured a predominantly black cast and won many awards. The fascination with black culture and family histories underscored the power and scope of television. . . . August 10: David Berkowitz is captured after committing eight murders. The serial killer known as "Son of Sam" claimed a demon inside his neighbor's dog Sam told him to kill. . . . August 16: Elvis Presley dies at forty-two of cardiac arrest from prescription drug and other abuses.

Annie Hall was Woody Allen's sixth film as a director. Prior to making this sophisticated new kind of romantic comedy, Allen pursued a joke-based style of humor rather than a character-driven narrative. Although the story is told by a male character not unlike Allen, the psyche of the title figure, played by Diane Keaton, is presented with complexity. Allen utilizes many cinematic devices in *Annie Hall*. He addresses the camera in a stand-up comic approach reminiscent of his earlier days in show business and a Brechtian, breaking-the-fourth-wall approach. Other characters talk to the camera as well; narration is utilized to move the story forward. Long takes are presented so the connection between the performance and the audience is unbroken. According to film editor Ralph Rosenblum, the material as scripted and photographed went through a substantial restructuring during editing, which would influence the Allen

John Travolta and Karen Lynn Gorney in *Saturday Night Fever. Universal Pictures/
Photofest © Universal Pictures*

films to come. Whereas earlier Allen films were shot in a less than artful manner, this first of many collaborations with cinematographer Gordon Willis, best known for his work on *The Godfather*, brings a textured, light, and clean compositional style to *Annie Hall*. Mel Bourne, the production designer, defines the characters with detailed settings and realistic backgrounds that root the comic situations. Woody Allen also makes a leap in pursuing his Jewish identity by connecting the character Alvy Singer in *Annie Hall* with his own persona, an approach he would apply in future films. With a distinctive structure and form all its own, this film would develop into a style that became a template for many future Woody Allen films. At the Academy Awards, it won Best Picture and Best Director, but Allen did not show to accept them. Also, Diane Keaton won for Best Actress and Allen and Marshall Brickman received the Oscar for original screenplay.

After *Annie Hall*, Woody Allen directed his first drama, *Interiors* (1978), inspired by the films of his cinema idol Ingmar Bergman. This family situation surrounding three sisters is somber and aesthetically controlled by an environment created by their mother, who commits suicide during the story. It was a turning point in Woody Allen's career as a director; he was now considered a serious film artist by critics and many of the filmgoing public. He was no longer just a director of inventive comedies but a well-rounded filmmaker. *Manhattan* (1979) is a black-and-white romance that was part of the evolution in Allen's work; it is an open question as to whether it is a comedy or a drama about the romantic age barrier and cultural lifestyle of New York City in the seventies. At this point, audiences came to expect anything from Woody Allen. In *Manhattan* (1979) Allen's character, Isaac Davis, a forty-two-year-old comedy writer, dates a seventeen-year-old girl, Tracy (Mariel Hemingway). In Allen's view, she is the smartest and most mature of the characters that inhabit the story, including Mary Wilke, played by Keaton, who is having an affair with a college professor played by Michael Murphy—the message here is that age does not always bring wisdom.

Diane Keaton can be eccentric, funny, very bright, and deeply dramatic. She was inspired to become an actress by her mother, who won a pageant for homemakers, and Katharine Hepburn, an actress who always played strong, independent women. She studied acting at the Neighborhood Playhouse in New York City. Keaton's first film role was in the independent comedy *Lovers and Other Strangers*, released in 1970, in which she plays a woman considering a divorce from her husband. In 1972 she played Linda Christie, a married woman who falls in love with Allan Felix, a man who wishes he was Rick in the movie *Casablanca*, played by Woody Allen in *Play It Again, Sam*, based on his Broadway play. Also in 1972 Keaton burst into superstardom as Kay Corleone in *The Godfather*. In 1973 Keaton was in *Sleeper*, playing Luna Schlosser, an artist from the twenty-second century who falls in love with Miles Monroe (Allen), who is transported from the twentieth century to the twenty-second century. *The Godfather: Part II*, released in 1974, is the sequel to *The Godfather*, in which Keaton reprises her role as Kay Corleone. In *Love and Death* (1975), Keaton continued her relationship with Woody Allen as Sonja, who marries her twice-removed Cousin Boris. *Harry and Walter Go to New York* is a period comedy with Keaton, Elliot Gould, James Caan, and Michael Caine, directed by Mark Rydell. *Looking for Mr. Goodbar* (1977) is an adaptation of the bestselling novel by Judith Rosner, directed by Richard Brooks, in which a young woman explores night life and her sexuality, unaware that she is in danger. In 1978 Keaton played one of the three sisters in the Woody Allen drama *Interiors*. She worked again with Allen in *Manhattan* (1979) as the mistress of a married man.

The origins of *Saturday Night Fever*, a film that introduced disco dancing and its culture to America and the world, began when *New York* magazine published the nonfiction article "Tribal Rites of the New Saturday Night" in its June 7, 1976, issue, written by Nik Cohn. The writer had just arrived in the United States and wanted to cover American working-class subculture. One night he traveled to the 2001 Odyssey club in Bay Ridge, Brooklyn, to explore the disco scene. After a fight broke out as he was about to enter, he decided to fictionalize the story rather than research the article, which he did not tell the magazine until 1996.

Impresario Robert Stigwood produced *Saturday Night Fever*. He first hired John G. Avildsen, who directed *Rocky* (1976), but fired him three weeks into preproduction over a script dispute and hired John Badham, who had directed only one feature, *The Bing Long Traveling All-Stars & Motor Kings*. The screenplay was written by Norman Wexler, who had written *Joe* (1969). The star of the film was John Travolta as Tony Manero, the young actor's third performance in a movie. *Saturday Night Fever* made Travolta an international star for his depiction of the talented working-class kid who wanted to be admired. His acting is real and his dancing is breathtaking, especially his long solo number, which is mesmerizing and influenced practically anyone who attempted to disco dance. The film was shot on location in Brooklyn in the famed 2001 Odyssey club. The glamour of the dancing is contrasted with the outside activities of Tony and his friends including rape, racism, and suicide. This provides some gravitas to the story. The music by the Bee Gees was a major bestselling soundtrack album, and the movie became a time capsule of life in the seventies when a subculture gained the attention of the mainstream.

Eraserhead is an independent, experimental horror film in black and white directed by David Lynch, a painter who attended the American Film Institute beginning in 1970 and became a filmmaker. The surrealistic characters and narrative follow Henry Spence, a sad-faced young man with extremely tall hair. His romantic life is disturbed and involves a sick "baby" who looks like a chicken and makes bizarre crying sounds. Henry encounters a beautiful, mysterious woman next door who seems to appear at will. Other characters are equally strange, including eel-like creatures. The film was a cult sensation when it first appeared and played the midnight movie circuit. The low-budget oddity took time to make due to funding issues and Lynch's meticulous approach to filmmaking. *Eraserhead* has a sound design by Lynch and Alan Splet that is as impactful, sometimes more so, than the stark, evocative images. Lynch is a surrealist, so the actions and happenings do not always make immediate sense, but the film is an event with its own logic. Not easy to watch, *Eraserhead* is scary on a human level rather than on a traditional horror plane. It can't be classified successfully, but because it was David Lynch's first feature film, the term *Lynchian* later applied.

Two essential collaborators on *Eraserhead* were cinematographer Fred Elmes, who took over when Herb Cardwell had to leave, helping the visionary director realize the story in his strange and imaginative head, and sound designer Alan Splet, a master of creating atmospheric tones and sonic effects. Lynch accomplished his design on the picture because of the minuscule budget and the fact that it was impossible for him to totally communicate how the film should look to anyone on the crew.

Sequels are made when films yield big box office profits and make a major impact on audiences. A sequel can begin where the original film ended or pick up a narrative thread connected to the original. *The Exorcist* was not only a box office bonanza but a cultural phenomenon, a new kind of horror film with extremely high production values and a polished narrative based on a bestselling book. *The Exorcist II: The Heretic* barely connects to *The Exorcist* with the noted exceptions of the now-teenage Regan, the character played again by Linda Blair, and Kitty Wynn, reprising her role as assistant to Regan's movie star mother, in a larger part that concludes with an eruption of flames. *The Exorcist II: The Heretic* is an obtuse title, but as the film begins, it becomes clear that it involves a priest who has lost his way in terms of his religion. Also from the beginning, the film is presented in a high-tech, futuristic manner with too much focus on an electronic device used to put Regan into a trance in sync with her therapist. The fine director John Boorman seems bent on going on a different route, away from commercial filmmaking toward an edgy, risky narrative style including a locust infestation and an African theme. Rather than place the film in a reality that is disrupted and threatened by the devil as in the original, Boorman fills the film with too many subplots and themes. Regan's mother is not portrayed in the film because she is out of town. Richard Burton seems overburdened with his spiritual crisis and dealing with the devil, who here takes a different form than in the original. Audiences like sequels to make sense in terms of the original or to go in a new direction that makes equal sense. The storyline of *The Exorcist II: The Heretic* is hard to follow because it does not logically connect to *The Exorcist* for a general audience. Audiences had big expectations for this sequel, but it is not long after the story unfolds that the viewer understands the filmmakers and the film are not up to the task due to several wrongheaded decisions. *The Exorcist* grossed $441.3 million on a $12 million budget; the sequel grossed $30.7 million on a $14 million budget.

The Hills Have Eyes is a cult classic written, directed, and edited by Wes Craven based on the legend of cannibal Sawney Bean, the supposed head of a forty-eight-person Scottish clan who murdered and cannibalized a thousand people. It involves a family on vacation who becomes stranded in the Nevada desert and is terrorized by cannibal savages. Looking for unusual casting, Craven found Michael Berryman, an actor with twenty-six birth defects, to play Pluto. Janus Blythe won the part of Ruby because she ran faster than the other actresses tested. The film was shot in 16mm on cameras borrowed from a pornographic filmmaker. Conditions were difficult for the actors, who were paid minimum wage. Temperatures during the daytime were more than 120 degrees and the nighttime lows were in the 30s. The crew was largely those who had worked on Roger Corman movies. A dog carcass was obtained and used in the movie. The initial rating given to *The Hills Have Eyes* was X, then some of the violence was trimmed. On a budget of around $350,000, the film grossed a surprising $25 million. Its cult status is due to the unusual situations it depicts and its metaphors on the human condition and the viciousness of man.

Looking for Mr. Goodbar was adapted from a bestselling book that was based on a true story. It reflected life in mid-seventies New York with barhopping and free sex. Richard Brooks—a long-established Hollywood writer/director known for *Blackboard Jungle* (1955) and *Elmer Gantry* (1960)—made a pre–New Wave movie, *In Cold Blood* (1967), also based on a true story, which captured the times and was rendered in a New Hollywood manner. Although Brooks was older than sixty when he made *Looking for Mr. Goodbar*, it was his approach that negatively affected the film rather than his age. The story takes place in New York, but the city in the film is generic and not effective or believable. Records state that the film was shot in Los Angeles and Chicago, and many shots clearly look like they were staged and shot on a studio backlot. The film is old fashioned, the aesthetics more Old Hollywood than not. The song score is effective, but the musical score is tired and obvious. The film was a hit because of the book and its star Diane Keaton, but it stands out among seventies movies as not keeping up with the times.

Smokey and the Bandit ranks among the most popular and successful film of the decade, making Burt Reynolds a good-ole-boy hero for the masses. The plot concerns the illegal transport of Coors beer to a race site and its pursuit by an oversized sheriff played by Jackie Gleason and a Trans Am–driving bandit portrayed by Reynolds. The film is the directorial debut of legendary Hollywood stuntman Hal Needham. It was originally planned as a low-budget film starring Jerry Reed, but he showed the script to his buddy Burt Reynolds, who said he would star. The film became a mainstream production because Reynolds was the number one box office performer at the time. In his autobiography, the actor revealed that the script, which at the time was written on legal pads, was the worst he had ever read but he agreed to it anyway. The dialogue was mostly improvised during shooting. Sally Field was not considered attractive enough for her part, but Reynolds supported her; she also remembers the film being mostly improvised.

Sorcerer was considered a monumental flop that cost too much and prioritized action over substance. Director William Friedkin claimed it wasn't a remake of the Clouzot film *Wages of Fear* (1953), although to many it seemed to be a reboot of that classic film. The basis of the story is similar—men are assigned to transport dynamite over difficult terrain by truck—but Friedkin's narrative is not as comprehensible. During the late seventies, audiences and critics began to feel that important directors such as Friedkin, Scorsese, and Coppola were going too far with their personal visions. Friedkin had trouble working with his crew and felt that his star, Roy Scheider, who was second to Popeye Doyle in his *The French Connection*, had become difficult to direct and work with. The initial budget, already a sizable $15 million, grew to $22 million and was a major box office flop. Friedkin would make another film soon after, *The Brink's Job*, released in 1978, which was more traditional and based on the legendary robbery, but it also would fail at the box office.

Roy Scheider was a fresh face of the seventies, appearing in only three sixties films. He had been a boxer then began to act in movies, on television, and on the stage. He was a character actor liked by audiences. He was versatile and original in his instrument and was a hardworking and prominent actor during the decade. In 1970 he was in *Loving*, which starred George Segal. Also in 1970 he appeared in *Puzzle of a Downfall Child*, Jerry Schatzberg's directorial debut. In *Klute* (1971) Scheider played a vicious pimp. In 1971 Scheider had the high-profile role of Buddy Russo, Popeye Doyle's partner in *The French Connection*. In *The Seven-Ups* (1973), directed by Phil D'Antoni, who produced *The French Connection*, Scheider heads a squad of plainclothes policemen who use any method necessary to get the bad guys. In 1975 Roy Scheider was put on the international map as Chief Brody, the central role of a major blockbuster: Steven Spielberg's *Jaws*. In 1976 he costarred with Dustin Hoffman in *Marathon Man* as the main character's brother who is dangerously embroiled in international intrigue. After *Sorcerer*, Scheider reprised his role as Chief Brody in *Jaws 2*. In 1979 he played Joe Gideon, based to a great extent on director Bob Fosse's life in *All That Jazz*.

Star Wars—later known as *Star Wars IV: A New Hope*—along with Spielberg's *Jaws* were catalysts that led to a new era in American filmmaking: away from the personal films of the American New Wave and toward blockbuster entertainment. Science fiction films were made in the fifties, sixties, and seventies based on a forward approach to the genre.

One of the factors of the *Star Wars* phenomenon was Lucas's backward approach, akin to the science fiction of the *Flash Gordon* serials of the 1930s, the use of a narrative crawl, and characters and situations from a bygone era. *Star Wars* started a major franchise, and it was common knowledge at the time that this first film was really the fourth in a larger cycle. *Star Wars* would be embraced by more than one generation and influence an enormous number of young filmmakers. *Star Wars* was a complete break with the content, style, and intent of the American New Wave. It was a cultural event with the potential franchise second only to the still-running James Bond 007 series. Merchandising, box office, and a place in the American lexicon were beyond any other movie in the seventies. *Star Wars* accomplished success in all. George Lucas, the director and creative mind of *Star Wars*, became the Walt Disney of his time; Steven Spielberg would follow. Spielberg would later collaborate with Lucas on *Raiders of the Lost Ark*, which, like *Star Wars*, became a franchise that dominated cinematic attention. Lucas created a company to improve visual effects, founding Industrial Light and Magic in 1975, and Skywalker Ranch for film sound for his own projects and the works of others, a major contribution to the art of film.

Twilight's Last Gleaming is a thriller focused on a crazed U.S. general who wants to take control of the country's missiles. Director Robert Aldrich was not known to use split-screen technique, but because this film had so much simultaneous action, he wanted the audience to see everything without intercutting, which would eliminate some of the action. He also felt it was the only way to tell the story in a reasonable amount of screen time. Shooting all that material and putting it together in the editing room took six months. *Twilight's Last Gleaming* was edited on film, so all the planning, structuring, and lab work was meticulous and time consuming. Apart from Brian De Palma, who regularly used split-screen technique in his movies, Aldrich's bold and appropriate use of it here didn't inspire many others.

Robert Aldrich was a maverick who took on difficult, controversial content and was an inventive storyteller. He also took strong financial and creative risks by creating his own movie studio in which he made his later films. In the fifties he made Westerns, war movies, and intense dramas. Aldrich directed many films in the seventies including *Ultzana's Raid* (1972), a highly regarded Western, especially by *Village Voice* critic Andrew Sarris, who labeled Aldrich an auteur. The film was interpreted by some as an allegory for the Vietnam War, still raging at the time. In 1973 he directed *Emperor of the North Pole*, which focused on hobos during the Great Depression era. In 1974 Aldrich directed *The Longest Yard* starring Burt Reynolds, a prison picture in which the inmates play football against the guards. Robert Aldrich remained independent in his choice of material, usually offbeat stories that kept the audience on their toes, and in the way he approached the filmmaking process.

The story of *Wizards* is set two million years after the Earth has been devasted by terrorists in a nuclear war. Only a handful of humans survive, and farriers, elves, and dwarfs have surfaced. Ralph Bakshi, director of this animation feature, long had interest in fantasy and drew artwork in that style. In 1967 he had an unproduced television series, *Tee-Witt*, that he developed and pitched to CBS, from which *Wizards* originated. In 1976 he pitched *War Wizards* to 20th Century Fox. Bakshi returned to his childhood drawings for inspiration and set out to prove he could make a family picture as successful as his adult films. The film made $9 million on a $2 million budget. The result is not a family film, but rather one with some violence and sexual titillation, although it was tame compared to his racier and more aggressive movies.

In *Cross of Iron*, Sam Peckinpah proved he could stage and film combat in a World War II film as well as in a Western. He used slow motion in a similar way: to graphically depict violence in detail. The point of view here—from the German side—is not unheard of but it is uncommon. The film's narrative is deliberately challenging; viewers try to comprehend what is happening as bombs continually drop. The more the battles intensified, the more crazed and complicated the characters become. Like Sam Fuller, Peckinpah served during World War II and saw that violence firsthand.

The Kentucky Fried Movie directed by John Landis is a sketch film. Some of the segments include parodies of movie genres. It poked fun at a morning news show with an anchor who, unable to hear the correspondents, starts scratching inappropriately. A couple in their underwear follow along with a sex instruction record. There is a parody of blaxploitation films. *The Kentucky Fried Movie* is *Saturday Night Live* without the television rules that restricted that show.

At twenty-one years old, John Landis directed his first feature film, *Schlock* (1973), a tribute to monster movies. The long association between the director and makeup wizard Rick Baker, who made a gorilla suit for the picture, began on *Schlock*. An assistant to Universal executive Thom Mount recommended Landis to direct *National Lampoon's Animal House*. Landis found the screenplay extremely funny with a dark edge like the magazine. The 1978 release had a $3 million budget and grossed an astounding $141.6 million. The college humor in the film was crass and the movie became what is known as a gross-out comedy. A standout in the picture was John Belushi, who was a regular cast member of television's *Saturday Night Live* but had not yet broken into the movies. The dumbed-down humor struck a chord with audiences, making the film one of the comedy highlights of the seventies.

After graduating Carnegie Mellon University in Pittsburgh, George A. Romero began making commercials and short films. He did a segment for *Mister Rogers' Neighborhood* in which the host had a tonsillectomy. In the late sixties Romero and nine friends formed Image Ten Productions. In 1969 Romero made horror film history with *Night of the Living Dead*, a low-budget horror film that became a cult classic. It was made for $114,000 and took in $30 million at the box office. In 1971 Romero directed one of only a few of his films not in the horror genre—the romantic comedy *There's Always Vanilla*. His next film was released in 1973; it was made under the title *Jack's Wife*, originally released under the title *Hungry Wives*, and known as *Season of the Witch*. The story focuses on a suburban wife who becomes interested in witchcraft. The distributor cut parts of the film and marketed it as a softcore porn movie, at one point trying to get Romero to make two sex scenes in the film pornographic but he refused. In 1973 Romero made *The Crazies*, a science fiction horror film in which a small town accidentally gets exposed to a military biological weapon. In its time the film was a failure but has since become a cult movie. *Martin* (1978) is a psychological horror film about a young man who feels he is a vampire. In 1978 *Dawn of the Dead*, an independent zombie movie, was released and became a huge hit at the box office. George A. Romero is considered a modern master of horror. His films were always highly original and scary in a way that Romero instinctively understood would frighten and delight his audience.

Short Eyes is a prison picture set in New York where the incarcerated population is black and brown. A white middle-class man is jailed, accused of the rape of a young girl. For the other prisoners, a pedophile is the lowest form of criminal. One older prisoner doesn't feel this way, and the man tells him that he doesn't remember raping the girl but confesses to raping other children. The legal case against him is shaky and unless the authorities are told about the confession, the man will go free, which puts the older man in a moral bind. Meanwhile the other prisoners plan to get rid of the child rapist by their own means. *Short Eyes* is based on a play by Miguel Piñero, who in 1972 at twenty-five years old was imprisoned at Sing Sing for second-degree armed robbery. He began to write in prison and based the play on an experience he had there. Theater impresario Joseph Papp saw the play at the Riverside Church and moved it to Broadway, where it was acclaimed and nominated for six Tony Awards. The play was adapted into a film by Pinero, who also had a part in the production, and it was directed by Robert M. Young and filmed in the Manhattan House of Detention for men, better known as the Tombs. Prison movies were a staple of the Classical Hollywood Studio System, but they rarely showed prison life in all its desolation and with internal rules that were often deadly.

After *Short Eyes* Robert M. Young directed *Alabrista!* (1977), about a Mexican farmer whose father is missing. *Rich Kids* (1979) is about two twelve-year-olds trying to make sense of their parents' lives and their own feelings.

Steven Spielberg had been a science fiction fan since his youth. Because so many prior films in the genre had aliens from a faraway planet come to Earth to take it over or destroy it, Spielberg wanted to make a film that went the other way. Also because of his childlike nature and bright outlook, he created *Close Encounters of the Third Kind.* The film stars Richard Dreyfuss as a man drawn to the sight of a mothership landing and also includes Melinda Dillion, who believes her young son is abducted, although it turns out that he was chosen to go to a new planet for a better life. The casting coup was French New Wave icon François Truffaut as a French government scientist who is an expert in UFOs. The plotting and directing are strong and the special effects dazzling. Audiences were thrilled by the journey of the characters and awestruck by the visuals and the use of sound as a communication tool between the Americans and the aliens. The film budget was $19.4 million and it grossed $306 million, making it a megahit and Spielberg's second blockbuster.

Martin Scorsese is America's film director/film historian. His films contain quotes and references to American and international pictures. After directing three films including *Mean Streets*, considered by some to be a film noir, and *Taxi Driver*, a modern retelling of the director's beloved *The Searchers* directed by John Ford (1956), Scorsese attempted a relationship film presented as an Old Hollywood–style musical. He named it after his home—*New York, New York*. Scorsese had been married several times and because of those experiences believed that it might be impossible for two creative artists to live successfully as a couple. He combined the American musical with an edgy story about a sax player performed by Robert De Niro and a singer played by Liza Minelli who meet in a scene that is two or three times as long as the viewer would expect. They marry and have difficulties generated mostly by De Niro's selfish needs. Anger, jealousy, and a near-maniacal temper drive the character's behavior. They separate and continue to create art on their own. De Niro's performance is way over the top. Minelli is wonderful and entertaining as the gifted songstress. The film was shot on soundstages and the design is deliberately artificial since Scorsese thought it would impart a sense of Old Hollywood to the story. *New York, New York* is long, tedious, and barely entertaining. The film did poorly in its original release but better when rereleased with the original ending intact. The production numbers play like a film unto themselves and are a platform on which Minelli can sing "New York, New York" and "Happy Endings." Scorsese was off his game here, a personal filmmaker with a personal theme but in an inappropriate format. Scorsese was brought up on musicals and knows the form, but his experiment combining an edgy relationship and artifice was another signpost that seventies American cinema was heading down a wrong road.

10

1978

April 2: The CBS television network launched in prime time the first nighttime soap opera titled *Dallas*, a show that revolved around the Ewings, a feuding Texas family, and created a new television genre that quickly spread among the networks. Many critics considered it a step backward for television culture and American culture itself. . . . June 28: The Supreme Court ruled in the case of *Regents of the University of California v. Bakke* against the school and for Allan Bakke, who stated he was the victim of reverse discrimination. The decision redefined affirmative action and was a cultural landmark in race issues in the United States. . . . November 18: 909 inhabitants of a Jonestown cult in Guyana led by Reverend Jim Jones were forced at gunpoint to drink Kool-Aid laced with cyanide, causing the greatest single loss of life of Americans at the time.

In 1978 films about the Vietnam War began to be released in the United States in greater numbers. Some were set in Vietnam, others at home. This subject was still risky because the unpopular war was very much on the minds of Americans. The pro/antiwar split about Vietnam persisted; because of continuing controversy, audience attendance was not a guarantee.

Marquee names like Scorsese, Altman, and Ashby were still making movies but the superstar director theory was less in play. A director's name recognition no longer was a guarantee of a satisfying experience; instead, genre, stars, and subject matter were stronger deciding factors for studios, which believed those were the necessary components for viewer-

Christopher Walken in _The Deer Hunter_. Columbia Pictures/Photofest © Columbia Pictures

ship. A wider range of films were opening; blockbusters were strong draws versus the American New Wave. Traditional narrative films still dominated the American movie market, but less narrative forms appeared such as _Renaldo and Clara_ directed by Bob Dylan and _The Scenic Route_ directed by Mark Rappaport. American films that looked like European counterparts such as _The Driver_ and _Interiors_ showed their influence.

Partly based on the life of the director, John Milius, _Big Wednesday_ is a coming-of-age epic about three young California surfers. This was an A-team production with Milius and producer Buzz Feitshans; the two had met at American International Pictures while working on Milius's directorial debut, _Dillinger_. Feitshans was now an executive at Warner Bros., which distributed _Big Wednesday_. Costume designer Anthea Sylbert observed that Milius was hyper-egotistical and refused to listen to anyone as the movie steadily went over budget. He gave the impression that he was waiting for that big wave. By the time the film was released, the budget was exceptionally large—$11 million—and *Big Wednesday* was a big flop making only $4.5 million after quickly being removed from the theaters. Three good friends, Milius, George Lucas, and Steven Spielberg had agreed to exchange a percentage point of *Big Wednesday*, *Star Wars*, and *Close Encounters of the Third Kind* prior to the release of the three films.

Blue Collar was Paul Schrader's directorial debut after his accomplished screenwriting career. It is the story of three Detroit auto workers played by Harvey Keitel, Yaphet Kotto, and Richard Pryor. The narrative explores the nature of the working man and turns into a crime film with a less than successful bank robbery, a murder, and the dark side of unionism at the auto plant. The three actors were always arguing and fighting. At one point, Richard Pryor—thought to be high on drugs—pulled a gun on Schrader because of the number of takes required for a scene. Schrader reports he had a mental breakdown dealing with his unruly stars.

Paul Schrader began his career as a film critic who wrote about foreign films and challenging American movies. In 1972 his landmark book *Transcendental Style in Film: Ozu, Bresson, Dreyer*, Schrader found commonality among these directorial masters and a new way of looking at movies that transcended content and visual style. For most of the seventies Schrader was known as an unconventional screenwriter. In 1974 he cowrote *The Yakuza* with his brother Leonard for a big payday, which evoked a deep knowledge of Japan and the underworld, directed by Sidney Pollack. In 1977 Schrader cowrote the violent *Rolling Thunder*, directed by John Flynn, which follows the life of a prisoner of war after he returns home. After *Blue Collar* he wrote and directed *Hardcore* (1979), in which a teenage girl disappears and her religious father ventures into the world of pornography to find her. In 1979 he scripted *Old Boyfriends* for Joan Tewkesbury, which depicts a psychiatrist having an identity crisis who goes on a road trip to see three former boyfriends and find herself.

Jane Fonda, daughter of Henry and sister of Peter, was an ardent antiwar activist who participated in many activities expressing her outrage. She and her partner Bruce Gilbert with her production company IPC Films (Indochina Peace Campaign) made the film *Coming Home*, directed by Hal Ashby, who, despite the outward appearance of a hippie panhandler, was a master film editor, director, and prime player in the American New Wave. *Coming Home*, which starred Jane Fonda, Jon

Voight, and Bruce Dern, concentrated on the political, social, and cultural war at home: how women's lives and gender roles changed during this period and how the return of the men who fought in the war came back physically and mentally maimed. Actual Vietnam veterans were given speaking and background roles, which brought a documentary veracity to the controversial film. When Captain Bob Hyde (Bruce Dern) returns from Vietnam, he learns his wife Sally Hyde (Fonda) is emotionally and physically involved with a paraplegic veteran, Luke Martin, played by Jon Voight. The relationships and character studies are in-depth, intimate, and explicit. The movie is never preachy but is direct about the war and its impact on America and Americans. It is a film about the aftermath of the Vietnam War and about a strong woman coming into her own consciousness. Hal Ashby, a longtime fan of the Rolling Stones, created a song score using many of the band's songs, which provided background, specificity, and lyrical and textual connection.

The director of photography was a perfect fit for this project. Haskell Wexler was well-known as a political activist and a documentarian. His antiwar stance combined with Fonda's active role in the feminist movement were a seamless match. Production designer Michael D. Haller had worked with Ashby before and was a continuing member of the realistic location school. Editor Don Zimmerman had also worked with Ashby previously. Both Jane Fonda and Jon Voight received Academy Awards for their performances.

Night of the Living Dead (1968) was so successful and popular that a franchise grew out of it. *Dawn of the Dead* was the sequel. George Romero came up with a terrifying idea: what if zombies attacked a suburban shopping mall? A set was not built; rather, production took place at a real mall. The audience identified with this palpable and believable terror. Master effects creator Tom Savini, a Vietnam veteran whose experiences inspired his work, supplied the gore and the zombies. Originally the film received an X rating—not for sex but for excessive violence—and the brave decision was made to release it without a rating. Eventually it had a traditional release. *Dawn of the Dead* is a contemporary horror film that doesn't just go for scares, but inspires terror in the hearts of the audience. The zombie craze on television owes everything to Romero and his zombies. The metaphor for those who go through life without real feeling or emotion was intellectual and visceral in Romero's movies.

Days of Heaven is often cited as one of the most beautifully photographed films in seventies cinema. The look of this film, set in 1916, is a collaboration among director Terrence Malick, production designer Jack Fisk, and cinematographer Néstor Almendros. The story involves a destitute couple who go to Texas to work as day laborers for a wealthy farmer. They present themselves as siblings but they are actually lovers. The woman marries the landowner to enhance their lot, and the couple tries to keep their relationship secret. A scene in which a swarm of locusts destroys the landowner's wheat crop is legendary, dramatic, and epic. The entire project has an austere nature, and the music from the seventh movement from *The Carnival of the Animals* by Camille Saint-Saens added to Ennio Morricone's score creates a haunting atmosphere. *Days of Heaven* is a stunning achievement as seventies art cinema, and Terrence Malick would grow as he pursued his personal form of art cinema.

Directed by Michael Cimino in his second outing, *The Deer Hunter* is a dramatic and controversial film about the Vietnam War that takes place both at home and in Vietnam. The screenplay was cowritten by Cimino and Deric Washburn, although this collaboration has never been settled since neither man agreed on their contributions. The cast includes Robert De Niro, Meryl Streep, Christopher Walken, John Savage, and John Cazale. The story follows three friends and their journey from the working-class town of Clairton, Pennsylvania, to the jungles of Vietnam, the latter scenes photographed in Thailand. Shortly after the release of *The Deer Hunter*, a long and key scene in the movie was criticized and challenged. After the three soldiers are captured, they are imprisoned in a murky, watery area below a hut where they are forced to engage in Russian roulette by Vietnamese soldiers. Experts in the Vietnam War who saw the movie claim this practice never took place. Although *The Deer Hunter* provided drama that sustained the audience's terror, this question contributed to its lack of believability and realism. Russian roulette is also a key element later in the film, when a drug-addicted Christopher Walken succumbs to the game played repeatedly by Vietnamese mobsters for profit. The performances are of the highest level; Meryl Streep received her first Oscar nomination and Christopher Walken won the Oscar for Best Supporting Actor. Michael Cimino won Best Director and the film took home the best picture prize. For many audiences, *The Deer Hunter* expressed what had been occurring in Vietnam and the impact the war had on the home front. It is not totally accurate history, but full and powerful story-telling.

Michael Cimino moved to Los Angeles in 1971 to become a screen-writer. In 1972 Cimino cowrote the science fiction drama *Silent Running* directed by Douglas Trumbull. In 1973 he coscripted the Dirty Harry film *Magnum Force*. Clint Eastwood was so impressed with Cimino's 1974 script for *Thunderbolt and Lightfoot* that he asked him to direct the film; it became his directorial debut. This is a successful buddy movie with a road picture element. In 1979 he made screenplay contributions to *The Rose*, a rock 'n' roll movie directed by Mark Rydell starring Bette Midler, loosely based on the life and times of Janis Joplin. Cimino was even going to direct *The Rose*, but instead moved on to *Heaven's Gate*, a movie that in every way would top what he had done before; further, it would damage him, the studio, and seventies cinema itself.

Christopher Walken, who played Nick in *The Deer Hunter* as one of the three soldiers who go to fight in Vietnam, acted in nine films during the seventies. They include *The Sentinel* (1977), directed by Michael Winner, a supernatural horror film in which he plays Detective Rizzo; *Roseland* (1977), directed by James Ivory, in which he shows off his dancing skills; and *Last Embrace* (1979), directed by Jonathan Demme, a thriller in which he plays a government agency supervisor.

During the seventies, John Savage, also one of the three soldiers in *The Deer Hunter*, appeared in *Bad Company* directed by Robert Benton (1972), *Steelyard Blues* directed by Alan Myerson (1973), and *The Killing Kind* directed by Curtis Harrington (1973).

In crafting the sparse, existential screenplay for *The Driver*, Walter Hill, who was also the director, gave a nod to *Two-Lane Blacktop* by not giving traditional names to his characters but instead using words or phrases that defined their roles: the Driver, the Detective, the Player, the Connection. The story is about a man who steals cars for use in getaways after committing crimes. The action is pared down with little dialogue. Hill's goal was to write a genre film in a pure fashion without Hollywood conventions. Steve McQueen was targeted to play the Driver but turned it down because he was in *The Getaway* (directed by Sam Peckinpah, screenplay by Hill) and wanted to move away from movies centered on cars and driving. Charles Bronson was contacted but he was angry at Hill for not sufficiently featuring his wife, Jill Ireland, in Hill's *Hard Times*, in which the actor also appeared. Ryan O'Neal was cast after contacting the production through his agent to express interest in the part. The film's experimental approach to the genre was effective, but at this point in the decade audiences preferred conventionality. *The Driver* did poorly at the box office.

Walter Hill worked his way into the film business as a screenwriter and assistant director. In 1973 Hill scripted a Cold War spy thriller *The Mackintosh Man*, starring Paul Newman and directed by John Huston. After directing *Hard Times* and *The Driver*, Hill was involved in writing the contemporary classic horror/science fiction film, *Alien*, directed by Ridley Scott. Also in 1979 Hill cowrote and directed *The Warriors*, a stylized gang movie. It made money and became a cult film because of the fantasy element Hill brought to the table.

FM takes place at a progressive rock radio station. The focus is on conflicts that arise among the staff. Throughout the seventies there were movies with song scores. Due to the nature of *FM*, the story and setting allowed for a constant song score. The music reflects the sounds of the times. Tracks include "Night Moves" by Bob Seger, "Life in the Fast Lane" by the Eagles, and "More Than a Feeling" by Boston. The movie did not do well but the soundtrack album was a major hit and won a Grammy.

Fingers tells the story of a young man with a double life who functions in two distinctly different worlds. His mentally ill mother has the gift of playing classical piano, which he has inherited, but he also is an expert at delivering damaging, violent messages to people who owe money to his mobster father. Harvey Keitel gives a startling performance as a conflicted individual obsessed with music—including classics and rock 'n' roll like the song "Summertime, Summertime"—and theories about them. Often, he is manic and out of control. James Toback wrote and directed the film, which was highly regarded by François Truffaut, but barely seen during its short release. *Fingers* contains an upsetting and violent sequence played by former football great Jim Brown, who slams together the heads of two young women.

Jim Brown is an African American sports figure, a former football star, and an action movie actor who played a man elected sheriff in the rural South who deals with extreme prejudice in *Tick, Tick, Tick* (1970), directed by Ralph Nelson. Later he appeared in a number of blaxploitation films: *Black Gunn* (1972), *The Slams* (1973), *I Escaped from Devil's*

Island (1973), *Slaughter* (1974), and *Three the Hard Way* (1974). In 1975 Jim Brown appeared in the spaghetti Western *Take a Hard Ride*.

Girlfriends was directed by Claudia Weill. The story is about Susan Weinblatt, played by Melanie Mayron, a photographer who makes the leap from shooting baby pictures and bar mitzvahs to serious work and a gallery show. This project started out as a thirty-minute film funded by a grant from the American Film Institute. Weill concluded that she wanted to explore what happened next in the narrative. In the end, the material in the short became the first seven minutes of the feature film. Funding came from the National Endowment of the Arts and New York State, which totaled $80,000. Principal photography ran for six and a half weeks, but in reality, it took longer because the production kept running out of money, causing pauses in production. After the grant funds were depleted, Weill, who also produced the film, looked for private investors. When *Girlfriends* was complete, Weill went to Hollywood, where she sold her first feature film to Warner Bros. The studio was so impressed with Weill that they signed a contract with her for two more features. *Girlfriends* was an independent film directed by a woman, which was not a common occurrence in the seventies.

Go Tell the Spartans, directed by Ted Post, is an early Vietnam War movie that was set in Vietnam and starred Burt Lancaster. It was based on the 1967 novel *Incident at Muc Wa* by Daniel Ford. It features so-called U.S. military advisers in 1964, when the author was a correspondent in Vietnam for *The Nation*. The title comes from a phrase by the Greek poet Simonides, an epitaph to three hundred soldiers who died fighting Persian invaders. In 1977 the producers asked the army for assistance with the production, but the army would participate only if the script was rewritten and the characters were modified. The army viewed the characters depicted as losers. The film was shot on a limited budget of $1.5 million in Valencia, California. When the money ran short after thirty-one days, Lancaster put in $150,000 to complete the film. After its initial release in 1978, it was rereleased in 1992, then on VHS in 2005, and on a limited edition Blu-Ray in 2016.

Ted Post started his career as a movie theater usher, a director of summer theater, then in feature films during the sixties such as *Hang 'Em High* (1968), which starred Clint Eastwood. In 1970 Post directed the second sequel to *Planet of the Apes* titled *Beneath the Planet of the Apes*. In 1973 he directed *Magnum Force*, a sequel to *Dirty Harry*, working with actor Clint Eastwood again. Also in 1973 Ted Post directed *The Harrad Experiment*, about a school where sexuality and erotic experimentation are explored. In 1975 Post directed Elliot Gould in *Whiffs*. The plot centers on a military private who is the subject of biological and chemical weapon experiments. As a result, he robs a bank. In 1978 Post helmed *Good Guys Wear Black*, an action film starring Chuck Norris.

Halloween was at the forefront of the new horror film, which evolved during the seventies. John Carpenter cowrote and directed this relentless scary film with producer Debra Hill. The low-budget film cost around $300,000 and made as much as $70 million at the box office. Although it was released at the end of October, traditionally in time for Halloween, it transcended the holiday and reinvented the genre conventions of horror films that preceded it. The story features Michael Myers, who had stabbed his sister when he was six years old and escapes from an institution to return to his hometown and continue his killing spree. There is a solid cast in the film, and Carpenter found a way to link his film to Hitchcock's masterpiece of horror, *Psycho*. *Psycho* starred Janet Leigh, whose character Marion Crane is stabbed to death in a running shower. The lead in *Halloween* is the seventeen-year-old Laurie Strode, played by Janet Leigh's daughter, Jamie Lee Curtis. The narrative takes place during the day on Halloween and at night, which puts children in their costumes and their babysitters, like Laurie, at risk. There are many bravura camera shots executed by director of photography Dean Cundey and his camera operator Ray Stella, often taken with a Panaglide camera, which allowed fluid movement. Directors of horror films have used many devices to frighten their audiences, some complex and involved, but John Carpenter used the basic film frame to keep the audience off balance and ready to jump when he wanted them to. Shots were framed to keep the viewer on edge, looking all around the frame to see if Myers was about to appear. Most of the times he didn't, but when he did, it left the audience shocked, drained, and not quite ready for the next scare. Carpenter provided the music, which was stripped bare and full of tension. *Halloween* is categorized as an early slasher film and has created a lucrative franchise.

John Carpenter attended University of Southern California, where he made student films. *The Resurrection of Bronco Billy* was cocreated with producer John Longenecker and won the Oscar for Best Live Action Short Film. Carpenter's first feature was *Dark Star* (1974), a science fiction comedy on which he collaborated with Dan O'Bannon, who went on to write *Alien*. Heavily influenced by studio-era auteur Howard Hawks, Carpenter took on contemporary filmmaking in the spirit of less is more—vintage Hawks. After *Assault on Precinct 13* and *Halloween*, John Carpenter became an A-list filmmaker in the horror, science fiction, and action genres.

Jamie Lee Curtis, daughter of Janet Leigh and Tony Curtis, made her debut as an actress in John Carpenter's *Halloween*. After appearing in a series of horror films, she became known as the Scream Queen. She has acted in six *Halloween* films in addition to comedies and other genres.

I Spit on Your Grave has a reputation of being the vilest movie ever. A young short story writer captures the attention of a group of violent men who seek her out, abduct her, and rape her. She plans her revenge and manages to murder each one. Four thousand women auditioned for the female lead Jennifer Hills. Actress and model Camille Keaton got the difficult part, which included a lot of violence, nudity, and stage blood. The worst feature of *I Spit on Your Grave* is that it wholly exploits the physicality and gender of the lead character. Writer and director Meir Zarchi could not find a distributor for his film, so he distributed it himself. It ran in some drive-ins but only for short runs, and he just barely made enough to cover the cost of advertising the movie. In 1980 it was picked up by the Jerry Gross Organization. Considered by some to be the worst movie ever made, *I Spit on Your Grave* has been banned and arguments about whether it is a feminist film have been made. At the very least, there is universal agreement that *I Spit on Your Grave* is poorly written, acted, recorded, and realized on film.

Interiors is Woody Allen's first serious film. At the center of the film, which was inspired by the works of Allen's hero Ingmar Bergman, are three daughters and their father who leaves his wife, an interior decorator, who then commits suicide. He is renewed by finding love with a totally different kind of woman, of whom his daughters do not approve. The writing is strained, but the actors manage to bring life to the story. The family home is impressive and designed to perfection. Production designer Mel Bourne reglazed the windows to clarify the many reflection shots and redid the putty in perfect lines, which is what he and Allen felt the mother would have done. *Interiors* does appear to be forced at times in narrative, dialogue, and actions of the characters, but it was considered a brave and weighty step for Woody Allen's development as a total film-maker.

Killer of Sheep was directed, written, edited, and produced by Charles Burnett. The film was shot during 1972 and 1973. It was originally given to the UCLA School of Film in 1977. It premiered at the Whitney Museum of American Art in New York in 1978, but there was no general release because Burnett had not paid for the rights to the music used in the movie. For a long time, the film existed only on old 16mm prints. Partially due to a donation from director Steven Soderbergh, *Killer of Sheep* was restored and blown up to 35mm. The music rights were purchased for $150,000. In March 2007 *Killer of Sheep* appeared in select theaters and later that year was released on DVD.

Killer of Sheep involves the lives and culture of African Americans in the Watts district in Los Angeles, California. The narrative embraces a vignette style of storytelling in a manner reminiscent of Italian neorealism. The film is a highly regarded feat unto itself, let alone a legendary film of the seventies that practically no one saw for decades.

The Last Waltz is a concert film directed by Martin Scorsese celebrating the Band's last concert. It has been widely considered by critics as the greatest rock movie ever made. Scorsese storyboarded the film in preproduction and for the one-time-only live shoot, he used top experienced production designer Boris Leven, whose many accomplishments included *West Side Story* (1961) and *The Sound of Music* (1965). The all-star camera crew included Michael Chapman *Raging Bull* (1980), Vilmos Zsigmond, and László Kovács. Performing acts include the Band, Bob Dylan, Eric Clapton, Van Morrison, and Joni Mitchell.

Midnight Express won the Oscar for Best Adapted Screenplay. The screenwriter—Oliver Stone—was virtually unknown until the eighties, when he became a premier American filmmaker who took on difficult and dicey topics, as he did in *Midnight Express* with drug smuggling. The project was based on the true story of Billy Hayes, who was incarcerated in a Turkish prison for trying to move a large amount of hashish out of Turkey. Brad Davis played Hayes and British filmmaker Alan Parker directed. The score was composed by Giorgio Moroder, who stood out in the seventies for his use of synthesizers and keyboards. Like many dramatic films during the decade *Midnight Express* is dark and relenting. The filmmakers were unafraid to explore inhumanity and morality. *Midnight Express* was a big success, grossing $35 million on a budget of $2.3

million, proving that audiences were still interested in adult-themed films.

Renaldo and Clara has an unconventional structure made up of documentary footage, concert footage, and dramatic vignettes that reflect Bob Dylan's music and lifestyle. American playwright Sam Shepard worked with Dylan on the script. The cast of actors and musicians is large. They include T-Bone Burnett, Roger McGuinn, Arlo Guthrie, Ronee Blakely, Joni Mitchell, and Harry Dean Stanton. The movie was filmed prior to and during Dylan's Rolling Thunder Revue. Originally it was released with a four-hour running time in select theaters, but overwhelmingly negative reviews led to it being pulled at that time.

The Scenic Route is a nontraditional feature film written and directed by Mark Rappaport, who historically has been considered an avant-garde/experimental film artist. This is one of his most famous films about two sisters and the man who married one and then becomes involved with the other. The film is narrated by the older sister, and her thoughts take up a lot of the film's narrative time. If characters speak while she is narrating, the voices are not just low but nonexistent. Dialogue, when it occurs, is sparse. The story contains many cultural references to opera, Greek myths, and photography. There is a television soap opera quality to *The Scenic Route*, but unlike that TV form, it amplifies the nature of the relationship and the actions of the characters during pauses, in between dialogue exchanges, and before and after scenes are presented. Color is specific and limited. The great majority of scenes has no interscene editing. Imagery is sparse and often defies reality.

Superman is an early superhero movie of the contemporary era. Director Richard Donner and his team put great effort into how Superman would fly without the clichéd techniques of the past. Christopher Reeve was the ideal Superman with his rugged good looks and chiseled physique in the classic costume. Margot Kidder plays Lois Lane with some quirks and resilience. The larger-than-life quality in general suits a comic book hero. *The Godfather*'s Mario Puzo was one of the screenwriters; John Williams wrote the triumphant music.

An Unmarried Woman was written and directed by Paul Mazursky, who continued to make comedy/dramas that resonated in their time. The film made Jill Clayburgh a certified star of the seventies. Her character, Erica Benton, gets divorced after she learns that her husband is leaving her for a younger woman. Divorce rates during the seventies were high, and the meaning of marriage and monogamy were newly examined themes. *An Unmarried Woman* deals with women's liberation and the sexual revolution, both movements affecting society during the seventies. The film was a major success because of its realistic, in-touch quality. Adult audiences had a growing need to see mature films that reflected their lives.

Up in Smoke was at the forefront of the stoner comedy genre. It stars the counterculture comedy team of Cheech Martin and Tommy Chong. The story follows the exploits of the two main characters, with most of the material coming from ten years of comedy routines laden with drug references and humor. *Up in Smoke* resonated with a young audience and reflected the drug culture, especially marijuana use, that was predominant across the country. The sensibilities of the sixties supported the story and the audience who came of age with recreational drugs.

Philip Kaufman was involved in the counterculture movement and then traveled around Europe. He decided to become a filmmaker after watching independent films by creators such as John Cassavetes and Shirley Clarke. In 1972 he wrote and directed *The Great Northfield Minnesota Raid*, a Western shot in a cinema verité/direct cinema style. In 1974 he directed *White Dawn*, a film about the cultural divide between Europeans and Inuits. In 1978 he made an updated color remake of the black-and-white science fiction classic *Invasion of the Body Snatchers* (1956). In 1979 Kaufman directed an adaptation of the Richard Price novel *The Wanderers*, which took place in the Bronx in 1963. It was a dramedy about rival gangs.

Moment by Moment is a romantic drama about an older rich woman living in Beverly Hills, played by Lily Tomlin, and her complex relationship with a younger drifter played by John Travolta. It was written and directed by Tomlin's romantic and professional partner Jane Wagner, who came to film from painting and writing. The project continued to show that women directors were often interested in women's issues, which attracted a larger female audience than films from a male point of view, and that female lead actresses did not have to fit a particular Hollywood mold.

In 1978 Jack Nicholson directed and starred in *Goin' South*, a comic Western with Mary Steenburgen and John Belushi. Nicholson played the lead, a horse and cattle thief who escapes hanging through a marriage offer. The off-kilter humor didn't help it with the critics or audiences.

11

1979

March 28: A partial meltdown of a reactor at the Three Mile Island Nuclear Generating Station in Dauphin County, Pennsylvania, caused a subsequent radiation leak. . . . July 12: A local disc jockey who rabidly hated disco was engaged for a baseball promotion at Comiskey Park in Chicago, Illinois. He told listeners to bring disco records in order to destroy the collected mass with an explosion as an expression against the popular seventies music genre. A crowd of twenty thousand were expected—five thousand more than a typical Chicago White Sox game—but best estimates suggest fifty thousand people showed up. Some of the crowd hadn't handed in their records but flung them onto the exploding mass. Thousands stormed the field and riot police were called. . . . November 4: A diplomatic standoff between the United States and Iran involved fifty-two Americans who would be held hostage until January 20, 1981, totaling 444 days.

Sally Field won a well-deserved Oscar for her portrayal of a single mom working in a poorly run cotton mill who becomes a highly effective union organizer in *Norma Rae*, directed by Hollywood veteran and activist Martin Ritt. Her transition into the role of mother and primary breadwinner further revealed a first-class actress who was once known for *Gidget* and *The Flying Nun* and came to prominence as a film actress during the seventies.

A landmark horror/science fiction movie directed by Ridley Scott, *Alien* is the beginning of a long franchise of monster movies with an intellectual bent. *Alien* is an ingenious film because it concerns a creature

Dustin Hoffman and Justin Henry in *Kramer vs. Kramer*. *Columbia Pictures/Photofest*
© *Columbia Pictures*

that keeps reimagining itself and targeting the crew of a spaceship one at a time. The audience becomes increasingly frightened with each attack and is engaged in trying to understand how and why the creature makes its multiple transformations. Culturally *Alien* is meaningful because of the diversity of the crew and because a strong woman, Ripley, played by Sigourney Weaver, becomes the leader of the spacecraft and defeats the alien—at least until it returns in the sequel. In earlier times horror and science fiction films were not usually directed by A-list filmmakers. Ridley Scott brings a tremendous sense of craft, design, and drama to *Alien*. The movie also has a memorable and effective tag line used in the marketing: "In space no one can hear you scream."

All That Jazz is an autobiographical film, although the movie's director, Bob Fosse, denies it. At times abstract, the narrative at many points reflects Fosse's life and work. The main character, Joe Gideon, played by Roy Scheider, is a director/choreographer who burns the candle at both ends in his female relationships and his professional commitments on stage and screen and it affects his heart, eventually fatally. Bob Fosse was heavily influenced by Federico Fellini, especially *8½*, as both are about film directors searching for love and a creative artistic summit. *All That Jazz* is a musical within a musical in progress. Visually the film is exciting and experimental in design. The dance and vocal numbers are angular, structural, and full of vocal ingenuity. The editing by Alan Heim won an Oscar and constantly moves the film in unusual and energetic ways, and the cinematography by Giuseppe Rotunno, who had worked with Fellini, is eye-catching, capturing the lively spirit of this picture.

Apocalypse Now is a movie about the Vietnam War that takes place in Vietnam, but the way the war is conducted and the manner in which the soldiers behave are not in the standard ways that armed conflicts were portrayed in any prior Vietnam War movie. During and shortly after the Vietnam War, there was detailed coverage of extreme drug use among soldiers, including psychedelics such as LSD, which impacted the actions and caused behavioral changes of the fighting men. *Apocalypse Now*, in content and structure, portrays a psychedelic war through the use of colored streams around the helicopters by Oscar-winning cinematography master Vittorio Storaro. The sound design by Walter Murch synthesizes the sounds of the helicopter so that they are no longer realistic but hallucinatory. This and other cinematic factors make *Apocalypse Now* an experiential movie in which the viewer watches the film while in the middle of the action as well.

John Milius wrote the screenplay for *Apocalypse Now* by framing the narrative around Conrad's masterwork *The Heart of Darkness* in extracting the main action of one man traveling a river to find another man who he believes is exceptional. In the film, this theme is transformed into Captain Willard's (Martin Sheen) assignment to seek out the once brilliant Colonel Kurtz (Marlon Brando) with orders to terminate Kurtz with extreme prejudice. George Lucas was to direct the film but eventually it fell in the hands of Francis Ford Coppola. The budget was high—$31 million—extreme weather in the Philippines, where it was shot, destroyed sets; time was lost; and casting was tedious—Steve McQueen turned the film down because of money and schedule. Martin Sheen was given the lead role but shortly thereafter had a heart attack, closing down production while he recuperated. Coppola had a breakdown. He could not figure out how to end the picture and shot several endings. Editing was untraditional in hopes that it would best capture the confusion of the

Vietnam War. A team of editors put scenes into a cut, then Coppola would work with the team producing a different version, then again this was handed to the next editor, and the process would happen all over again. Over the decades new versions appeared as Coppola tried to perfect his film. It is a masterpiece because it reinvented the war film genre, not just in its visualization but in the telling of a cinematic narrative.

Harrison Ford began in the sixties with four films, two of them uncredited. In 1970 he played an airport worker in Michelangelo Antonioni's critique of America, *Zabriskie Point.* In 1973 George Lucas gave Harrison Ford a big break by casting him as Bob Falfa, a hot rod driver looking for a race in *American Graffiti.* In 1974 he played a mysterious corporate assistant in Coppola's *The Conversation.* In *Apocalypse Now* he played Colonel G. Lucas, an aide to Lieutenant Colonel R. Corman, played by G. D. Spradlin (the monikers are a nod to George Lucas and Roger Corman), who provided background to Captain Willard before the dangerous mission. In 1977 he played Han Solo in *Star Wars.* In 1979 in *The Frisco Kid*, Ford played a bank robber who befriends a Polish rabbi. Also in 1979, Harrison Ford appeared in the sequel to *American Graffiti, More American Graffiti.*

Best Boy won the Oscar for Best Documentary. Director Ira Wohl had a fifty-two-year-old cousin named Philly who was mentally handicapped and unable to take care of himself. Wohl convinced Philly's parents, his aunt and uncle, to prepare Philly for when he would be without assistance. They agreed and Philly received training for self-sufficiency in a sheltered living facility. Philly's father died during production and Ira's involvement in Philly's life became the film's purpose.

Cinematographer and head of postproduction of *Best Boy* Tom McDonough had worked only on the TV series *The Big Blue Marble* before shooting the Academy Award–winning documentary *Best Boy.* Director of the film Ira Wohl was also an editor of *The Big Blue Marble.*

During the seventies movies were especially risky in sexual content and violence. One of the most challenging movies to address cultural morality was *Hardcore*, written and directed by Paul Schrader. Schrader was known for his deep trips into the dark side with his screenplays for *Taxi Driver* and *Raging Bull* (1980). *Hardcore* focuses on a religious father whose daughter suddenly disappears. Schrader made dangerous choices. The father, led to believe his daughter might be in the world of pornographic movies, disguises himself as a producer planning to make a hardcore film in hopes of uncovering information as to her whereabouts. There is nudity in the film, but Schrader finds ways to imply hardcore activity in the movie. There is a snuff film in which a person, usually female, is murdered on camera. The very title and the subject matter of *Hardcore* spelled danger to audiences. Schrader's narrative tested the morality of a devout man and what he would do to find his teenage daughter whom he no longer understood.

George C. Scott was an actor who gave powerful performances on stage, television, and in the movies. In 1970 he won an Oscar for *Patton* but refused to accept it. In 1971 in *They Might Be Giants*, directed by Anthony Harvey, Scott played a man who slips into fantasy after his wife's death, believing himself to be Sherlock Holmes. Also in 1971 Scott appeared in *The Hospital*, an outrageous attack on that institution from an original screenplay by Paddy Chayefsky. In 1972 George C. Scott directed himself in the lead role of *Rage*, the story of a man and his son exposed to nerve gas by the government. Later in 1973 he directed and starred in *The Savage Is Loose*, a dangerous film in which a father and son lust after their wife and mother when they crash on an uncharted island. In 1978 he was in *Movie Movie*, which contains two films, a boxing picture and a musical comedy, directed by Stanley Donen.

Divorce had been a part of movies since the Classical Hollywood Studio System. The breakup of a relationship between a man and a woman makes for good drama and an understanding of how couple relationships work and don't work. Seventies society saw many divorces across the country and in movies addressing the painful personal and cultural aspects of marriage. In 1979 Robert Benton directed *Kramer vs. Kramer* costarring Dustin Hoffman and Meryl Streep. This film examined an aspect of divorce scarcely explored. In *Kramer vs. Kramer*, the mother walks out and the father must continue to work and raise their young child. When the mother decides she wants her son back, a custody trial ensues and the father loses on the grounds that it's a mother who should have primary responsibility for raising a child. On the day the boy is to go with his mother, she has a change of heart and recognizes that the father is the parent best suited for the job. The film's production is handsome and the acting is realistic and compelling—Benton's adaptation of the book by Avery Corman is smart and knowing.

Manhattan is a romance written and directed by Woody Allen in which his character, Isaac Davis, a forty-two-year-old television comedy writer, dates Tracy, a seventeen-year-old high school student, played by Mariel Hemingway. Allen considers the teenage girl smarter than all the adults in the film. Whether Allen's assessment is correct is an open question, nevertheless *Manhattan* is considered Woody Allen's masterpiece and one of his most thoroughly realized films.

Over the Edge was written by Tim Hunter and Charlie S. Haas based on a 1973 article in the *San Francisco Examiner* titled "Mousepacks: Kids on a Crime Spree by Bruce Koon and James A. Finerock." Director Jonathan Kaplan led a strong group of teen actors including Matt Dillon (in his motion picture acting debut) and Vincent Spano in this story about kids living in a planned middle-class community who turn to sex, violence, and drugs to combat their boredom. Legendary character actor Harry Northup plays the law trying to clean up a gang of problems. The character portrayals are strong and the visualization of a modern living facility that goes nowhere is realistic without Hollywood trappings. Social problems such as teen issues were dealt with for decades in Hollywood, especially in B movies of the Roger Corman variety, but *Over the Edge* appeared realistic—the kids could have lived next door—and the detachment between parents and teens reflected the new generation gap that unfolded in the seventies.

Quintet directed by Robert Altman took place in a future ice age in which a game called *Quintet* is played. Paul Newman stars along with a strong international supporting cast including Bibi Anderson, Vittorio Gassman, and Fernando Rey. The film received negative notices, and few saw it in first run. It was considered confusing and without purpose or meaning.

The Rose stars Bette Midler as Mary Rose Foster, a sixties rock 'n' roll singer clearly based on Janis Joplin. It was directed by Mark Rydell and written by Bo Goldman and Bill Kerby. The film is a drama about rock 'n' roll life and the tremendous toll it takes on the body and psyche. Midler gives a go-for-broke performance. Midler's acting is emotional; she particularizes the songs and makes them her own.

The Warriors directed by Walter Hill is a gang movie set in New York City. It is based on the novel by Sol Yurick and has a large cast of the gang members portrayed in the film. There have been numerous movies about street gangs, but *The Warriors* is significantly different and audacious in two ways. The names and nature of the gangs are unique and over the top. The style of the film—and the abundant action—is like a cartoon or more appropriately a graphic novel. The film became a cult favorite precisely because it was hyper-realistic.

In what must be the ultimate haunted house picture, *The Amityville Horror* is based on what a real family claims they experienced living in a new home purchased in Amityville, New York. The true story angle heightened the excitement for audiences. The film was a surprise blockbuster produced for $4.7 million and grossing an astounding $86.4 million. It was written by Sandor Stern adapted from the book *The Amityville Horror* by Jay Anson and directed by Stuart Rosenberg.

During the 1970s horror films continued to push the envelope. Director Abel Ferrara was part of a New York underground, a filmmaker who went where few would follow. In *The Driller Killer*, he plays the lead under a pseudonym as an artist who goes mad and kills derelicts on the street by drilling into their heads. The line between the horror genre and extreme violence that reflected contemporary society continued to be tested and became part of movie content in the seventies.

It often takes time for a Broadway play to translate to the movie screen. The movie *Hair* was based on the seminal sixties stage production that began in downtown New York and appeared on Broadway in 1968. On film it was more than ten years late. It no longer was for just the baby boomers but for younger audiences as well. Czechoslovakian-born director Miloš Forman was miscast in this assignment. Twyla Tharp's choreography is distinctive but does not relate to the spirit of the play. Overall *Hair* was cast and performed well, but the narrative is so changed that it is nearly unrecognizable. It is closer to 1978 than 1968 in tone, when the youth revolution of the late sixties dazzled audiences.

During the seventies there was a roller-skating trend in discos and clubs. *Roller Boogie* is a feature film starring Linda Blair, grown up since her appearance in *The Exorcist*. It was directed by Mark L. Lester. The plot was thin, heavy on the skating and disco music. Other films in this genre include *Skatetown USA* (1979) with Patrick Swayze.

Saint Jack is a film directed by Peter Bogdanovich that lifted him up from the bottom, where he found himself earlier in the seventies with movies that had an Old Hollywood vibe. Here the director embraced a contemporary story and the exotic locale of Singapore with Ben Gazzara as a low-level entrepreneur who sets up a brothel and runs into formidable interference from crime figures.

Originally the *Star Trek* television show was a failure that ran for seventy-nine episodes over three seasons (1966–1969). Later it returned in syndication and became a huge hit. Fans who became known as Trekkies watched episodes over and over and created a lore and a mythology. *Star Trek* creator Gene Roddenberry convinced Paramount to continue the show in the form of a feature film. In 1975 writers tried to create a *Star Trek* screenplay but Paramount was unhappy with the results. In 1977 movie plans were scrapped when Paramount decided to do a sequel to the TV show. However, when they saw that *Close Encounters of the Third Kind* was a big success, they canceled plans for the television series sequel and returned to the *Star Trek* feature film idea. In 1978 Paramount announced with fanfare that the highly accomplished filmmaker Robert Wise would direct that film. Wise was familiar with the science fiction genre, having directed *The Day the Earth Stood Still* (1951) and *The Andromeda Strain* (1971). The project assembled original cast members and crew from the television series. It received mixed reviews and didn't totally live up to fan expectations, likely an impossible feat. The budget kept expanding to a final $46 million and it brought in $139 million. *Star Trek: The Motion Picture* started a motion picture franchise that as of 2016 totals thirteen movies. There are four television spinoffs.

Director Steven Spielberg had two megahits—*Jaws* (1975) and *Close Encounters of the Third Kind* (1977)—when he made *1941.* The film was not so much a World War II service comedy as a large-scale epic with physical comedy featuring gags, explosions, pratfalls, blunt jokes, and over-the-top performances with some juvenile antics as seen in a *Three Stooges* short. It was the kind of comedy that caused raucous laughter in the earlier days of Hollywood but fell flat in the seventies. The screenplay is by Robert Zemeckis, who became an A-list director in the eighties and nineties, and his writing partner Bob Gale. The executive producer was John Milius, who also contributed to the story. Steven Spielberg's *1941* takes place right after the attack on Pearl Harbor, when the sighting of a Japanese submarine causes chaos in Los Angeles. The large cast includes John Belushi, Dan Ackroyd, Ned Beatty, Christopher Lee, Tim Matheson, Nancy Allen, Toshiro Mifune, Warren Oates, and Robert Stack. The attention to scenes with model shots and large effects—such as a house slowly pushed off its foundation as it crashes into a mountain and falls in pieces into the sea—makes the viewer worry about the director's awareness of the characters. The film is loud, in bad taste, and has more than its share of racist jokes. Audiences around the country and media film critics strongly disliked *1941*. Some said it was unpatriotic, making fun of World War II when so many died in defense of the country. Others laid blame on Spielberg's infatuation with the television phenomena *Saturday Night Live,* which at that time had been on NBC for four years. The film did feature cast members from *SNL* and at times seemed to be part of a sketch from the show. There were some clear messages to some in- and outside the film industry that auteurist cinema was going too far, not only because *1941* wasn't a hit, but because it was excessive and narratively out of control. Spielberg admitted publicly the film was a total failure and then moved on.

Culturally, the movie *10* continued an old sexist position toward women on screen and in society during a decade when there were seeds of change. In *10* a middle-aged man played by Dudley Moore falls head over heels for a young woman he has seen but not met. In this part was Bo Derek, the wife of actor/Svengali John Derek, portraying the Svengali. Writer, director, and producer Blake Edwards's image of a woman at the top of the scale was projected onto the standards of moviegoers. Dudley Moore's acting exceeds comic standards. Bo Derek has little acting skill and technique. Slow motion photography and a long musical track of Ravel's *Boléro* are gimmicky and obvious, but in terms of popularity *10* totaled a $74.8 million gate on a $7 million budget. The cultural damage done by *10* is that, for some men, Bo Derek became a benchmark of beauty against which to compare their wives, girlfriends, or women passing by on the street.

In the 1960s Blake Edwards established himself as a deft director of comedies, especially with *The Pink Panther* (1963), the first in a successful series of Inspector Clouseau comedy mysteries. In 1970 Edwards directed *Darling Lili,* an original film musical often cited as contributing to the end to the Old Hollywood Studio System. It starred his wife, Julie Andrews, and Rock Hudson. Set during World War I, the movie featured an English music star who is actually a German spy. The budget for *Darling Lili* was $25 million but the film grossed only $3,250,000, a devastating loss of money that illustrated a lack of interest and faith in Old Hollywood and the now-dying form of the movie musical. In 1972 Edwards directed *The Carey Treatment,* the third film directed by Edwards during the seventies that was seriously reedited by the studio without his involvement. His next three films were part of the Pink Panther franchise: *The Return of the Pink Panther* (1975), *The Pink Panther Strikes Again* (1976), and *Revenge of the Pink Panther* (1978).

12

1980–1987

Seventies motion pictures did not end on the last day of December 1979. By the middle of the seventies, the upward trajectory of the American New Wave movement was starting to falter and shift downward. The A-list members of the Wave were not always making noteworthy films and the B and C groups were touch and go. Significant numbers of seventies filmmakers were dropping off the radar.

For the most part, the original American New Wave directors were not maintaining their artistic standards. The directors selected projects they were interested in exploring, but the content and aesthetics were not equal to the audience experiences during the seventies cinema revolution. Many of the big names such as Robert Altman and William Friedkin struggled with a hit-and-miss pattern.

Cruising, directed by William Friedkin (1980), was a tactical mistake from genre, content, and artistic standpoints. It was a cop picture, starring Al Pacino, but unlike the clearly defined and portrayed Popeye Doyle (Gene Hackman), the policeman in *Cruising* becomes increasingly unsure of his sexual identity. The center of the film questions whether a straight undercover cop investigating gay murders in New York's Greenwich Village can navigate the sadomasochism scene while maintaining his sexuality and sense of self. The theme is plausible and Friedkin worked with an adaptation of Gerald Walker's 1970 novel. The film's approach realistically exposed the rough trade clubs situated in New York's meat-packing district and contained explicit sequences a bit more than a soft-

Brad Dourif and Jeff Bridges in *Heaven's Gate. MGM/Photofest © MGM*

core adult film. Friedkin was always a risk taker, but the material and controversy were too much for audiences.

The production was riddled with protests. There were actual disruptions during the exterior location shooting with large angry groups making so much noise that it was impossible to use location sound. The director was forced to dub large parts of the film during the editing process. These hands-on demonstrations with the goal of severely impairing the film were devastating.

When *Cruising* was submitted for rating consideration, the board stamped an X. It was the Motion Picture Association of America's practice not to specify exactly what was offensive in the film. It can be assumed that the violence and the especially sexual depictions were the problem. Friedkin has stated that the film was submitted for rating consideration as many as fifty times, which cost the production as much as $50,000 in shooting and postproduction costs. More startling is that William Friedkin, collaborating with film editor Bud Smith, deleted as much as forty minutes from the cut that was first submitted.

Cruising was released on February 15, 1980. The critical notices were overwhelmingly negative. Protests continued, and the gay community was deeply negative about a movie they found unfair and prejudicial. They labeled the director homophobic.

Auteur cinema continued to take a hit and the industry began to tire of personal films. Studios were concerned about giving auteur directors full control and worried about films resulting in a short-end payday. After his overwhelming success with the Oscar winner *The Deer Hunter*, Michael Cimino could write his own ticket. United Artists saw him as a savior who could get them back in the game with a blockbuster movie by a director with major name recognition. For his project with United Artists, Cimino demanded creative control and decided to direct an earlier script he had written about the historic Johnson County War in Wyoming that began in the late 1880s, in which immigrants were slaughtered by U.S. military forces who believed they were taking jobs, money, land, and livestock away from natural-born Americans.

The production quickly fell behind schedule and went overbudget due to Cimino's obsessional work methods and dictatorial attitude. Working with his cast and crew on location in Montana, there were overruns everywhere. He shot take after take on most scenes, overcovering them for more control in the editing room. The cast was put through a series of lessons about ballroom dancing and roller skating that prepared them for period accuracy. A town was built from scratch, the sound was recorded for total realism, rendering some scenes nearly impossible to decipher. The film was unmanageable at its extreme length of three hours and thirty-nine minutes. The acting was uneven, and although Vilmos Zsigmond's cinematography was breathtaking, *Heaven's Gate* failed miserably with its cryptic dialogue and confused narrative. United Artists premiered the film in one theater. The reviews were devastating and centered on Cimino's self-indulgence and inability to make a coherent movie. United Artists quickly pulled *Heaven's Gate* and it was reedited to 149 minutes. In 1981 it was put into wide release with equally bad reviews and audience reaction. Shortly after, the film disappeared. United Artists was unable to withstand the losses from Cimino's *Heaven's Gate* and went out of business. Although Cimino made a few more films, his career was forever damned. He was known as the filmmaker responsible for one of the greatest disasters of the twentieth century; *Heaven's Gate* demolished a studio that extended back to the early days of Hollywood. In the end United Artists spent $44 million on *Heaven's Gate* and took in $3.5 million. The message was clear: an auteur director was given full rein and the result was not only a bad movie, but one that no one wanted to see, personal vision or not.

In 1982 Francis Ford Coppola embarked on a project he likened to a romantic comedy in the spirit of a Neil Simon play or movie. *One from the Heart* was written by Armyan Bernstein (*Thank God It's Friday*, 1978) and Coppola. It is the story of a couple, Frannie, played by Teri Garr, and Hank, portrayed by Frederic Forrest, who live in Las Vegas and are celebrating their fifth anniversary on the Fourth of July. They begin to quarrel and break up, going their separate ways. Frannie plans to go to Bora Bora with Ray, played by Raul Julia, a handsome musician who turns out to be a waiter. Hank is romancing Leila, played by Natassja Kinski, a high-wire circus performer. What started out as a contained relationship story began to grow exponentially. Coppola had financed his own studio, which was set up as a modern-day version of Old Hollywood. Working with the Sony Corporation, he developed what he dubbed an electronic cinema, in which he could visualize the film before shooting it. He directed the film from inside a well-equipped trailer so that he could give directions to cast and crew without being on the studio floor. Lavish and expensive sets were built, including a Vegas street with storefronts and casino marquees adorned with countless lightbulbs. The look of the film imagined by Coppola and rendered by production designer Dean Tavoularis and cinematographer Vittorio Storaro was breathtaking, but it totally overwhelmed the story of the four characters. The budget began to grow, as did the production, from $15 million to $26 million. The style of *One from the Heart* was both theatrical and cinematic. It wasn't realistic and used some stage techniques and also employed deeply saturated camera techniques that transformed it into a dreamlike state, although it was set in a real place that most viewers knew of or knew about—Las Vegas. Coppola also made a mistake by showing an unfinished version of *One from the Heart* to critics and journalists. They sent out the word that Coppola had an expensive turkey on his hands, dimming box office potential. When the film opened on February 12, 1982, few went to see it, plunging Coppola into debt and forcing him to sell his twenty-three-acre Zoetrope Studios. The gross on the film was $636,796. The distinct message was that another major auteur—an original American New Wave filmmaker, the first out of film school and a figure who inspired so many Wavers and filmmakers of the decade—had gone down in flames.

Ishtar was released in 1987 by Columbia Pictures. It was written and directed by Elaine May and starred Dustin Hoffman and Warren Beatty. The budget was $51 million, and the gross was $14.4 million.

Elaine May was considered an auteur filmmaker. She also was known to be difficult and would do anything to protect her films—including taking reels of film from the editing room and hiding them from the studio. She did many takes on her films and let the actors improvise until there was agreement that they could move on. *Ishtar* was inspired by the road movies that starred comedian Bob Hope and the crooner's crooner Bing Crosby. *Ishtar* finds Warren Beatty and Dustin Hoffman as a song-writing team who write really bad songs and sing them even worse in public. They run into trouble and are forced to relocate overseas. One bad singing performance might be tolerable or even funny, but Beatty and Hoffman, neither of whom could sing well, perform many songs through-out the picture; it is excruciating. Most Hollywood movies with consider-able budgets need name stars to mount and sell a film. Here Beatty and Hoffman were top draws, but it strained the audience to see such stellar talent in roles as down-and-out bad performers. Some may argue that what makes it funny is precisely the fact that it *is* Beatty and Hoffman; otherwise, it would not be funny. During postproduction on *Ishtar*, the film was running long. Elaine May told the editors to remove a scene. Then she screened the entire movie to decide if the film played well. If she decided that the scene should remain, it was put back and another scene was taken out and the film was run again in its entirety. This process continued until she was pleased with the results. *Ishtar* received bad word of mouth, critics called it the worst movie ever made, and its title became synonymous with a bombed movie. This was another blow for auteur cinema and films that pleased the maker more than the audi-ence.

The seventies was a time that broke with filmmaking of past. Filmmakers were interested in now, not in how history would judge them. I was there and saw all I could in first run. I knew I was witnessing not only some-thing fresh and new, but the reinvention of the movies.

NOTES

I. HOW OLD HOLLYWOOD BECAME NEW HOLLYWOOD

1. Roger Ebert, "Warren Beatty and Julie Christie and the Map to Presbyterian Church," RogerEbert.com, August 1, 1971.
2. Ignatiy Vishnevetsky, "Paul Schrader on Staying Creative and Being Bored by Strip Clubs," https://film.avclub.com/paul-schrader-on-staying-creative-and-being-bored-by-st-1798253803, November 2, 2016.
3. Unsigned, "Samuel Fuller (Director)," cine-scope.com, March 28, 2018.

3. 1971

1. Pauline Kael, "Straw Dogs: Peckinpah's Obsession—Review by Pauline Kael," *The New Yorker*, January 29, 1972.

SELECTED BIBLIOGRAPHY

Bach, Steven. *Final Cut: Dreams and Disaster in the Making of Heaven's Gate.* New York: William Morrow, 1985.

Biskind, Peter. *Easy Riders, Raging Bulls: How the Sex-Drugs-and-Rock 'n' Roll Generation Saved Hollywood.* New York: Simon & Schuster, 1998.

———. *Star: How Warren Beatty Seduced America.* New York: Simon & Schuster, 2010.

Bordwell, David, Janet Staiger, and Kristin Thompson. *The Classical Hollywood Cinema: Film Style & Mode of Production to 1960.* New York: Columbia University Press, 1985.

Bouzereau, Laurent. *The DePalma Cut: The Films of America's Most Controversial Director.* New York: Dembner Books, 1988.

Boyer, Jay. *Bob Rafelson.* New York: Twayne Publishers, 1996.

Carney, Raymond. *American Dreaming: The Films of John Cassavetes and the American Experience.* Berkeley: University of California Press, 1985.

———. *Cassavetes on Cassavetes.* London: Faber and Faber, 2001.

Clagett, Thomas D. *William Friedkin: Obsession and Reality.* 2nd ed. Los Angeles: Silman-James Press, 2003.

Compo, Susan. *Warren Oates: A Wild Life.* Lexington: University Press of Kentucky, 2010.

Cook, David A. *Lost Illusions: American Cinema in the Shadow of Watergate and Vietnam 1970–1979.* History of the American Cinema, edited by Charles Harpole, vol. 9. Berkeley: University of California Press, 2000.

Coppola, Eleanor. *Notes.* New York: Simon & Schuster, 1979.

Corman, Roger, with Jim Jerome. *How I Made a Hundred Movies in Hollywood and Never Lost a Dime.* New York: Random House, 1990.

Cowie, Peter. *Coppola: A Biography.* New York: Da Capo Press, 1994.

———. *The Apocalypse Now Book.* New York: Da Capo Press, 2000.

Dawson, Nick. *Hal Ashby Interviews.* Jackson: University of Mississippi Press, 2010.

———. *Being Hal Ashby: Life of a Hollywood Rebel.* Lexington: University of Kentucky, 2011.

———. *Dennis Hopper Interviews.* Jackson: University of Mississippi Press, 2012.

Deeley, Michael. *Blade Runners, Deer Hunters, and Blowing the Bloody Doors Off.* New York: Pegasus Books, 2009.

Elsaesser, Thomas, Alexander Horwath, and Noel King, eds. *The Last Great American Picture Show: New Hollywood Cinema in the 1970s.* Amsterdam, Amsterdam University Press, 2004.

Fine, Marshall. *Accidental Genius: How John Cassavetes Invented the American Independent Film.* New York: Miramax Books, 2005.

Folsom, Tom. *Hopper: A Journey into the American Dream.* New York: itbooks, 2013.

Fonda, Peter, *Don't Tell Dad*. New York: Hyperion, 1998.

Fonda, Peter, Dennis Hopper, and Terry Southern. *Easy Rider: Original Screenplay*. New York: New American Library, 1969.

Friedkin, William. *The Friedkin Connection: A Memoir*. New York: HarperCollins, 2013.

Friedman, Lester. *Bonnie and Clyde*. London: BFI Publishing, 2000.

Gabler, Neal. *An Empire of Their Own: How the Jews Invented Hollywood*. New York: Crown Publishers, 1988.

Gelmis, Joseph. *The Film Director as Superstar*. Garden City, New York. Doubleday, 1970.

Gilbey, Ryan. *It Don't Worry Me: The Revolutionary American Films of the Seventies*. New York: Faber and Faber, 2003.

Goodwin, Michael, and Naomi Wise. *On the Edge: The Life and Times of Francis Coppola*. New York: William Morrow, 1989.

Gray, Beverly. *Roger Corman: An Unauthorized Biography of the Godfather of Indie Filmmaking*. Los Angeles: Renaissance Books, 2000.

Harris, Mark. *Pictures at a Revolution: Film Movies and the Birth of the New Hollywood*. New York: Penguin Press, 2008.

Haskell, Molly. *Steven Spielberg: A Life in Films*. New Haven, CT: Yale University Press, 2017.

Hill, Lee. *Easy Rider*. London: British Film Institute, 1996.

Hogan, Ron. *The Stewardess Is Flying the Plane: American Films of the 1970s*. New York: Bulfinch Press, 2005.

Jacobs, Diane. *Hollywood Renaissance*. New York: Dell, 1977.

Jones, Brian Jay. *George Lucas: A Life*. New York: Little, Brown, 2016.

Keesey, Douglas. *Brian De Palma's Split-Screen: A Life in Film*. Jackson: University of Mississippi Press, 2015.

King, Geoff. *New Hollywood Cinema: An Introduction*. New York: Columbia University Press, 2002.

Kolker, Robert. *A Cinema of Loneliness: Penn, Stone, Kubrick, Scorsese, Altman*. 3rd ed. Oxford: Oxford University Press, 2000.

Krämer, Peter. *The New Hollywood: From Bonnie and Clyde to Star Wars*. London: Wallflower, 2005.

Laderman, David. *Driving Visions: Exploring the Road Movie*. Austin: University of Texas Press, 2002.

Lev, Peter. *American Films of the 70s: Conflicting Vision*. Austin: University of Texas Press, 2000.

Lewis, Jon. *Whom God Wishes to Destroy . . . Francis Coppola and the New Hollywood*. Durham, NC: Duke University Press, 1995.

LoBrutto, Vincent. *Selected Takes: Film Editors on Editing*. New York: Praeger, 1991.

———. *By Design: Interviews with Film Production Designers*. Westport, CT: Praeger, 1992.

———. *Sound-on-Film: Interviews with Creators of Film Sound*. Westport, CT: Praeger, 1994.

———. *Principal Photography: Interviews with Feature Film Creators*. Westport, CT: Praeger, 1999.

———. *Stanley Kubrick: A Biography*. New York: Donald I. Fine Books, 1999.

———. *The Encyclopedia of American Independent Filmmaking*. Westport, CT: Greenwood Press, 2002.

———. *Martin Scorsese: A Biography*. Westport, CT: Praeger Publishers, 2007.

Lynch, David, and Kristine McKenna. *Room to Dream*. New York: Random House, 2018.

Mazursky, Paul. *Show Me the Magic*. New York: Simon & Schuster, 1999.

McBride, Joseph. *Steven Spielberg: A Biography*. New York: Simon & Schuster, 1997.

McDougal, Dennis. *Five Easy Decades: How Jack Nicholson Became the Biggest Movie Star in Modern Times*. Hoboken, NJ: John Wiley and Sons, 2008.

McGilligan, Patrick. *Robert Altman: Jumping off the Cliff: A Biography of the Great American Director*. New York: St. Martin's Press, 1989.

———. *Jack's Life: A Biography of Jack Nicholson*. New York: W. W. Norton 1994.

———. *Clint: The Life and Legend*. New York: St. Martin's Press, 1999.

Meade, Marion. *The Unruly Life of Woody Allen: A Biography*. New York: Scribner, 2000.

Michaels, Lloyd. *Terrence Malick.* Urbana: University of Illinois Press, 2009.
Monaco, James. *American Film Now: The People, the Power, the Money, the Movies.* Rev. ed. New York: New American Library, 1984.
Mordden, Ethan. *The Hollywood Studios: House Style in the Golden Age of the Movies.* New York: Simon & Schuster, 1988.
————. *Medium Cool: The Movies of the 1960s.* New York: Knopf, 1990.
Petrou, David Michael. *The Making of Superman the Movie.* New York: Warner Books, 1978.
Phillips, Gene D. *Godfather: The Intimate Francis Ford Coppola.* Lexington: University Press of Kentucky, 2014.
Phillips, Julia. *You'll Never Eat Lunch in This Town Again.* New York: Random House, 1991.
Pye, Michael, and Lynda Myles. New York: Holt, Rinehart and Winston, 1979.
Schatz, Thomas. *The Genius of the System: Hollywood Filmmaking in the Studio Era.* New York: Pantheon Books, 1988.
Schickel, Richard. *Clint Eastwood: A Biography.* New York: Knopf, 1996.
————. *Woody Allen: A Life in Film.* Chicago: Ivan R. Dee, 2003.
Schumacher, Michael. *Francis Ford Coppola: A Filmmaker's Life.* New York: Crown, 1999.
Segaloff, Nat. *Hurricane Billy: The Stormy Life and Films of William Friedkin.* New York: William Morrow, 1990.
Sherman, Eric, and Martin Rubin. *The Director's Event: Interviews with Five American Film-Makers: Budd Boetticher, Peter Bogdanovich, Samuel Fuller, Arthur Penn, Abraham Polonsky.* New York: Atheneum, 1970.
Sigoloff, Marc. *The Films of the Seventies: A Filmography of American, British and Canadian Films 1970–1979.* Jefferson, NC: McFarland Classics, 1984.
Sterritt, David. *Robert Altman Interviews.* Jackson: University Press of Mississippi, 2000.
Stuart, Jan. *The Nashville Chronicles: The Making of Robert Altman's Masterpiece.* New York: Simon & Schuster, 2000.
Taubin, Amy. *Taxi Driver.* London: BFI Publishing, 2000.
Thompson, David, ed. *Altman on Altman.* London: Faber and Faber, 2006.
Tonguette, Peter. *The Films of James Bridges.* Jefferson, NC: McFarland, 2011.
Townsend, Sylvia. *Bumpy Road: The Making, Flop, and Revival of Two-Lane Blacktop.* Jackson: University Press of Mississippi, 2019.
————. ed. *Peter Bogdanovich Interviews.* Jackson: University of Mississippi Press, 2015.
Tzioumakis, Yannis, and Peter Krämer, eds. *The Hollywood Renaissance: Revisiting America's Most Celebrated Era.* United Kingdom: Bloomsbury Academic, 2018.
Wake, Sandra, and Nicola Hayden. *The Bonnie & Clyde Book.* New York: Simon & Schuster, 1972.
Wasson, Sam. *A Splurch in the Kisser: The Movies of Blake Edwards.* Middletown, CT: Wesleyan University Press, 2009.
————. *Fosse.* Boston: Houghton Mifflin, 2013.
Weddle, David. *"If They Move . . . Kill 'Em!": The Life and Times of Sam Peckinpah.* New York: Grove Press, 1994.
Winkler, Peter L. *Dennis Hopper: The Wild Ride of a Hollywood Rebel.* Fort Lee, NJ: Barricade Books, 2011.
Wurlitzer, Rudy, and Will Corry. *Two Lane Blacktop: Screenplay.* New York: Award Books, 1971.
Zuckoff, Mitchell. *Robert Altman: The Oral Biography.* New York: Knopf, 2009.

INDEX

ABOUT THE AUTHOR

Vincent LoBrutto was an instructor of editing, film history, and other courses at the School of Visual Arts in Manhattan for three decades. He is the author of numerous books on filmmaking including *Stanley Kubrick: A Biography* (1999), *The Encyclopedia of American Independent Filmmaking* (2002), *Becoming Film Literate: The Art and Craft of Motion Pictures* (2005), and *Martin Scorsese: A Biography* (2007). LoBrutto is the recipient of the Robert Wise Award for Journalistic Illumination of the Art of Editing.